WAITING
FOR CHINA

*The Anglo-Chinese College at Malacca, 1818–1843, and
Early Nineteenth-Century Missions*

by

BRIAN HARRISON

HONG KONG UNIVERSITY PRESS

ISBN 962-209-011-7

Printed by
LIBRA PRESS LTD.
56 Wong Chuk Hang Road 5D, Hong Kong

'All the various tribes of men have equal rights, and every system . . . has a right to be heard. When this shall be the case, mighty Truth shall prevail.'

(Robert Morrison, *To the public*, 1823)

'Thus does the son of a Malacca peasant derive an enlightened education denied to the son of the Emperor of China.'

(Charles Marjoribanks, commenting on the Anglo-Chinese College at Malacca, 1831)

'China, one of the fairest portions of the globe; the most ancient, the most populous, the best skilled in the management of human nature, of any country under heaven . . .'

(Robert Morrison. *To the public*, 1823)

Contents

ILLUSTRATIONS (between pages 114 and 115)

1. Robert Morrison, D. D. as President of the Anglo-Chinese College. Drawn by J. Wildman, engraved by T. Blood. *From the Collection of historical paintings of the Hong Kong Museum of Art.*

2. Dr & Mrs Milne. Drawn by G. Baxter. From Robert Philip, *The life and opinions of Rev. William Milne, D. D., missionary to China.* London, John Snow, 1840.

3. Malacca. From *Missionary Sketches*, no. LIV, July 1831.

4. The Anglo-Chinese College at Malacca. Drawing by Capt. P. J. Begbie, watercolour by J. Gantz. From Capt. P. J. Begbie, *The Malayan Peninsula.* Madras, 1834.

5. Bird's eye view of the Anglo-Chinese College-House at Malacca. From *Missionary Sketches*, no. XXVIII, January 1825.

6. Claudius Henry Thomsen, member of the College staff, 1818–22. *From the Council for World Mission Collection, School of Oriental and African Studies Library, University of London.*

7. Walter Henry Medhurst, member of the College staff, 1818–20. Drawn by W. T. Strutt. *From the Council for World Mission Collection, School of Oriental and African Studies Library, University of London.*

8. Rev. William Milne, D. D. From *The Indo-Chinese Gleaner*, no. 1, May 1817.

in all parts of the world, vol. 8. London, Longman, Hurst, Rees, Ormes and Brown, 1808–14.

19. Dr Legge and his three Chinese students. Painting by H. Room. From Helen E. Legge, *James Legge, missionary and scholar*. London, The Religious Tract Society, 1905.

Preface

THE image of the missionary is not what it was; it has lost much of the aura of sanctity and self-sacrifice that once surrounded it. This, no doubt, is largely because the record of Christian missions has come to be identified with that of European colonialism, itself now stripped of much of its former glory. But as the age of colonialism and the missionary movement associated with it recede further into the past we may perhaps begin to see both in clearer perspective. In time nineteenth-century colonialism may come to be judged as something more than the crude system of economic exploitation and political repression with which it is still often simply equated; in the long run of history it may even come to be seen as on the whole a liberating and creative force rather than a repressive one. Similarly, the Christian missionary of the age of colonialism may in time come to be rated as something more than a narrow-minded and presumptuous agent of religious and racial propaganda; for he could indeed be very much more—a vitally important, if unconscious, instrument of social and cultural change.

This study is concerned with the missionary as innovator in the educational and cultural spheres rather than with the religious aspects of his work. It focuses on the educational ideas and achievements of the first Protestant missionary to China, Robert Morrison—an outstanding personality—and some of his fellow-workers in Southeast Asia. In particular, it deals with a lesser-known aspect of their educational work in the creation and development of a remarkable early nineteenth-century cultural institution at Malacca (now Melaka) on the Malaysian peninsula, the Anglo-Chinese College founded by Robert Morrison and sponsored by the London Missionary Society.

In tracing the story of this enterprise, the study seeks to identify a theme which is still one of great significance for today—that of the problems raised by the meeting and interaction of different cultural traditions. While the main focus of attention is on the work and fortunes of the Anglo-Chinese College at Malacca, on the part it played in the early history of modern education in Malaysia, and on its contribution to the development of Chinese and Southeast Asian studies, an attempt is also made to relate the story of the College itself to issues of wider historical significance— the Western image of China, the missionary approach to the world of East Asia, and the general relationship between missions and colonialism.

Those who have told the story of Christian missions to China have tended to draw a clear line of division between the earlier Catholic missionaries of the seventeenth and eighteenth centuries with their generally humane and scholarly approach, and the later Protestant missionaries of the nineteenth century with their comparatively narrow and intolerant attitude towards the Chinese cultural and intellectual tradition. In accordance with this rather arbitrary division, Robert Morrison and his co-worker William Milne have been regarded as representative of the later approach, as being the first of the narrow pietist, fundamentalist evangelical missionaries of the nineteenth century.[1] My study of the documentary sources (mainly contained in the archives of the former London Missionary Society) has led me to differ from that view, and to see Morrison and Milne as very much nearer in spirit to their Catholic predecessors than to their Protestant successors in their missionary approach to China. To a large extent indeed they shared much of the attitude which the earlier Jesuit missionaries showed towards the Chinese social and cultural tradition—an attitude of informed, if restrained, admiration.

In Malacca as in southern China during the years covered by the present study (1807–1843), the Protestant missionaries achieved only minor practical success in winning souls to Christianity. But that, after all, was not their immediate purpose; their basic approach was much more an indirect one. Their aim was rather to set in motion a whole process of educational and cultural change within the indigenous societies in the hope that new conditions favourable to the acceptance of Christianity would thereby be created in the long run. If in the end the results of the work of Morrison, Milne and their associates at Malacca were of small account in the strictly missionary field, the educational and cultural assumptions underlying the approach to their work may still be seen as having some lasting validity in the sphere of intercultural relations. And if the work of their successors in the missionary field of China itself was likewise narrowly limited in immediate effect, the long-term influence of the Protestant evangelical missionary movement as a whole may be seen as in essence a revolutionary influence, as a significant factor in the ultimate liberation of China from her past.[2]

Besides Robert Morrison, whose main life-work was concentrated at Canton on the south China coast, a number of prominent missionaries, teachers and officials operating in Southeast Asia at the time are introduced in relation to the central topic of this book. No attempt has been made, however, to provide full-length portraits of the major personalities involved such as Robert Morrison himself, or his closest colleague William Milne; and such figures as Stamford Raffles and 'Munshi' Abdullah are here treated as merely incidental to the main story. If the book has a hero it is the Anglo-Chinese College itself, as a unique experiment in cultural transfer.

For help in the protracted and wide-ranging search for
materials for this study, grateful thanks are due to the members
of the staffs of the London Missionary Society's Library (since
transferred to the Library of the School of Oriental and African
Studies, University of London), the India Office Library, and the
Royal Commonwealth Society's Library in London; Algemeen
Rijksarchief in The Hague; the National Library and the University Library in Singapore; Arkib Negara in Kuala Lumpur; Arsip
Nasional in Jakarta; and the University of Hong Kong Library.
The Council for World Mission, successor to the London Mission-
ary Society, kindly gave permission to publish material used from
their archives.

Thanks are also due to the Canada Council for a research
award in 1970–71; to the University of British Columbia for study
leave in 1972–73; and to the School of Oriental and African
Studies, University of London, for a senior visiting fellowship in
1972.

A special word of thanks is due to the Rev. Carl T. Smith of
Chung Chi College in the Chinese University of Hong Kong for
his helpful co-operation. Permission to reproduce material from
my article 'The Anglo-Chinese College at Malacca, 1818–1843' in
C. D. Cowan and O. W. Wolters (eds.), *Southeast Asian history and
historiography*, Cornell University Press, 1976, is also gratefully
acknowledged.

B. H.

CHAPTER ONE

The Indirect Approach

ONE of the passengers arriving at New York by ship from London on 20 April 1807 was a young Anglo-Scottish missionary named Robert Morrison. He was on his way to China, on a journey that was to last over seven and a half months. Had the choice been open to him he would have taken the much shorter sailing route direct from England to the East via the Cape of Good Hope. But the English East India Company, with exclusive control of British shipping to China as well as India, was not in favour of introducing Christian missionaries into the Eastern world at this time. Besides, England was at war with France; it would be wiser to sail well out over the north Atlantic to the United States and then continue on from there to the East in a neutral vessel. So, after a stay of about three weeks in New York and Philadelphia, Morrison continued on the second stage of his journey in an American ship. Recrossing the Atlantic, rounding the Cape, and then sailing across the Indian Ocean and the South China Sea, he arrived at length on 4 September 1807 at Macao, the old Portuguese settlement on the south China coast.

Thus from the start Morrison's approach to China was an indirect one. And so it was to remain; for in twenty-seven years of living and working in Macao and Canton, he was never to succeed in finding a way of approach to the Chinese people other than one that was both narrowly restricted and indirect.

Born near Morpeth in Northumberland in 1782, the young Morrison had grown up in an age of revolutionary change. One of the major influences for change in the England of that day was a powerful movement of thought in which humanitarian, evangelical and missionary ideas were all closely interrelated. The Evangelical movement, activist and enthusiastic, had generated a new missionary urge to carry the message of Protestant Christianity across the world for the supposed benefit of mankind. The two great missionary societies that were founded in the last decade of the eighteenth century, the London Missionary Society (1795) and the Church Missionary Society (1799), represented each in its own way a predominantly evangelical outlook.[1]

Robert Morrison joined the London Missionary Society in 1804. Two years earlier, at the age of twenty, he had decided to enter the ministry of the Presbyterian Church. At the beginning of 1803 he commenced his theological training at Hoxton Academy in London, one of the 'Dissenting academies' then offering a university-type education to Nonconformists—who were still effectively debarred from admission to Oxford or Cambridge. It was while studying at Hoxton that Morrison determined to become a missionary.

Accepted as a trainee by the London Missionary Society with China in view, he went first in May 1804 to a missionary academy at Gosport in Hampshire;[2] then returned in August of the following year to London for a further sixteen months of intensive study—in medicine at St. Bartholomew's, in astronomy at Greenwich, and in Chinese under a young Cantonese tutor, Yong Sam-tak, who happened to be in London at the time. On completion of his training Morrison was ordained, and on 31 January 1807 he sailed for China.

The decision of the London Missionary Society to train a young recruit for service among the Chinese at this time may call for some explanation. For hitherto India had been the main objective of Protestant missionary interest in Asia, despite the East

India Company's official discouragement of missionary activities in its Indian territories. The English Evangelicals, bringing a fresh impetus to the missionary movement, had tried to effect a change in the official attitude towards missions and education in India when the Company's charter came up for renewal by the British Parliament in 1793. Though they failed in that attempt, they did manage to draw public attention to their point of view: that Britain had missionary and educational responsibilities in Asia, and that Indian society—which they regarded as thoroughly corrupted by Hinduism—could only be reformed by the infusion of Christian faith and Western education.

Such 'enlightened' ideas were in the air when the London Missionary Society was founded in 1795. The Society soon tested the East India Company's policy by proposing to send a group of its missionaries to Bengal, but permission for this was refused. It was not in fact until 1813 (six years after Morrison had sailed from England) that the Company's charter was to be amended so as to permit independent missionary and educational activities in India.[3]

Meanwhile, however, the London Society had begun to look further afield. It had become attracted to the idea of commencing work among the Chinese in Southeast Asia. Here presumably, as distinct from India, no overt opposition by the East India Company was anticipated. The first reference to plans for a 'China mission' appears in the Society's annual report for 1805, where mention is made of a possible mission base on Prince of Wales, or Penang, Island, lying off the north-west coast of the Malaysian peninsula. Penang, which had been obtained by the East India Company from the Sultan of the neighbouring mainland state of Kedah in 1786, had a growing population of emigrant Chinese as well as Indians and Malays, and was closely linked to Britain's expanding trade with China. At this time, prior to the founding of Singapore in 1819, Penang was regarded as a new centre of great potential for Western trade and influence in the Malaysian region. Indeed in 1805, the year of the Missionary Society's report, the island was

newly designated by the British admiralty as a naval base and at
the same time elevated by the Company from a subsidiary settlement to the status of a Presidency.[4] The Society's plans may well
have been influenced by these developments. At any rate it was
announced in 1806 that two missionaries, Morrison and Brown,[5]
had been selected to train for work among the Chinese, apparently
at Penang. Later Brown was to withdraw, and so Morrison was
sent out on his own—though not now to Penang as originally
intended.

For by the time of Morrison's actual departure from England
early in 1807 there had been a further change of plan. The
directors of the London Missionary Society had now become
convinced that an essential tool for sustained missionary work
among the Chinese people must be provided in a new scholarly
translation of the Bible into their language. Morrison, with his
Chinese language training already well advanced, seemed the
obvious person to undertake such a work; moreover China itself,
rather than any centre of overseas Chinese settlement in Southeast
Asia, seemed the proper place for him to carry it out. So the Penang
project was shelved for the time being, and Morrison was sent off
alone on the long journey to China.

Arriving at Macao in 1807 as the first Protestant missionary
to China, Morrison was clearly faced with a formidable task. Not
that the Chinese had hitherto shown any marked hostility to
Christian teaching as such. Indeed China in the past had been
notably tolerant of imported religious ideas such as those of
Buddhism, Islam and Christianity. The efforts of Western Catholic
missionaries to convince them of the truth and value of Christian
doctrine had been generally respected, though also largely ignored,
by the Chinese for centuries—from as far back as the middle ages
of European history, and the time of the so-called 'Tartar Peace'
when Mongol rule over the whole of Central Asia had permitted
a comparatively free overland movement of missionaries as well as

merchants (including William of Rubruck and Marco Polo among many others) between Europe and China.

Then with the coming of the Portuguese to East Asia by sea in the sixteenth century, Jesuit missionaries from Portugal and other Catholic countries of Europe had begun to enter China through the port of Macao, eventually becoming accepted in Peking itself—though not, it is true, for their religious teaching so much as for their scholarship and for their technical and artistic skills—and occupying influential positions as advisers to the imperial court. The famous Ch'ien Lung emperor of the eighteenth century made regular use of Jesuit scholars and technicians at his court.

Now, however, with the arrival of Morrison—Ma Li-sun or 'polite, humble horse' as the name might sound to Cantonese ears—there stood at the gates of China for the first time a new brand of Christian missionary. He was neither a Catholic nor an Italian, Portuguese, Frenchman or German, but a Protestant and an Englishman—a less familiar breed of barbarian from the outer seas, not hitherto associated in the minds of Chinese officials with missionary or scholarly activities but rather with hard commercial dealing. Ironically—in view of the English East India Company's attitude to missions in India—but inevitably in the circumstances, an English missionary newly arriving in south China at this time was bound to be linked in the Chinese mind with the commercial Company, the sole official body representing Britain in the area.

With the steady growth of Britain's China trade in the eighteenth century—the age when tea became firmly established as the English national drink—the East India Company had consolidated its position as the leading association of foreign merchants trading with China. It had possessed a permanent 'factory' or warehouse and business office since 1715 at Canton—thirty miles or so up-river from Macao and the only Chinese port open to foreign trade—where it dealt mainly in the export of Chinese tea and silk in exchange for cotton textiles and payments in silver. By the end of the eighteenth century this thriving business had expanded enormously. At the same time it had come to depend heavily for the stimulus of its cash supply on the proceeds of a busy smuggling trade in opium that was carried on in the Canton river area by private merchants trading between India and China. Mounting profits were made out of opium by Chinese as well as foreign merchants, while regular denunciations of the illegal trade came from the government in Peking, concerned as much by the growing loss of foreign exchange through the outflow of silver in payment for opium, as by the physical and moral harm to its people which the opium imports were thought to cause.

Altogether this was hardly the most favourable environment in which to start a new religious mission. And it was rendered even less promising by the tight controls imposed by the Chinese authorities at this time not only on the conditions of foreign trade at Canton but also on the day-to-day relations between individual foreigners and Chinese there. Such restrictions included, for example, a requirement that the foreigners must withdraw from their Canton factories to Portuguese Macao at the conclusion of the trading season in April each year, and also a strict prohibition against the teaching of the Chinese language to non-Chinese.

In his first days at Macao, Morrison met with a predictably cool reception from the officials of the East India Company stationed there. But from the head of the American merchants and his colleagues he soon received an offer of accommodation in their Canton factory, which he gladly accepted.[6] From these beginnings Morrison, moving to Canton shortly afterwards, was able gradually to win general acceptance by the foreign merchants of his strange presence in their midst. For a time he followed the example which had been set by the pioneer Jesuit missionary of the early seventeenth century, the Italian Father Ricci,[7] by dressing in Cantonese style, wearing a 'pigtail' of hair and letting his finger-nails grow long like those of a Chinese scholar. At the same time Morrison showed that he was a serious scholar-missionary, devoting long hours day after day to the study of Chinese in both the Peking (Mandarin) and Cantonese dialects. The English Company officials now began to thaw, and before long their chief merchant not only succeeded, surprisingly, in obtaining a language tutor—a young Roman Catholic Chinese from Peking—for Morrison, but gave him also some assurance of financial support for his new project of a Chinese-English dictionary. By the end of the year 1808, barely sixteen months after his arrival, Morrison had translated part of the New Testament and completed a Chinese grammar, in addition to making progress on the preparation of his dictionary.[8]

But there must have been times when, raising his head from his desk, he would see in his mind a distracting picture of Penang. Had the Missionary Society really made the right decision in sending him to Canton, in choosing it as their base for a Chinese mission? Here in Canton it was indeed possible for him to do good work on the quiet, in language study and translation, but in face of official restrictions and popular indifference there seemed little prospect that other missionaries who came out would be able to make any real progress in the equally important work of preaching and teaching. Should the Society after all have chosen Penang?— or possibly Malacca, the English-held port on the west coast of the Malaysian peninsula?

Not long after his first arrival in China, Morrison had begun to raise such questions as these in his letters to England. 'With respect to a person coming out to join this mission', he wrote from Canton, 'I wish that whoever comes would explore Penang and Malacca.' That would be worth doing, he thought, 'chiefly with regard to the Chinese who are there, having also a reference to the Malays'. He himself might go to Penang if compelled to leave Canton; he might even go there voluntarily so as to 'be able to decide on which place to make the seat of the mission—Canton or Penang'. After months of study in Canton and Macao, Penang

was still very much in his mind as he wrote, early in the year 1809:
'I think it likely that I shall remove to Penang in order to print a
grammar which is compiled, and in due time to commence the
dictionary.' And at the end of the same year he took up the
question of Penang again, writing to the Missionary Society: 'I
wonder that you have not sent a missionary to Prince of Wales
Island. . . . Make it a stepping-stone to China, embracing at the
same time the Malays. It appears to me exceedingly desirable to
have a missionary establishment there—as ships from every part
of India pass that way—which would form a centre of communication between all your missionaries in these parts.' Thus gradually
Morrison's ideas for a missionary base in Southeast Asia were
beginning to crystallize.[9]

But whatever the decision with respect to Penang or Malacca
might be, a radical change now occurred in Morrison's personal
situation which made it unlikely that he would soon leave Canton.
In February 1809 he married Miss Mary Morton, daughter of an
Irish doctor then on a visit to Macao; and at the same time he was
offered and accepted the post of Chinese Secretary and Translator
to the English Company's factory at Canton at a salary of £500
a year. Having thus gained the status of a Company servant,
Morrison was now reasonably assured of being able to continue to
reside and work in Canton and Macao. His commitment to the
London Missionary Society still stood—particularly in respect of
the Chinese translation of the Bible, on which he continued work
for years—but his new post, with the financial security it brought,
was to give him a greater sense of independence in his dealings
with the Society.

These events marked a turning-point in Morrison's career. The
missionary had joined the ranks of the merchants. It was an
arrangement that possessed obvious practical advantages, and the
Missionary Society heartily concurred in it. But inevitably there
was to be criticism, both then and later, of the dual role which
Morrison had assumed. He himself was well aware of, and highly

sensitive to, such criticism. 'It is thought that . . . my serving the Company and being a missionary are not compatible with each other. If this be pushed much further, a separation must take place,' he wrote. At such times too he had hinted strongly at the possibility of his settling the whole question 'by removing to Malacca or Java'.[10]

But if, as seemed more likely, Morrison did not really intend now to move from Canton, and if his still undefined ideas for a Southeast Asian mission base serving as an indirect approach to China were ever to take shape, he would need more practical information, more concrete facts about existing conditions at such possible mission centres as Penang, Malacca and Java. And if he were not to visit those places himself, he would need to have some reliable witness to observe and report on his behalf.

Considerations such as these helped to sharpen the pleasure that Morrison felt on hearing the news that the London Society was sending out another missionary, William Milne, to join him.

CHAPTER TWO

The Road to Malacca

FROM his first days in Macao and Canton, Morrison had been constantly urging the London Missionary Society to send out more workers to widen the bridgehead he had formed in East Asia. 'I still desire to have assistance sent from you to this place, or as an auxiliary mission to Penang or Java', he wrote from Macao in January 1811. The Society did in fact have both those places in mind as possible mission bases at the time; but when in 1812 a suitable young man became available for service in the general East Asian field, it was decided to send him out to join Morrison in Canton. And so William Milne, newly appointed 'missionary in the East', sailed from England in September 1812 for China.[1]

Milne's repute as an early nineteenth century scholar-missionary in the East has become largely overshadowed by that of his senior colleague Morrison, yet he was very far from being a figure of minor significance. He was once described as a man 'of unusual gifts, of great force of character, and of an intense spirituality'. Though of poor health from the start, he filled a short life with a burning intensity of purpose. 'A man so intent on great objects . . . , so severe with himself', was how Morrison was to describe him later. These two men were to co-operate closely as missionary partners for almost nine years. They were to share the task of translating the whole of the Old Testament into Chinese. And together they were to design and build the Anglo-Chinese College at Malacca as a Southeast Asian academic centre as well as a training base for the missionary approach to China.

Born in the parish of Kennethmont in Aberdeenshire in 1785— and so only three years younger than Morrison—Milne seems to have endured a hard youth. Only six years old when his father died, he is said to have worked for years as a shepherd or farmhand. As a young man he became an active member of the Congregational Church at Huntly, a small town forty miles north-west of Aberdeen. Deciding about the age of twenty to become a missionary, he was accepted some five years later by the London Missionary Society, and sent for training to the Gosport academy in Hampshire in 1810. After two years of study there he was ordained in July 1812. In the following month he married Rachel Cowie of Aberdeen and together they sailed from England on 4 September 1812, having managed to obtain a passage as far as Cape Town on the first stage of their journey to China.[2]

The Milnes had a long wait at Cape Town and another delay in Mauritius before obtaining onward passages. With apparently little or no special language training so far, Milne made good use of the time 'working on Chinese characters and reading'. On 15 June 1813, over nine months after their departure from England, they reached Malacca, the historic seaport town around which so much of Milne's later career was to revolve.[3]

Malacca, the old river-port city on the west coast of the Malaysian peninsula, had by this time lost much of its former importance both as a commercial and cultural centre of the Malaysian world, and as an outpost of Western trade and empire standing guard over the strategic sea-lane of the Straits of Malacca. Founded about the year 1400, it was captured from its Malay Sultan in 1511 by the Portuguese, then taken from them in 1641 by the Dutch. In 1795 the city was occupied by the English as a temporary colonial prize in the global war being waged at that

time—the long war that was not to end until the fall of Napoleon
and the peace of 1815.

Under the English East India Company's wartime occupation
beginning in 1795 and continuing on into 1818, Malacca suffered
from being regarded as merely a temporary prize in the Straits
area as compared with the permanent possession of Penang,
acquired earlier in 1786. To reduce the strategic value of Malacca
to a minimum in the possible event of its abandonment at the end
of the war, the fine old fortress, built up over the years by the
Portuguese and Dutch, was almost completely demolished, and
the town itself was generally neglected. But Malacca, as Milne
first saw it from the deck of his ship in 1813, had managed to retain
something of the atmosphere of an international trading port, yet
also an air of quiet dignity and charm, with its central hill topped
by the ruins of an ancient church, its neat colourful houses,
tree-shaded seafront, and pleasant surrounding countryside of
Malay villages, coconut plantations and green rice-fields. 'Town
much the appearance of a country village in England', Milne
briefly noted.[4]

During this first short visit of about thirty-six hours, Milne
strolled through the cosmopolitan town, saw the main Chinese
temple and the Malay mosque, noticed several Chinese schools, in
which he could hear the 'children all speaking aloud at once', and
then paused for a shave by a Chinese barber, 'without soap, and
with a two and a half inch razor'. Later he called on the English
military commandant, Major William Farquhar, who had been in
charge of Malacca since 1803. During their conversation Farquhar
assured Milne that should he and Morrison ever be compelled to
withdraw their mission from Canton they would be made welcome
in Malacca.[5]

Milne was to return to Malacca before very long, but meanwhile, continuing their eastward journey, he and his wife arrived
at last at Macao on 4 July 1813. Morrison, who was there for the
summer months, joyfully came to meet them and installed them

in his residence. But almost immediately the Portuguese civil and religious authorities, deciding that two Protestant missionaries were more than enough for Macao, ordered that Milne should leave within ten days. 'Mr. Milne must go up to Canton', wrote Morrison in his diary on 7 July, and on the 16th Milne went off secretly on his own in a Chinese boat up the Canton river. He managed by changing boats more than once to reach the European factory area outside Canton, where he found rooms and before long settled down to a daily routine of intensive study of the Chinese language.[6]

'I have been labouring hard on the very difficult and peculiar language of China', Milne wrote home in September 1813; 'I am now working on the Mandarin dialect.' After a further four months of concentrated language study he had to admit: 'My progress is very small . . . , but I am not cast down.' He went on to explain later with wry humour that a mastery of the Chinese language— 'the study of which I love'—was only for those with 'bodies of brass, lungs of steel, heads of rock, hands of spring-steel, eyes of eagles, hearts of apostles, memories of angels, and lives of Methuselah!' 'Still', he added cheerfully, 'I make a little progress.' On Sundays, putting aside his language study, he would hold a religious service in the foreign factory area, preaching a sermon before a small congregation of merchants and seamen, 'principally Americans, and a very few English officers of ships'. 'The Americans', Milne commented, 'were constant, attentive and polite.'[7]

But Milne's future position in the Canton-Macao area remained very unsure. The English factory officials were not prepared to afford him even nominal recognition as Morrison's assistant in Canton, and the Portuguese authorities again refused him permission to reside in Macao. However, Milne's difficulty turned out to be Morrison's opportunity. Even before Milne went up to Canton from Macao, Morrison had noted in his diary on 7 July: 'His last resource will be to go to Java or to Malacca'. By September

Morrison had put the idea of a Southeast Asian mission to Milne himself, who however was at first 'very unwilling to leave this place', as Morrison reported to the directors of the Missionary Society, adding that he himself thought there was 'a wide field for labour at Java among the Chinese there'. By November Milne had come round to the idea of making a preliminary reconnaissance of the region, and 'after much deliberation', as he wrote to the directors, had agreed to go on a missionary tour of Java, Penang and Malacca.[8]

The objects of Milne's tour as he himself summed them up in January 1814 would be to distribute copies of Morrison's recently completed translation of the New Testament and other religious literature in Chinese, and to find out what facilities for Chinese printing were available in the places visited; to make a comparative assessment of the likely missionary opportunities among the Chinese people in those places; and 'to look out for a place of residence and seat of the mission, as there is no opening at present in China'. Morrison wrote an open letter of introduction requesting assistance for Milne from any civil authorities concerned, giving an assurance to all that there was 'no design, no sinister nor political motive' behind the journey.[9]

Milne sailed from Canton for Java on 14 February 1814 in a 'country' ship (that is, one independently owned but licensed to trade by the East India Company), taking with him his tutor, a printer, and a servant. His tutor-assistant ('his name is Ho-ye-che, and we call him Seën-sang, i.e. teacher, by way of courtesy') had been a transcriber in the Li-pu, or Board of Ceremonies, at Peking and an unsuccessful candidate in the Chinese imperial civil service examinations. The Chinese printer understood typecutting as well as printing in both English and Chinese; he would be employed during the course of the journey on occasional printing and would also make an assessment of the printing facilities available at the different centres. Special attention would be paid to any opportunity for printing Morrison's new *Chinese and English dialogues,* a phrase-book intended for English-speaking students of Chinese. Milne mentions, almost casually, that he committed this whole work to memory before his departure in case the manuscript should become lost.[10]

Soon after sailing from Canton Milne found an early opportunity of meeting a sample group of Chinese emigrants to Southeast Asia, for his ship was carrying over four hundred and fifty of them, bound for the island of Bangka (off the south-eastern coast of Sumatra) to work in the tin-mines there.[11] When they reached the island, then under British wartime occupation, Milne went ashore and met the English officer in charge, Major M.H. Court, from whom he learned that there were upwards of five thousand Chinese then on Bangka island and in the adjacent town of Palembang on Sumatra, and that thousands more were expected to follow.[12]

Milne's ship arrived at Batavia (the present-day Jakarta), capital of Java, on 10 March 1814. At this time Java and other Indonesian islands such as Bangka were under the rule of the English East India Company, having been taken from the Dutch by a British-Indian expeditionary force despatched from Madras and Malacca in 1811. This expedition was itself a consequence of the French occupation of Holland in 1795, which had exposed all Dutch overseas possessions to British naval action during the long Anglo-French contest that was to last until 1815. It was as part of a whole series of wartime moves on the global chessboard at this time that Britain took over such former Dutch colonial possessions as Cape Town, Ceylon, Malacca and Java.

Milne spent nearly five months in Java (March-August 1814) collecting information about the country and its inhabitants, especially the Chinese settlers, and travelling extensively over the island. He was provided with much useful information by Stamford Raffles, the wartime Lieutenant-Governor of Java. Raffles, who thought Milne 'a liberal, well-informed, excellent man', invited him to stay at his official country residence at Buitenzorg (Bogor) outside Batavia, and lent him some of his personal notes and papers on Malay and Indonesian subjects. Raffles also arranged free transportation for a six week tour by Milne of central and eastern Java and the island of Madura, during the course of which he was presented to the Susuhunan or Javanese 'Emperor' of Mataram at Solo (Surakarta), slept a night in the palace of the Sultan of Madura, and visited most of the larger towns and villages where Chinese lived. 'The Chinese', Milne wrote, 'are my chief object'; but he found much interest also in the Javanese—'said to be a good-natured and civilized people'—and in their religion and culture. He 'travelled among the people unarmed and without fear'. Altogether Milne was most favourably impressed by the island of Java, 'in which', he observed, 'the botanist, the mineralogist, the antiquary, the linguist, the historian, and the missionary have each an immense field'.[13]

The next objectives of Milne's tour were the Malaysian ports of Malacca and Penang. After a week's sea crossing from Java he reached Malacca on 11 August 1814. There he stayed at the residence of the officer in charge, Major William Farquhar, whom he had met on his previous short visit a little more than a year before. Milne remained for over a week this time, studying the local conditions and surveying the possibilities for a Chinese mission base.

Malacca had been an important centre of overseas Chinese settlement and commerce for centuries—one of the oldest in Southeast Asia. Under successive Malay, Portuguese, Dutch and English regimes, the Chinese merchants (mostly Hokkien-speaking, from the south China province of Fukien) had always provided the essential elements of capital and skill in Malacca's traditional exchange trade, dealing in such varied key commodities as Malaysian tin, Indian textiles, Burman timber, Thai rice, Indonesian pepper and Chinese silk. Malacca's trade had its ups and downs over the years, and at this time, with the town under British occupation, it was suffering from the effects of political uncertainty and wartime disruption as well as from the competition of the neighbouring port of Penang. Malacca had seen its best days, but its Chinese merchant families lived on in their solid, cool, heavily shuttered houses by the river and along the seafront, doing what business they could and hoping for better times.

On his previous visit in 1813 Milne had been informed that the population of Malacca town was about seventeen thousand, of whom some nine or ten thousand were Chinese. He now estimated that the total population of the town and surrounding rural areas might well amount to as much as twenty thousand, though the Chinese community would form a smaller proportion of the whole, amounting to perhaps five thousand or even less. However, the Chinese inhabitants were mainly concentrated in the town proper and so would form, Milne thought, an excellent basis for a mission, offering the added advantage of ready communication through them with other Chinese communities in the general region. Moreover, he now realized, the Malacca Chinese enjoyed a special position of prestige among their fellow countrymen in Southeast Asia, not only for their known business acumen but also because there were always some amongst them who had kept the cultural tradition of their homeland alive. 'The Chinese here seem more intelligent than on Java and have preserved their own language better; there are not a few learned men and poets among them', Milne observed.[14]

After Java and Malacca, the next stage of Milne's tour was to have included a visit to Penang. But by now he had become weary of travel and exhausted by the oppressive heat and humidity of the climate. He was beginning to tell himself that however important it might be to start a mission in Southeast Asia, he was not the right person to do so. 'I still feel my mind binding me to China itself', he wrote, thinking especially of the close union already formed between Morrison and himself in Canton, and of his own need of further time for language study there. He was therefore able to persuade himself that, 'seeing it was late in the season and no certain prospect of getting on soon', he should forego a visit to

Penang at this time and return without further delay to China. And so he did, sailing from Malacca on 19 August and reaching Macao on 5 September. He had been on his travels for nearly seven months, covering several thousand miles. 'Am feeling effects of the fatigues of my summer's excursions', Milne wrote about three weeks after his return. But even so he was immensely cheered by the fact that this time the Portuguese authorities had raised no objection to his presence in Macao.[15]

CHAPTER THREE

Malacca Beginnings

DURING Milne's absence Morrison had been developing his own ideas about a Southeast Asian mission base. Pending the opening of China's doors to Protestant missions, such a base, he considered, should form a missionary headquarters for the whole area lying between India and China. It should also provide not merely a training centre for specifically missionary purposes, but something more than that—a centre of higher education generally for the region as a whole. Morrison had outlined these broad ideas as early as December 1812 in a letter to the directors of the London Missionary Society. 'I wish that we had an institution at Malacca for the training of missionaries, European and native, and designed for all the countries beyond the Ganges,' he wrote. 'There also let there be that powerful engine, a press. . . . We want a central point for our Asiatic missions; we want organized co-operation; we want a press; we want a committee of missionaries.'[1]

Justifying this concept of a training centre located at Malacca rather than in England, Morrison expressed the conviction that 'the final triumphs of the Gospel will be by means of native missionaries and the Bible'. And with that view Milne was to agree, while under no illusion as to the length of time it could take for 'the final triumph' to be achieved. 'We are fully persuaded', Milne wrote, 'that the evangelizing of the Chinese will be a work of ages. . . . We think a seminary for native Chinese missionaries will be the most likely means of effecting the work.'[2]

For the moment, Morrison was careful to stress the purely missionary aspects rather than the more widely educational character of his proposed 'institution', as being more likely to win the Missionary Society's backing for the overall plan. The Society did not respond to his proposal at once, but it showed sufficient interest to have a memorandum of information on Malacca drawn up (based mainly on William Marsden's authoritative *History of Sumatra,* first published in 1783); and by February 1815 it had arrived at the decision to send a new missionary out to Malacca, though for work among the Malays rather than the Chinese there.[3]

By this time, however, Morrison and Milne had come to an independent decision to open a mission at Malacca mainly, though not exclusively, for the Chinese. Discussing the whole question after Milne's return from his tour in Southeast Asia, they first considered the respective merits of Java and Malacca as potential mission centres. Both places now seemed likely to be restored to Dutch rule with the ending of war—Britain had in fact agreed to return these and other overseas possessions to Holland by the London Convention of August 1814—but as Milne felt confident that the restored Dutch authorities would raise no objection to the setting up of a Protestant mission in either place, there was nothing to choose between them on that score. Java appeared at first to possess distinct advantages, with its comparatively large though scattered Chinese population and its frequent direct sea-communication by trading junk with China. At Malacca on the other hand, although the Chinese population of the town was quite small by comparison, it possessed a certain quality of distinction all its own, and the potential range of communications from the seaport seemed wider and more varied, embracing both India and China as well as the countries of mainland and island Southeast Asia. Moreover, Malacca was 'a quiet place', and it was also thought to be much healthier than Batavia.[4]

Penang seems to have dropped out of the reckoning at this stage. Milne had not visited it on his tour, and besides it was generally known that the life of the island had lost much of the stimulus associated with its elevation to naval base and presidency status in 1805, a combined move that had proved disappointingly unproductive; whereas Malacca, though now bereft of its ancient fort—demolished by the English caretaker administration in 1807—had managed to retain something of its air of distinction and its quiet serenity.

The choice of Malacca was finally agreed on between the two missionaries, and Milne had been persuaded to go there to open the mission by January 1815. Morrison wrote to the London Society justifying the decision. The Chinese government had been unusually hostile, he explained; any unofficial communication between Chinese and foreigners in Canton was strictly prohibited, and to preach the Gospel there was quite impracticable. Milne would go to Malacca in the confident expectation that the Society would agree to make it 'a central point, a well-supported missionary station, supplied with good missionaries and a press or presses—Chinese, Malay and English—, undertaken however without ostentation or much publicity'. Morrison concluded by reminding the Society of his earlier suggestion of a training college, as he wrote: 'Let Malacca be the seat of your missionary college for training both natives and Europeans to the work of the ministry in the countries beyond the Ganges.'[5]

Before Milne's departure from China on his new Southeast Asian assignment the two missionaries proceeded to draw up a detailed programme of activities for the Malacca mission, amounting in sum to 'preparations . . . for entering China with more effect, as soon as it shall please God to open a door for us'. Elementary education, religious instruction, and printing and publishing in Chinese would be major priorities, and the general emphasis of the programme would be on work amongst the Chinese in the immediate area. At the same time, however, the mission at

Malacca would attempt to serve a wider area embracing all the
countries lying between India and China; in this aspect it would
be the general headquarters of an 'Ultra-Ganges Mission'—a name
which should be regarded, Morrison explained, 'rather as pointing
to the scene of our labours than intimating that we consider
ourselves as sole possessors of the field'.[6]

Morrison was now most anxious that these plans should be put
into effect without further delay. Though apparently unaware of
the Missionary Society's intentions with regard to Malacca, he
may well have wanted to see his friend and ally Milne installed
there as senior incumbent before the arrival of some unknown
missionary sent out fresh from England. Accordingly, Milne and
his wife with their young daughter began rapid preparations to
leave from Macao in early March 1815. Even so, they missed the
the first suitable ship and had to wait over a month for the next
opportunity of sailing in April. Then, after five days at sea, in a
vessel without a medical doctor, Mrs Milne gave birth prematurely
to twin boys. A month later, on 21 May, the Milne family,
accompanied by Milne's tutor-assistant and a Chinese printer,
arrived at Malacca.[7]

The inhabitants of Malacca, amongst whom Milne had now
come to work as a Christian missionary, had long been charac-
terized by an ethnic diversity that was fully reflected in a corres-
ponding variety of religious beliefs. Islamic mosques, Confucian,
Buddhist and Hindu temples, Christian churches—all had their
faithful supporters. The indigenous Malays, mostly fishermen and
smaller farmers living on the outskirts of the town and in rural
villages, were Mohammedans. As a people they had absorbed
Islamic beliefs and practices through cultural and commercial
contacts with Sumatra and India from the fourteenth century
onwards. In that process, and in the further dissemination of Islam
throughout the Indonesian islands, Malacca had been a major
influence during the century or so before its sultanate fell to the
Portuguese in 1511. The memory of the sultanate and its past glory

had survived in Malay literature and oral tradition, but the Malacca Malays in general had long become reduced to a subordinate position in a multiracial community since governed by successive Portuguese, Dutch and English colonial administrations which were always closely associated with local Chinese and Indian commercial enterprise.

Of the Malacca Chinese—merchants and contractors, shopkeepers and petty traders—most had preserved almost unchanged the complex set of Confucian-Buddhist socio-religious beliefs and practices brought with them by their forefathers from China; some, a mere handful, might be Moslems or Christians. Among the Indians—merchants, shopkeepers, junior officials and clerks in the administration—whether a man was a Hindu, a Moslem, a Buddhist or a Christian usually depended on his place of origin (or that of his forebears) in the Indian subcontinent itself.

The main body of the small Christian community at Malacca was composed of Portuguese and Dutch Eurasians (the latter group including some fairly well-to-do merchants and property owners), and official members of the civil and military branches of the East India Company's administration. The Portuguese Eurasians were Roman Catholics, the Dutch Eurasians belonged to the Dutch Reformed Church, and the Company officials might be members of the Church of England or Nonconformists of some kind. Christianity in Malacca, though prominent in regard to the number and position of its church buildings, was the religion of a small minority associated with European rule, past and present.

Milne came to this mixed community prepared to undertake a well-defined range of activities that included preaching, teaching, language study and translation, printing and publishing. He threw himself into these various tasks without delay.

The basic task of an evangelist was of course to spread the Gospel by preaching and by distributing the holy scriptures. Besides preaching a Sunday sermon in the Dutch church before a small Protestant congregation, Milne in these early days at

Malacca would take up a stand in the streets of the town several
times a week, addressing all who passed by in Cantonese, Mandarin
or English—or in a mixture of all three—and distributing copies of
the New Testament and other religious works in Chinese until a
curious crowd collected. Or sometimes he would go from house to
house, from shop to shop, or among the sailing boats and junks
offshore, talking to the Chinese and handing out testaments and
tracts. On their part the Chinese, as Milne himself observed, were
remarkably tolerant and patient towards this strange figure among
them. Milne's description of his weekly visit to the main Chinese
temple in Malacca[8] illustrates the point. 'I sit down before the
altar, preach the Gospel, and condemn idolatry in the presence of
the idol and its votaries', he wrote. 'Sometimes, on great days,
I am obliged to sit before pots of smoking incense, cups of tea, and
burning candles of an immense size, placed on the altar in honour
of the deity whose worship it is my aim to overthrow.' On a visit
to Penang in 1816 Milne recorded in his diary: 'Went to the
temple of the goddess Kwan-Yin, whither a great number of
Chinese followed. I stood up on the altar, addressed them, and
gave away many tracts.'[9]

In the field of education Milne made a modest beginning at
Malacca by opening a boys' school in a small building in the
grounds of his residence on 5 August 1815. It was a free school in
which a Chinese master taught reading, writing and arithmetic
through the medium of Hokkien, the dialect of the majority of
Malacca's Chinese. The following year a similar school for
Cantonese-speaking pupils was opened, and by the middle of 1816
the total enrolment in the two schools had risen to about eighty.[10]

Milne soon began to encounter some of the complex educational
problems inevitably associated with a plural society such as that
of Malacca. Besides the obvious problem presented by a variety
of languages and dialects, there were the more subtle difficulties
related to patterns of social behaviour within the different ethnic
communities. Because up to this time few women emigrated from

China, overseas Chinese males living in Southeast Asia customarily married the women of the country, whether Burmese, Thai, Vietnamese, Indonesian, Filipino or Malay. In Malacca such intermarriage had resulted in the gradual emergence of a community of mixed Chinese and Malay blood, the so-called Babas, who possessed a distinct identity of their own, regarding themselves as Chinese and retaining the essentials of the Chinese social and cultural tradition while partly adapting to Malay style of dress and speech habits. Thus the first language spoken by Chinese boys who came to Milne's school would be a Malay patois; yet they would not have learned to read in Malay, for such reading as they had been taught at home would have been in Chinese.[11]

While making an early start in education, Milne was at the same time preparing the ground for a programme of printing and publishing. He had brought a Cantonese printer, Leang Ah Fah, with him to Malacca, and on 5 August 1815—the same day that the new school opened—they produced the first number of a monthly publication, *The Chinese Magazine*. Designed 'to combine the diffusion of general knowledge with that of Christianity', it contained articles and essays in Chinese, many written by Milne himself, 'chiefly of a religious and moral kind, although interspersed with a few simple essays on astronomy, instructive anecdotes, etc.' Five hundred copies were printed monthly during the first three years of publication and circulated free of charge 'through all the Chinese settlements of the Eastern Archipelago, also in Siam, Cochin-China, and part of China itself'. Here Milne's earlier comment aptly applied: 'Malacca is a small place, of importance not so much for its own sake as for the opportunities it affords of communicating with other places.'[12]

All during this first year at Malacca Milne was also busily engaged in language study and translation. He was preparing a joint translation of the Old Testament into Chinese in co-operation with Morrison. Before the end of 1815 he had completed an English translation of a Chinese classic, the K'ang Hsi emperor's

The Sacred edict,[13] which he dedicated to Stamford Raffles. 'The days are spent in study of the language, translating and composing, correcting and revising', Milne wrote. Some time was reserved each day for study of the Malay written language, but Milne admitted: 'Every moment taken from the Chinese I seem to grudge.'[14]

Although, with the long-term objective of China in view, the work of the Malacca mission was to be directed primarily to the Chinese, the intention from the start was that efforts should also be made to engage the interest of the Malays and to publish in the Malay language. However this branch of the mission's activities only began to come alive with the arrival of Claudius Henry Thomsen in September 1815. Originally from Holstein in Lower Saxony, Thomsen seems to have been selected by the London Missionary Society specially for work among the Malays. At any rate on arrival at Malacca he concentrated on the study of the Malay language under the tuition of a prominent local teacher and writer, Abdullah bin Abdul Kadir, who was Milne's Malay tutor as well. Thomsen opened a school for Malay children in 1816. Later in that year, however, he and his wife became so ill that they departed in September on sick leave, first to Java and then back to England. Mrs Thomsen died at sea on the way home, but Thomsen eventually recovered and was back at Malacca by the end of 1817.[15]

Thomsen's absence meant that the Malay school was closed for over fifteen months and the mission's newly-started Malay programme had suffered a setback. But Milne, though left on his own again, managed to keep up his admittedly secondary interest in the Malay language and his tutorial sessions with the 'munshi' Abdullah.[16] On this side of his work Milne had some interesting comments to make:

'I have been paying some attention to the Malay language. . . . I begin to read Malay books with some degree of pleasure, and by the help of a native

assistant with tolerable facility. I also write a little. I think the Malay a fine language. . . . It has, however, no fixed standard of orthography, even common connective particles are sometimes spelled in three or four different ways. I have been at some pains and expense to obtain Malay books, which must, as you already know, be all transcribed; this is a very tedious and expensive process, but there is no alternative. Mr. Thomsen's Malay books were all obtained in this way. Those I am collecting will be fixed as the property of the Mission Library. I am fully persuaded that nothing can be done to purpose without native books. . . . *No method can be more detrimental to a missionary's object than that of making himself completely dependent on European helps. . . . But I seem to grudge every moment that is not devoted to the* Chinese.'[17]

CHAPTER FOUR

Planning a College

WITH Milne's various activities going so well the Malacca mission had made a promising start, but it still lacked something that was essential for further growth and development; it needed a focal point, a physical base. To remedy this, Milne decided to visit Penang in January 1816 to petition the presidency government there for a grant of land at Malacca. Following exploratory discussions with the Governor, the Hon. William Petrie, over breakfast on Penang Hill, Milne presented his petition on 19 January and a week later received an official reply. The Penang government, it stated, could not make an outright grant of land at Malacca in view of the expected restoration of that settlement to the Dutch, but it would allot the Malacca mission a piece of waste ground there under a conditional grant to be confirmed later by the new Dutch administration. Permission was granted meanwhile for the establishment of a mission printing-press.[1]

Back in Malacca in early February, Milne found that the only waste ground in fact available under government grant was situated some distance from the town, at St John's Hill. However, a little over a month later he had effected an exchange of a plot of land obtained there for a smaller though much more convenient property belonging to a local South Indian merchant, Tamby Ahmad Sahib, situated on the seafront just outside the western, or

Tranquerah,[2] gate of the town. An old building on the property was made ready to provide a mission house with living quarters for Milne and Thomsen and their families, who moved out from the town to the new premises in August 1816. That summer they built a stone wall across the seafront and began the construction of a range of outbuildings along one side of the property, to contain a printing house, paper store and printers' quarters, which was completed in January 1817. A similar range of outbuildings, parallel to the first, was completed along the other side of the premises in June of the same year, thus providing in effect two printing houses, Chinese and Malay, with auxiliary storage and living space for each.[3]

With land of its own, the mission could now hope to grow and to develop into a regional headquarters with an active printing press, a library, a language school—and ultimately a training college. In particular, the new land and buildings made expansion possible on the Chinese printing and publishing side, a major priority.

The first edition of Morrison's *New Testament* in Chinese was now exhausted; a second edition seemed definitely called for, and a grant of £1000 towards printing was obtained from the British and Foreign Bible Society in 1816. The first edition had been an expensive undertaking, printed in large octavo size—'in conformity with the most respectable editions of the *Sze-choo*[4] and other Chinese classical books', as Milne explained; and so the second edition was planned in a smaller duodecimo format. It was decided to have the printing done at Malacca, and in the spring of 1817 Morrison sent down from Canton six printers, a large quantity of metal type, and sufficient paper for a printing of about ten thousand copies—all of which Milne installed in the second range of outbuildings then nearing completion.[5]

The first row of new outbuildings to be constructed on the mission site was already occupied by English and Malay presses. Morrison had requested the London Missionary Society several times from November 1815 onwards to send out a master printer (not necessarily a missionary) as well as a press to Milne at Malacca. At the same time, not being too hopeful of the Society's willingness or ability to respond, he had advised Milne to see if he could secure a press from India. Milne did so and obtained early results: printers, a press, and founts of English and Arabic (for Malay) type arrived from Bengal in November 1816. Milne had asked for two printers and they sent him six. Then a month later the London Society informed Morrison that in response to his earlier request they were now sending a printer and a press to Malacca.[6]

Milne had to cope with this onrush of printers and presses on his own, for Thomsen was still absent on sick leave. In desperation he put the printers from Bengal to work on new editions of English theological works such as 'Bogue's *Essay on the New Testament* and Doddridge's *Rise and progress of religion in the soul*'.[7] But before long he had them also working on a new project of his own, a quarterly periodical in English, *The Indo-Chinese Gleaner,* which first appeared in May 1817. This journal was designed to contain accounts of mission activities, 'general intelligence, and miscellanea'. Milne was both editor and main contributor. Announcing the first number, he wrote in his finest style: 'Important questions may be discussed; useful essays will now and then appear. . . . Periodical publications are calculated to excite the mind to profitable reflections. In the intellectual wastes which missionaries generally inhabit, thought rusts, mental energy languishes, and sentiment, destitute of the necessary support, degenerates . . .; but if a publication combines religion and philosophy, literature and history, there is something to inform the understanding. . . .' However, *The Gleaner* never paid its way, though it was later described as an 'excellent publication' which had 'gained considerable celebrity among the *literati* of Europe'. Morrison wrote in support of the new journal that 'some such religious and moral publication is much wanted in these countries—let us make a trial'; and then, always quick to discern the matter of principle involved, he added: 'Our Society will, I am persuaded, in its usual liberal manner, grant full liberty of the press and freedom of opinion.'[8]

The new man sent out from London by the Missionary Society to superintend the printing presses arrived at Malacca in June 1817, bringing with him a new fount of English type. He was Walter Henry Medhurst, described as a young man 'of wiry frame, good health, and unfailing cheerfulness'. Born in 1796, Medhurst had received a classical education at St Paul's School and theological training at Hackney College, London, where he displayed 'an unceasing activity of mind and a remarkable gift for languages'. Becoming attracted to the art of printing, he had developed sufficient skill in that direction to impress the Missionary Society most favourably when he offered his services in 1816 at the age of twenty. 'A very superior youth', they reported; 'he can not only print well, but has a taste for languages and an ability to attain them with ease'; and to Morrison they announced with enthusiasm the appointment of this 'very ingenious young man' to the mission at Malacca.[9]

Milne was both delighted and relieved at Medhurst's arrival. There was now a regular mission staff of about twenty persons whose work needed to be organized and supervised—printers, translators, language assistants, teachers in the junior schools outside—and Milne had been in sole charge since Thomsen's departure on sick leave nine months before. Milne himself had been far from well, his illness 'occasioned it is supposed by a chronic liver complaint'; yet in addition to the duties of general planning and supervision he had kept up work on his own numerous tasks—writing and editing, language study and translation. He had hoped to go to Canton for a change of climate during the winter months of 1816–17—'have felt for some days past a very earnest wish to visit China', he wrote in his diary in August 1816—but Thomsen's departure had made that impossible. Now with Medhurst's arrival Milne felt justified in going on leave. His

wife, recovering from the loss of an infant daughter in April and
seriously ill with fever, sailed with the children for China on 1 July
1817 and he himself followed on 9 August, leaving the general
charge of the mission as well as the supervision of printing and the
schools to 'a young beginner', as Medhurst ruefully described
himself.[10]

'Milne is very poorly', remarked Morrison after meeting his
friend who arrived at Macao on 3 September. Morrison himself
had been going through a period of restless discontent which had
caused his thoughts to turn again to the idea of quitting Canton
and going to join the mission at Malacca. His visit to Peking in
August 1816 as Chinese secretary to the British embassy led by
Lord Amherst—an irresistible opportunity for seeing inside China
—the embassy's subsequent dismissal by the Emperor, and then the
long overland winter journey back to Canton, had left Morrison
dejected and self-critical.[11] From the start he had been torn by
doubts about the wisdom of joining a diplomatic mission to the
court of Peking, as he wrote to the secretary of the Missionary
Society: 'We expect an Embassy here; I feel great reluctance to
have anything to do with it—*(keep this inviolably secret)*'. Then
after his return from Peking to Canton in January 1817 Morrison
had resorted to self-mockery in describing his experience to the
same correspondent:

*'I dare say you do not often laugh; but I think that if you did not laugh
heartily you would at least have smiled to see me in my scarlet coat and cocked
hat, and a court dress sword by my side. This aberration from my proper
pursuits made me rather sigh than laugh; and I had pretty nearly determined
to leave this place on my arrival from the north. However I see the opinion
entertained by you is that I had better remain here. . . . You will suppose of
course that I was going to Malacca.'*[12]

A month later, still unsettled and uncertain, Morrison wrote
again from Canton: 'I wish to go to Malacca to aid the mission

there, at the same time that I pursue the Dictionary and my translations. . . . After ten years of anxiety here I wish to retire to a place of some quiet, where I may pursue my object openly. This is a tiresome place; a place, as far as religious society is concerned, truly solitary. . . . If I am obliged to go away I will endeavour to go to Malacca.'[13]

But the arrival of Milne later in that year, ill though he was, gave new life and confidence to Morrison. He had just completed a *Retrospect of the first ten years of the Protestant mission to China* which 'Mr. Milne will probably enlarge and print at Malacca'. Now together in Canton again, the two could look to the years ahead and discuss their plans and ideas in detail. Their joint programme of Old Testament translation was going well. Milne had completed the books of Deuteronomy and Joshua—'the translation is good and perspicuous', was Morrison's verdict—and while on leave in Canton he planned to finish his work on Judges, as well as writing 'an Exposition of the Lord's Prayer and a tract on the Folly of Idolatry'.[14]

Discussing the work in hand and future projects together during September and October 1817, the two friends decided that the time had now come to place their joint operations in Canton and Malacca on a more formal basis. Constituting themselves as the 'provisional committee of the Ultra-Ganges Missions', they first drew up a series of resolutions which they completed and signed at Canton on 2 November. These resolutions provided the rationale for the founding of the mission base at Malacca, placing it on record that it had been 'originally formed with an especial view to China, and as the best substitute for an actual residence in that country.'[15]

They then turned to the project which had been forming in Morrison's mind for a number of years, the idea of a college at Malacca for further education and training of both Chinese and European missionaries. By this time his original ideas on the subject had expanded to the point of envisaging an institution with

a rather broader purpose and wider appeal. His association with
the East India Company and his consequent semi-independent
status as a missionary—as scholar, too, rather than as preacher—
may have inclined him towards the broader concept of a college
of education, something perhaps on the lines of the English
'Dissenting Academy', that would be linked with, but not tied to,
the aims of a missionary centre. By the beginning of 1815 the
institution had taken shape in his mind as 'a Chinese College'; and
by October of that year he had clarified his ideas on the subject so
far as to draw up a statement of his proposals, addressed to a wide
public—'the benevolent Christians of Great Britain and Ireland'—,
for 'establishing by voluntary subscription an English and Chinese
College at Malacca in the East Indies'. The aims of the proposed
College were here stated in educational rather than missionary
terms. The immediate object would be 'to facilitate an amicable
literary intercourse between England and the nations in which the
Chinese written language is employed'. The ultimate object would
be to accomplish 'the hope that, under the blessing of Divine
Providence, the light of Science and of Revelation will, by means
of this Institution, peacefully and gradually shed their lustre on the
eastern limits of Asia and the islands of the rising sun.' On the
teaching staff of this institution—one which today might have
been described as an East-West Centre—there would be, to start
with, a European professor of English and Chinese, and two
assistant professors (one Chinese and one European); while provision would be made for six Chinese and six European students.[16]

The initial public response to Morrison's appeal for subscriptions cannot have been very encouraging, and the whole idea
seems to have lain dormant for a time until Milne's visit to Canton
in the winter months of 1817–18 now brought it back to life. Thus
on 2 January 1818 the two colleagues drew up 'additional resolutions' which dealt specifically with the college project. As a
provisional committee they would allocate a plot of land on the

mission premises at Malacca as the site for an 'Anglo-Chinese College'; and to get the scheme going Morrison would anonymously donate the sum of £1000 towards the cost of building, with a promise of £100 a year for five years towards recurrent costs. With Morrison's money and the mission's land, they could at least make a start.[17]

But both realized well enough—Morrison especially so—that tact would be called for in their dealings with the Missionary Society whose land they were thus proposing to earmark for their own special purposes. Morrison was therefore most careful to underline the missionary training aspects of the proposed institution while playing down its more secular character. 'I beg that you will (if you approve it) advocate the establishment of a College (or any other name that you may prefer) at Malacca, to train up persons for the diffusion of the Gospel by itinerating and preaching', he wrote to the secretary of the Society. And soon afterwards, putting the proposal to the directors, he wrote: 'We are about to erect a building at Malacca on the Society's premises, to be called the Anglo-Chinese College, for the purpose of teaching English and the principles of the Christian religion to Chinese youth, and particularly for the purpose of instructing missionaries and others in the language and literature of China.' This was immediately followed up by a letter explaining the details of the proposed arrangements, concluding with an appeal to the directors: 'Let me beseech you to deal kindly with the infant seminary, the Anglo-Chinese College. Its ultimate end . . . is the reign of Christ upon earth. Literature is the means, not the end.'[18]

But it would be some time before Morrison could know the reaction of the London Society to the whole idea. And meanwhile the plan had one serious weakness: Milne's health. A doctor in Canton feared that Milne could not survive much longer: 'Appearances are against him; his lungs are weak and he is greatly emaciated. Extreme weakness greatly impedes his labours; he is

quite unable to speak for any length of time.' 'If he be called away',
Morrison wrote despairingly, 'I know not what will become of the
Malacca branch of the Chinese mission. Where is there a
successor?'[19]

But William Milne was to battle on bravely for some years
longer.

CHAPTER FIVE

The Foundation

THE Milnes, 'somewhat improved in health' by their visit to Macao and Canton in the cool season, were safely back in Malacca soon after the middle of February 1818. The young Walter Medhurst, anxious to get on with his Hokkien language study, gladly handed over charge of the mission to Milne, though the responsibility of running it had already been greatly eased for him by the return of C. H. Thomsen at the end of the previous December.

Thomsen's return did something to restore a balance between the Chinese and Malay sides of the mission's activities at Malacca. He himself felt personally involved in the maintenance of such a balance, asserting that work among the Malays was 'a very essential part' of the mission's function. He soon reopened the Malay-English school originally started in 1816 and organized a new school for Malabari Indian children as well. He was busy too preparing material for publication in the Malay language. Two of his Malay tracts had been printed during his absence in 1817; others now followed (including one on 'Human Depravity'), and also a Malay spelling book (1818), described by Milne as 'the first Malay work of the kind we have heard of in the native character either by foreigners or Malays'.[1]

The need for a Chinese-Malay balance seems to have been kept in mind by the London Society itself in planning its operations

in the Malaysian region at this time. 'The missionary station at
Malacca is certainly a very important one; we shall strengthen it
from time to time', the Society's secretary assured Morrison in
December 1816; and the directors were able to announce in
November 1817 that they were sending out four new missionaries
to Malacca, some for eventual posting to other centres in the region
such as Penang. One of these, John Slater, came out towards the
end of 1817 to work on the Chinese side of the mission. He and
Medhurst between them had three Chinese schools in Malacca
under their supervision by the middle of 1818. Eventually, after a
brief spell in Canton for his health and for further language study,
Slater left Malacca in April 1819 to start a Chinese mission at
Batavia in Java, visiting en route the Chinese communities of
Singapore (newly founded as a settlement by Stamford Raffles at
the end of January 1819), the Riau-Lingga island group south of
Singapore, and the West Borneo river ports of Sambas and
Pontianak. Three more new arrivals to join the mission at Malacca
in September 1818 were Samuel Milton and John Ince on the
Chinese side, and Thomas Beighton for the Malay side. After
further language study all three moved on to other stations: Milton
to Singapore, Ince and Beighton to Penang. Thus the project of
a mission centre in Penang, originally intended as Morrison's first
assignment in 1806, was finally realized by 1819.[2]

To Morrison the Malacca mission was always primarily one
for the Chinese, essentially a launching site for the great eventual
mission to China itself. 'I incline to the greater part of the missionaries attending to Chinese; the field is vast—two or three people
are lost in attempting to cultivate it', he declared as he sent
additional language tutors from Canton to instruct the new
arrivals at Malacca. 'Our last ten years have been spent in
acquiring just notions of this people—of their language, history,
opinions, and so on', he wrote. 'We are perhaps nearly on a par
with the Romish missionaries as to knowledge of the Chinese, but
we are not at all equal to them in respect of agents. . . .' Therefore,

Morrison concluded, 'We must use every means to raise up *native missionaries*. Some great change must take place amongst these nations before European missionaries can have free access to them to preach the Gospel. I therefore beg to press again on your attention the *Anglo-Chinese College*.'[3]

Preparations for starting the College were going ahead meanwhile at Malacca. The *Indo-Chinese Gleaner* formally announced the scheme in its issue of February 1818. 'A friend of Christianity and of literature' (Morrison, of course) had donated a sum of money for setting up a college which was intended to serve 'the purpose of cultivating Chinese literature, general history, sacred criticism, Christian theology, etc., with a final view to the spread of Christianity in these parts, and to the promotion of general literature'. 'To native students the English language and other important branches of European literature will be taught,' the announcement continued. 'Though the building can hardly be expected to be ready for more than a year to come, yet an application in behalf of any pious young man, whether born in India of European parents, or a native Chinese, or a European, well recommended, will meet with due attention. . . .'[4]

For the moment, however, any arrangements for starting a college at Malacca could be no more than strictly provisional in view of the forthcoming postwar restoration of the town to the Dutch. Indeed the publication of the scheme and the preparations announced in *The Gleaner* anticipated not only the approval and support of the Missionary Society in London, but also the incoming Dutch government's approval of the Malacca mission itself as well as its confirmation of the tenure of the mission premises. However, with the long-awaited arrival of the Dutch commissioners appointed to accept the formal postwar transfer of Malacca in September 1818, it became at last possible to raise such questions as these for decision. Major Farquhar, the British Resident of Malacca, sent a written request to the Dutch commissioners on 16 September that they would 'favour and protect the Rev. Mr.

Milne of the Chinese Protestant Mission, and . . . confirm the
conditional grant of land made to it by the British government'.
Milne himself followed this up after the formal transfer of Malacca
on 21 September with a detailed statement of the history, aims and
activities of the mission, explaining that it was intended 'to diffuse
science, morals and religion through the Chinese dominions and
those islands and countries which lie between the island of Penang
and China'. Milne also outlined the plans for the Anglo-Chinese
College and the programme of the mission press, already 'printing
the Old Testament in Chinese and part of the Gospels in Malay'.[5]

A favourable response was given to these approaches by the
Dutch authorities, and preparations were soon in hand for the
ceremony of laying the foundation stone of the new college. In
readiness for the ceremony and to mark the occasion, a three-page
prospectus entitled *General plan of the Anglo-Chinese College forming
at Malacca* was prepared and printed for general distribution. This
informative document, dated October 1818, contained a detailed
statement of the objects of the whole scheme and of the systems of
administration, staffing and instruction proposed for the College.
It reflected the educational views of the two partners in the project
with regard to the particular social and cultural environment in
which they would be operating. It represented their estimate of
what would be required, in terms of both general educational
background and specific training and skills, in order to produce
out of the human material and the practical facilities available the
kind of end result they hoped to obtain: a corps of Chinese Christian
missionaries to the Chinese people. Most importantly, it also
revealed—and put in question too—some of their views and
assumptions concerning basic issues involved in the whole plan,
such questions as, for example, the relationship between missions
and education, or that between religion and culture.

The whole tone of the *General plan* suggested the broad aim of
an essentially liberal, secular institution. The first section of the
plan explained that the designation 'College' was considered to be

more appropriate than any other possible term such as academy or school. The second section announced the twin objects of the institution as 'the reciprocal cultivation of Chinese and European literature, and the diffusion of Christianity'—in that order. 'On the one hand', it continued, elaborating on the first aim, 'the Chinese language and literature will be made accessible to Europeans; and on the other hand, the English language with European literature and science will be made accessible to the Ultra-Ganges nations who read Chinese. These nations are: China, Cochin-china, the Chinese colonies in the Eastern Archipelago, Loo-choo, Corea, and Japan.' The second aim was then summarily described in terms that seemed almost to suggest no more than a remote possibility: 'It is hoped that this course of proceeding will finally have a favourable influence on the peaceable diffusion of Christian principles, and the general civilization of the eastern hemisphere.'

The next section of the *Plan* dealt with the facilities which it was proposed to offer. There would be 'an extensive Chinese Library', and a collection of European books relating to the language, history, manners, etc., of the Eastern countries mentioned. The staff would consist of 'European tutors of the Chinese language, capable also of teaching European learning', and 'native Chinese teachers'. A limited amount of student accommodation would be provided, though students would be free to 'lodge in the town, as is the case in Europe', and there would be a fund to assist poor students. The Chinese language would be taught to European students for whatever purpose they chose to apply it to, whether 'to religion, to literature, or to commerce'. Chinese students would be taught the English language, geography, history, arithmetic, 'and such other branches of learning or science as time may afford, together with moral philosophy, Christian theology, and Malay.' Finally, there would be English and Chinese printing presses.

The fourth section enumerated three broad categories of student that the College might admit. Firstly, persons of any

European nation or of the American continent, and belonging to any Christian communion, who were suitably recommended. Secondly, persons from European universities on travelling fellowships, Christian missionaries, and members of commercial companies or national consulates. And thirdly, 'native youths' of any of the Asian countries mentioned, whether self-supporting or sponsored by Christian societies or by private individuals; such students would not be required to profess the Christian religion or to attend Christian worship. Other sections dealt with the minutiae of the College organization and management. Finally, it was announced, any subscription from two dollars upwards would be thankfully received 'by the Rev. W. Milne, Malacca, or by the Rev. Dr. Morrison, China'.[6]

Morrison enclosed a copy of this *General plan* in a letter to the London Society's treasurer, W. A. Hankey, dated 28 October 1818. He wrote:

> '*I now send you a Plan of the Anglo-Chinese College; I will thank you to lay the plan before the Missionary Society, and advise such measures as appear to you right. I should be glad of your hearty concurrence and that you will be pleased to make it known to benevolent men in London or any other part of the British Empire. . . .*
>
> *The Missionary Society must furnish our European professors of Chinese. I hope they will see this to be perfectly in the way of their duty. . . .*
>
> *P.S.   I trust that the Missionary Society's not appearing in the Plan will be no objection. It wishes to do the good, let who will take the honour.*'[7]

Whatever the Missionary Society might think of it all, everything was now prepared at Malacca for the formal foundation ceremony. On 11 November 1818 the foundation stone of the Anglo-Chinese College was laid by the former English Resident and Commandant of Malacca, Major William Farquhar, in the presence of the new Dutch Governor, the Commandant of the Dutch troops, and the leading inhabitants. Only one name, that of Morrison, appeared in the Latin inscription on the plate attached to the stone, which read: 'Collegium Anglo-Sinicum, sub auspicio et impensa Roberti Morrison S.T.D. fundatoris, 1818'.[8]

Milne made an interesting speech at the foundation ceremony in which he stressed that the fundamental aim of the new institution would be to gain a greater knowledge and understanding of China.

'China, viewed as an object of literary and philosophical speculation, has scarcely been touched by Protestant countries,' he declared. 'There is scarcely any foreign country of more importance for the British nation to investigate than China. The proximity of British territory to that of China, and the very important commercial relations which subsist between the two countries, certainly make it a point of high political consideration to understand fully Chinese laws, opinions, and manners; and that can only be done effectually by a knowledge of the language. . . . This consideration gives the present humble Institution a peculiar claim on the support of the British nation.'

But if cultural, commercial and political considerations all seemed to point especially to the need for the study of China and her people, the countries of Southeast Asia were also important enough to be included in the scope of the College's interests:

'The other countries and languages of Ultra-Ganges India are also very important. The laws, manners, literature and religion of these countries likewise furnish ample subjects for investigation. The Malay language has indeed been long cultivated by the Dutch, and of late by the English; and several very interesting and useful books have been printed with a view to its illustration. But even here, there is still much to be done. The languages of the interior of Sumatra, of the Javanese, of the inhabitants of Borneo and the Celebes, of the Philippine Islands, of Japan, of Cambodia and Siam, are all (with the exception of some imperfect ideas of the Japanese given in Kaempfer's excellent History of Japan, *and* Thunberg's Travels) *untouched by Protestant nations, or in great measure so.'*[9]

But, for all that, the study of China would have first priority.
'It is intended in this Institution to unite the study of the languages
and history of these countries with those of China in so far as may
be practicable. But our settlement at Malacca . . . was intended
for China, and as a kind of substitute for a residence on the border
of that country, which we would have preferred had it been
attainable.' Therefore objects connected with China will hold a
chief place in the Seminary now proposed.'[10]

Milne had rightly taken advantage of the occasion to state the
academic case—with due regard to the higher practicalities
involved—for setting up what might have been termed a School
of East Asian Studies. To his hearers the whole idea must have
sounded eminently reasonable and enlightened. But the scheme
inevitably raised a number of questions that lay beyond the scope
of the immediate occasion. It raised one question in particular—
where did the London Missionary Society come in? The Society
had been informed some time ago of the College plan but so far
there had been no consultation, no two-way discussion. It was on
the Society's land, originally obtained through Milne in 1816, that
the College was to be built. Further, the Society was now being
instructed by Morrison, rather curtly it seemed, where exactly its
duty lay: it 'must furnish our European professors of Chinese'. Yet
it had not received even a passing mention in the published
College *Plan*, nor, it appeared, in Milne's speech at the foundation
ceremony. No reference had been made to it in the inscription on
the foundation stone standing on its land. The Society was being
treated in effect as an anonymous sponsor. It would have to be
satisfied, seemingly, with the cold comfort of Morrison's bland
assurance: 'It wishes to do the good, let who will take the honour.'

CHAPTER SIX

College and Mission

FOR the directors of the London Missionary Society the general tone of the Malacca College plan, the method of its presentation, and the style of the foundation ceremony all combined to raise major issues amounting to serious matters of principle. How far and at what levels should a missionary society become involved in education? To what extent did fundamental missionary aims require the support of educational systems and methods? It might be argued that involvement by a missionary society in educational activities of some kind and to some degree was inevitable, but where should the line be drawn? What should the cut-off point be, from the viewpoint of essentially missionary interests, between elementary education in the vernacular and, say, higher education in English? At what stage did the aims and methods of the educational process cease to be central and begin to become peripheral to basic missionary objectives? Clearly these were difficult questions which would not admit of simple or uniform answers. Much would have to depend on the circumstances of each case. But generally the view taken by the London Society was the practical one that within the limited resources available its interests should normally be restricted to the lower rungs of the educational ladder, to elementary and junior schools in which the rudiments of general education and Christian teaching would be offered in combination. If education at higher levels were to be undertaken at all, it should probably be envisaged in the form of the theological seminary offering quite specialized training for a missionary vocation rather than as a college of the liberal arts.

In this particular instance the central problem for the Missionary Society on the one hand, and for Morrison and Milne on the other, was how to establish and if necessary define the relationship between the Malacca mission and the College. A first clear warning of the problem's approach had been received by the directors of the Society in a letter written by Milne soon after his Canton discussions with Morrison in January 1818. The proposed Anglo-Chinese College at Malacca, Milne informed the directors somewhat tartly, was 'not to be considered as a mission-house; that, being of a more general nature, the Society must furnish. . . . It is to be considered a house devoted to the sole purposes of affording accommodation and instruction to those who study the Chinese language with a view to propagate the Gospel or to advance the interests of general literature.' 'Missionary objects', Milne went on severely, 'hold a very prominent, but not an exclusive, place in the plan of the founder. It is his wish that these particulars be distinctly understood, and that the College be not confounded with a mission-house, which is more comprehensive in its meaning. . . . I hope you will take the earliest opportunity of furnishing the College with proper students; missionaries will always have the preference.'[1]

The reaction of the Society's secretary to Milne's letter was that of the cautious administrator. 'As to the College', he wrote to his colleagues in London, 'we should inform Mr. M. we cannot be at much expense on account of it . . . I am a little afraid lest the word College should excite expectations which will not be answered, and we should avoid ostentation.' At a meeting of the Eastern Committee of the Missionary Society in London on 11 November 1818—the actual day of the foundation ceremony in Malacca—the resolutions passed by Morrison and Milne in Canton in November 1817 and January 1818, with the *General plan* of the College, and Milne's letter, were all read to the members. In the discussions that followed at that meeting and at a subsequent meeting of the full board of directors in February 1819, general concern was expressed on a number of points in the College scheme. While gratefully acknowledging 'the liberal proposals' of Morrison and Milne, approving the 'general design' of the College, and confirming the allocation of part of the mission land at Malacca for the projected building, the directors expressed concern that the new institution should be clearly given 'a decidedly paramount direction towards missionary objects'.[2]

As the plan stood, the directors considered the scope and variety of studies proposed to be needlessly wide, going well beyond strictly missionary requirements. On the other hand, they thought there was room for a much wider coverage of one very useful subject area—that of language study; and they therefore stressed the importance of enlarging the original plan, with its strong Chinese language bias, so as to make it embrace 'the study of all the languages requisite for the diffusion of the Gospel throughout the continent and islands situated eastward of Malacca'. Finally, while giving their consent to the establishment of the College— even though 'intended to embrace other subjects than such as are strictly missionary'—the directors warned against the dangers of bringing together in one and the same institution students with purely religious aims and those whose aims were primarily secular.[3]

Meanwhile Morrison in Canton, unaware of these developments, remained in the dark as regards the Society's general reaction to the whole scheme. It was well over a year since he had announced to the directors the definite intention of setting up the College at Malacca. Beginning to feel a little uneasy about the outcome, he thought it well to remind the directors, in a letter of February 1819, of his original instructions received before leaving England in January 1807. These, he pointed out, had included not only the translation of the scriptures into Chinese and the composition of a Chinese-English dictionary, but also 'the com-

munication of secular knowledge such as the Mathematics or the
English Language.' 'The last-mentioned', he explained, 'I consider
commenced by the Anglo-Chinese College at Malacca . . . I have
requested Mr. Milne to take the superintendence of the College,
and to teach in it the Chinese language, theology, Church history,
and the general history of China.' Then, a few days later, while
informing the treasurer and secretary of the London Society that
'there is now subscribed to the Anglo-Chinese College £2,422,
including my first grant to it', he added the querulous note: 'We
(Milne and I) wrote about the Anglo-Chinese College, . . . we
have received no answers.'[4]

An answer came, though not before another ten months had
passed, in a formal statement of the comments and criticisms
expressed by the directors at their meeting in February 1819, as
already described, when they had approved the scheme with some
reservations. Acknowledging their views in a letter of 21 December,
Morrison's reply was barely polite. 'I am glad you *approve generally*
of the College; you have however rather misapprehended the
nature of the foundation,' he wrote, adding the hope that the
printed report of Milne's speech at the foundation ceremony
might help them to understand it better. Then, in a scornful
reference to the directors' warning about mixing religious and
secular students together, he asked: 'If your missionaries cannot
bear contact with secular students, alas, how do you think they
will do to be sent into the wide world, surrounded by vicious
heathens and profligate Europeans and spiritual enemies, and in
exile from Christian society?'[5]

If only by implication so far, Morrison seemed to be challenging
the right of the Society to anything more than a formal jurisdiction
over the College and its educational policy, once the allocation of
land for the building had been agreed. His letter to the treasurer,
written a day later, left no room for doubt about his attitude.
'In as much as the College subscriptions thus far have been made
by persons who would not have subscribed to the Missionary

Society, its affairs cannot be put under the *exclusive* direction of that body. The Missionary Society is *invited* to *a large share* in the direction, for its success will depend much on their being its friends and patrons; and I hope this will appear all that reason and justice can demand.' So much for the management of the College; as for its character, Morrison went on: 'The subscriptions we have received here have been made to the object in a more enlarged view than your letter of last season seems to take.' Then, turning to the general principle involved, Morrison put forward a point of view that would become increasingly familiar not only to the directors of the London Missionary Society but also to the officials of the British Colonial Office during the course of the nineteenth century—the doctrine of the superior wisdom of 'the man on the spot'. 'You are in a place like that of a home government which must take the advice and opinion of colonial legislatures', Morrison wrote, and he continued with a certain note of condescension: 'It is difficult, if indeed possible, to form accurate views of circumstances in which we have never been placed, and which differ considerably from our usual experience.' Therefore, he concluded, the Society should 'attend much to the representations of their most experienced missionaries, and *invite* their opinions'.[6]

There the matter rested for the time being as far as Morrison was concerned, but the whole question was revived for him when he received a copy of the report of the Missionary Society's annual general meeting held in May 1819, at which the directors announced their 'cordial approbation' of the Malacca College plan, with the reservations already expressed to the effect that its general studies ought to be narrower in scope while its language training should be less exclusively Chinese. 'I regret that the Anglo-Chinese College does not meet with the unanimous and complete approbation from the Directors of our Society', wrote Morrison again in November 1820. Defending the strong Chinese bias in the curriculum, he went on: 'As to my making it more general, I still think it would not have been proper. China as an object of

Christian benevolence is important enough in itself for many
missionaries and many students, and the language and literature
of China constitute a large field of labour. Other fields adjoining
are open for other labourers to enter, and the preparatory schools
may be placed side by side. I would that they were numerous
enough to form an Asiatic University.' 'As to the Institution's
becoming a secular one, I see no fear of that', he went on.[7] Then,
turning to the attack, Morrison complained that 'no *actual*
donations nor subscriptions have occurred in the United Kingdom;
we want not large funds, but something more than verbal approbation would have encouraged more those concerned.' 'I am truly
astonished', he continued, 'at the suspicion and dislike with which
the Institution has been viewed. I hoped it did not, at this day,
require arguments to shew its utility. The Christians in England
have not yet done anything for it. My efforts in respect of the
College have been viewed with a degree of suspicion and coldness
which makes me feel greatly injured and most unjustly treated. . . .
The College is not a concern opposed to the Mission, but an agent
of it; it is not a mere tool of the East India Company.'[8]

At the heart of the acrimonious discussion of the nature and
aims of the College at Malacca there lay some of the most difficult
of all the problems to be faced at that time by an organization of
such wide intercontinental scope as the London Missionary Society.
They were problems, as Morrison had shrewdly remarked, very
similar in essence to some of those experienced by a colonial
system. Probably the root problem of all, in an age of painfully
slow communications, was that of distance. The 'tyranny of
distance' was a constant factor limiting the exercise of remote
control by the central authority over its local agents overseas.[9]
Distance greatly delayed both the outward transmission of instructions and the inward submission of information and proposals, so
weakening the impact of each when at length received. Because of
distance, a certain amount of discretionary authority had to be
allowed to 'the man on the spot', whether colonial official, com-

pany merchant, or missionary, so that he could act on his own initiative in the intervals between the arrivals of mail. In that age of sailing ships—the sole method of overseas communication—it could take, for instance, between four and six months, depending on weather conditions and onward connections at the Cape and in India and the Straits, for instructions from London to reach Canton. Such conditions tended to encourage a sometimes exaggerated spirit of independence, an impatience of interference and a resentment of criticism among those serving overseas; they tended at the same time to breed among the authorities at home an attitude of excessive caution, a suspicion of the overzealous enthusiast, and a dread of the *fait accompli*.

The man on the spot was often prone to self-dramatization, more especially perhaps when he went out as an apostle to the heathen. Modesty was not usually one of his weaknesses. His feelings might veer between illusions of grandeur and a conviction of divine right on the one hand, and a sense of hopeless frustration, cruel neglect and utter loneliness on the other. Likewise, the attitude towards the individual serving overseas on the part of the heads of the administrative machine in London, often distracted by a multiplicity of problems coming at them from every direction, might range between complete lack of interest, cautious approval, and weary exasperation.

By the very nature of his calling the missionary was even more independent, more on his own, than the civil servant or the merchant overseas; and of all missionaries the evangelical was likely to be the most independent, the greatest individualist. The spirit of individualism seemed to permeate the ranks of the London Society's missionaries. And if the directors found this something of a problem in their dealings with men like Morrison, he and Milne in their turn found it something of a nuisance when it came to dealing with the young missionaries who came out to Malacca. These men of God did not easily submit to human authority. There seems to have been much dissension, jealousy and bickering among them. 'At Malacca, as is usual with all our missionaries, much to their disgrace, there are murmurings and disputings', Morrison reported. The new men who had arrived in September 1818—Thomas Beighton, John Ince and Samuel Milton—were kept severely in their place by Milne, whose attitude they considered dictatorial. Thinking they had come out as trained missionaries, they found themselves treated as language students under college discipline. They felt that Milne was holding them back in favour of the earlier arrivals, Thomsen and Medhurst. But even Thomsen was to complain of 'the consequences of Mr. Milne's taking upon himself to act alone and without the concurrence of any other member whether junior or senior'; and Medhurst later broke with Milne and left for Penang, alleging that 'he was shut out at Malacca; that in consequence of the people believing Mr. Milne was his master he was treated with contempt'. Morrison, not surprisingly, took Milne's side. 'They accuse Milne of not consulting them, but doing everything himself', he wrote. 'They have been but a few months in the place, and want to direct its affairs!'[10]

The root of the trouble, in the opinion of one of the missionaries, was that Milne was so steeped in Chinese literature that he had come to model his behaviour on the traditional family head of China. 'As to the principle on which the Mission was conducted', wrote John Slater, who had moved from Malacca to Batavia, 'I believe it to be purely Chinese, gathered from the rules and maxims of the Four Books of Confucius, which is the principle of a father and his family, where the father alone has power to act and direct.' Milne, 'so severe with himself', as Morrison put it, was equally severe with others. There seems little doubt that he was authoritarian in method, and that he 'possessed naturally a very ardent, impetuous, determined mind', as Morrison was to comment later.[11]

But the root causes of dissension in the Malacca mission lay deeper. Not only the method but the very grounds of Milne's

authority were questioned by the junior missionaries. Basically
this was due to the fact that the original ambiguity concerning the
relationship between mission and College had remained unresolved.
To Milne, the mission *was* the College; he exercised authority over
it by virtue of his position as Principal of the College. But to the
younger missionaries the College was in a sense extraneous to the
mission; it belonged to Morrison and Milne; it was Morrison's
child and Milne was its foster parent. Moreover to the younger
men the College was not strictly speaking a missionary institution
at all. Beighton and Ince, the leading critics of Milne and the
College, who moved from Malacca to Penang in 1819, reported
to the Missionary Society: 'Milne openly declares that the College
is not under the direction of the Society; he declares that the
government of the College rests with himself; one man is sole head
and master . . .; the majority of the brethren are determined to
own no one as supreme; the Directors alone we consider as having
the right to dictate.' And—a more serious charge—: 'In the
College the propagation of Christianity is the secondary object.'[12]

There spoke the radical democratic evangelist, impatient of
worldly authority, critical of much in the collegiate ethos, with
its graded hierarchy and its devotion to scholarship, as being
irrelevant to the missionary's immediate purpose—that of 'going
to the people' and propagating the Gospel among them. Morrison
appreciated such criticism, but he would not accept it. 'There
seems an impression that the College does not bear enough on
evangelical objects,' he wrote. 'Colleges have degenerated—true;
and what mode of spreading knowledge is sure not to degenerate?
Let not the good that Colleges have done in preserving and
diffusing Divine Truth be forgotten. Though our institution is not
called a Mission College, its object is no less missionary for that.'[13]

But doubts and unease concerning the function and purpose of
the College were to remain, not only in the minds of the younger
missionaries in the region but also in those of the directors and
officials of the Missionary Society at home.

CHAPTER SEVEN

The Building

CONSTRUCTION work on the College building at Malacca commenced soon after the foundation ceremony of November 1818. The site chosen by Milne for the building lay directly behind the original mission house which had been acquired with the property in 1816. The property itself was situated to the west of Malacca town, just outside the gate of Tranquerah (described in 1826 as 'the only ancient gateway of the town now standing'). It consisted of a long and fairly narrow strip of land running inland for about half a mile from a frontage of something over 200 feet on the sea coast. The front, where the original mission house stood, faced on to the coastal road that ran from Tranquerah gate out to the point of Tanjong Kling. The rear limit of the property was formed by the right bank of the Malacca river as it ran parallel to the coast before beginning to bend southward and flow into the sea. The whole property was effectively divided into two parts by a wall and ditch that ran across it about half way between front and rear. The rear part, on the river side, consisted of low swampy ground and was uncultivated. The front part contained the old mission house facing the sea, with the site for the new College building immediately behind it, and a fenced garden planted with coconut and fruit trees behind that again. Along either side of the house and garden stood the row of outbuildings, erected since the property was acquired, which provided space for the printing presses, tutors' and workers' quarters, classrooms, and storage. Across the road opposite the mission premises was a small plot of ground which formed a kind of front garden, protected from the sea by a wall built along the shore.[1]

The College building was completed by about August 1820. Described as 'a plain substantial edifice', it was a two-storied building, ninety feet in length and thirty-four in breadth, with brick walls thirty-five feet high. A wide verandah supported by pillars ran right round the upper storey, and there was a Chinese-style tiled roof. Each floor had eight rooms and a central lobby. The ground floor space was divided into classrooms, a library and a museum. The upper floor was used as living quarters for the missionary staff and their families to supplement the limited accommodation provided by the old mission house. All the materials for building were produced locally except for the floor tiling, which was imported from China. The essential parts of the woodwork were made of *merbau* wood, which was exceptionally strong, durable, and proof against the attacks of white ants; the timber had been floated down the river to Malacca from forests in the interior. The total cost of the building was given in a final statement of account dated 8 September 1820 as slightly under 7,500 Spanish dollars.[2] 'A handsome building', was the judgment of two visiting commissioners from the London Society who saw it in 1826; indeed they thought it 'the best building in Malacca'. Its situation was by general agreement 'open and airy' and 'favourable to health and study', commanding a fine view across the Malacca straits. For a time, though, the view was partly obstructed by the original mission house in front, but in 1823 Morrison ordered the old building pulled down and a row of shady trees planted in its place. Finally, a front railing along the edge of the road, with a handsome Chinese-style triple gateway—also added by Morrison in 1823—completed an impressive setting for the College building.[3]

The contents of the library on the ground floor of the building had been gradually built up since the start of the mission at Malacca. Milne had asked the Missionary Society for help in obtaining 'books in all languages', supplying them with a detailed list of 'much wanted' items in December 1815. His list, reflecting something of the public taste and the current reference literature of the time, included such publications as 'Dr. Johnson's Dictionary, Encyclopedia Britannica, General History of Philosophy, Systems of General History, Natural History, Mathematics and Chemistry, Dr. Adams' Latin Grammar, Pinkerton's and Cooke's Geography, Mr. Scott's Bible, an Atlas, and a good system of Chronology', as well as *'Memoir de la Chine,* by the Jesuits, and *Lettres édifiantes et curieuses,* by the same'.[4] Milne was particularly anxious to build up the library's Asian holdings, not only in Chinese but also in Malay and Siamese. 'A considerable number of Malay manuscripts' had been acquired by 1823. In the same year it was reported that the College library contained about 3,380 volumes, of which 2,850 were in the Chinese language and the remainder in various Asian and European languages. By that time 'Rees's Cyclopedia and the Pantologia' had been acquired. In 1824 the library was to receive a windfall of about three hundred valuable books as a gift from 'a British nobleman', Lord Kingsborough, who had been very favourably impressed by the quality of the College publication, *The Indo-Chinese Gleaner*.[5] The same benefactor also offered the sum of £1,500 to the College if it would agree to publish an edition of *Notitia Linguae Sinicae*, a study of Chinese grammar and usage by the eighteenth-century French Jesuit missionary and sinologist, Joseph Henri Marie de Prémare. The offer was made to Morrison with the assurance that by publishing 'a work of this learned Jesuit—confessedly the most profoundly versed in the genius of the Chinese language of the Roman Catholic missionaries who visited China', the College would be 'doing a thing useful to the friends of science and creditable to themselves'. It must surely have been something of a challenge to the scholarly detachment of a Presbyterian evangelist to be asked to publish the work of a Jesuit sinologue; but fifteen hundred pounds was a handsome offer, and Morrison accepted it. The *Notitia* was published by the College press as a quarto volume in 1831.[6]

Morrison and Milne were both aware of the importance for missionary and educational aims of 'that powerful engine', the press. The printing and publishing of religious and scholarly literature were among the primary concerns of the Anglo-Chinese College. The printing presses—Chinese, Malay and English— flanked the College building on either side; nearby were the living quarters of the printers and their assistants, as well as the stores for paper and other printing supplies. The whole layout lent itself to smooth operation and effective supervision. The head Chinese printer, Leang Ah Fah, had come to Malacca from Canton with Milne in 1815. Other printers and typecutters were recruited by Morrison and sent down from Canton, along with supplies of Chinese metal type, from time to time. An English printer, P. P. Thoms, sent out to Canton by the East India Company in 1814 to supervise the production of Morrison's Chinese Dictionary, also acted as adviser and supplier to the Malacca mission press, which was named the Anglo-Chinese Press after the foundation of the College in 1818.[7]

Direct supervision of the press had been entrusted to Walter Medhurst from the time of his arrival at Malacca in 1817. Medhurst had quickly made himself sufficiently familiar with Chinese and Malay to be able to organize and supervise the printing work. But a man of his restless and dynamic nature was not likely to remain for long content with a single field of activity. As noted earlier, he turned to the study of the Hokkien dialect of Chinese so as to be able to supervise the three Chinese schools under the mission's charge in 1818, and before long he had commenced preaching in Hokkien four times a week in different parts of

Malacca town. Early in 1819 he went to Penang to start a Chinese school there, but was soon recalled to Malacca to cope with the mounting pressure of printing work. In the whole of the year 1819 the press printed about 43,000 copies of Chinese books; 12,000 copes of the *Chinese Magazine;* about 22,000 copies of sundry religious tracts in Malay; and about 3,000 copies of books and tracts in English. One of the books published in that year was written by Medhurst himself, a *Geographical catechism* in Chinese for use in schools, giving a brief description, with maps, of the principal countries of the world.[8]

On the Chinese side the press had a regular ongoing commitment in *The Chinese Magazine,* started by Milne and Leang Ah Fah in 1815. Medhurst in 1817 devised a new fount of small metal type suitable for the size of the magazine and for tracts. By 1819 the magazine's monthly circulation had grown from 500 to 1,000 copies, and Milne reported an increasing demand from all over Southeast Asia, especially from Java.

Of all the mission staff Milne, despite heavy administrative responsibilities and poor health, was by far the most productive writer for the press. His *Sacred edict,* completed in 1815, was published in London in 1817.[9] Now, while completing a *Retrospect* of the mission's history, contributing regularly to *The Indo-Chinese Gleaner,* and preparing a number of tracts, he kept up his joint work with Morrison on the translation of the Old Testament into Chinese, which was finished in November 1819. Then, released from intensive translation work, Milne went on to write within the next two years—in Chinese—a commentary on the New Testament, an essay on the immortality of the soul, a practical exposition of the Epistle to the Ephesians, and a brief sketch of all the kingdoms of the world! But the major responsibility of the head Chinese printer at Malacca, Leang Ah Fah, and his assistant, Kew Ah Gung, was the production of the complete Chinese version of the Old and New Testaments as translated by Morrison and Milne.

Leang remained on this task until he saw it completed, in twenty-one Chinese style volumes or *chüan* on 20 May 1823.[10]

The Malay publishing programme at Malacca was also an active if comparatively limited one at this time. Thomsen's tracts and hymns, his *Spelling book* (1818), a vocabulary and an arithmetic, as well as a *Malay Magazine* (1821) are all mentioned as issuing from the Malay press. The young 'munshi' Abdullah bin Abdul Kadir appears to have acted as assistant editor and printer for such publications, while also working as language tutor to Thomsen, Milne and other members of the College.[11]

A major periodical publication by the Anglo-Chinese press in the English language, already referred to, was the quarterly *Indo-Chinese Gleaner,* mainly a personal undertaking by Milne though other members of the College also contributed to it. Here again Abdullah was helpful, in one instance supplying Thomsen with information for an article on Malay demonology. An important work in English completed by Milne and published by the press at Malacca in 1820 was *A retrospect of the first ten years of the Protestant mission to China*. Actually Morrison wrote the first part of the work in 1817 to mark the tenth anniversary of his arrival in China, but he brought the account only as far as 1813, the year when Milne had come out a join him. Milne wrote the rest of the book from that point on, covering in fact the first twelve years of the mission's activities in both China and Southeast Asia up to the end of 1819.[12]

Medhurst remained in charge of the press until September 1820, when he moved to Penang (for the second time) shortly before the arrival at Malacca of his successor as superintendent of printing, George Henry Huttman. Medhurst, who had quarreled with Milne, left under a cloud, taking with him a portable Chinese press and type which belonged to the mission. But after his departure the production rate of the press dropped off, especially on the Chinese side. His successor, Huttman, started to learn Chinese on his arrival but soon gave it up. Over two years later

Morrison, to his intense disgust, was to discover that Huttman was 'totally ignorant of Chinese'. Morrison had little time for anyone who did not understand Chinese; he had no time at all for anyone who had started to learn it and then given up.[13]

Besides the College library, the ground floor of the new building also housed a small museum. Its contents, a curiously miscellaneous collection, reflected the interest of the College in both biblical and Chinese studies. Additions to the museum reported in 1820 included 'a fragment of stone broken off the Rock of Meribah; another from the Wilderness of Zin; ditto from the Cave of Moses on the top of Mount Sinai; a piece of cloth taken from an Egyptian mummy; three ancient Roman coins, one Roman-Egyptian, and one Grecian ditto'. Further contents noted in 1823 were 'Chinese drawings, maps and charts; Chinese anatomical plates; specimens of Chinese musical instruments, bronze figures, etc.; specimens of the rocks in Palestine; Birds of Paradise, Cups of Bacchus, and Petrefactions'.[14]

The original plans for the College also included a botanical department and garden. At one stage Morrison suggested that the Royal Horticultural Society in London should send out a young botanist to Malacca to learn Chinese, translate scientific botanical works into that language, and make a collection of the tropical plants of the Eastern archipelago. One of the missionaries, John Slater, claimed that he was well qualified to fill such a post, being 'the only person belonging to the Mission who had any scientific knowledge of botany', but apparently Milne would not agree to his appointment. According to one observer the scheme for a botanical garden failed from mismanagement, but it is doubtful whether it ever really got started.[15]

When the College building was nearing completion, in March 1820, Morrison decided that the time had come to draw up a deed of trust formally recording his donation of funds to found the institution. Intentionally or otherwise, he omitted to send a copy of the deed to the London Missionary Society, which only learned of its contents indirectly from a report on the College issued from Malacca three years later. Thus the relationship between the College and the Society continued to be cι riously ambivalent. Morrison always tended to treat the College as his personal property, keeping the Society at a distance as far as its internal affairs were concerned, yet at the same time expecting the Society to afford the College general support and encouragement. The College, after all, had been built on the Society's land and its officers were the Society's missionaries. Some liaison between College and Society there clearly had to be, but what little there was remained strangely hesitant and uneasy.[16]

With the trust deed completed, Morrison drew up a code of laws and statutes for the College. Milne, who admitted 'I feel myself extremely ignorant of the proper method of College management', drew up rules and regulations for the library and museum. Then in September 1820 Milne issued a pamphlet on the progress of the College plan, announcing the completion of the building and the commencement of teaching, and describing the general plan of studies. 'The building of the College House is now finished, the funds expended, and the work of tuition begun', he declared. Instruction in Chinese had been given daily as part of the curriculum since March 1818, before building had even begun. 'However humble in origin, this is the only Institution that has yet proposed the cultivation of Chinese as its chief literary object,' Milne claimed. The pamphlet concluded with an assertion of the College's academic independence, declaring it to be 'totally unconnected with any system of politics, or with any political body whether Asiatic or European'.[17]

CHAPTER EIGHT

Death of the Builder

THE Anglo-Chinese College had been successfully laun-
ched on its career. If it and the Missionary Society were
slightly uneasy bedfellows at Malacca they still managed
well enough to live together. The Society supplied the Principal of
the College and the other missionary teachers—making a donation
of £500 to the College funds in 1821 as well—but it refrained from
interfering in the internal arrangements. The College provided the
teaching facilities, and otherwise maintained an attitude of
independence while pursuing the general missionary aims of the
Society in its own peculiar way. It was a practical working
arrangement. Underlying questions as to the respective rights and
duties involved in the relationship only came to the surface in
moments of stress.

Changes in the teaching staff of the College arose both from
new appointments in London and from new postings within the
mission's sphere of operations in Southeast Asia. Medhurst and
Thomsen—one a specialist in Chinese and the other in Malay—
had worked together in Malacca as a pair from 1817; Ince and
Beighton, new arrivals of 1818, also paired off on the same basis.
Acrimonious debate then arose among all four as to which pair
should be given charge of the new permanent mission station to be
opened in Penang in 1819. Milne decided in the end in favour of
Ince and Beighton. Medhurst, smarting from a sense of injustice—

for it was he who had earlier prepared the ground for a mission at Penang—stayed on at Malacca until September 1820. Then, aided and abetted by Thomsen, he broke away from Milne and went again to Penang, as we have seen, taking some of the mission's printing equipment with him. Milne seems to have maintained a commendable coolness of judgment in these difficult circumstances. 'I have a great regard for him', Milne wrote of Medhurst; 'his knowledge of the language fits him for extensive usefulness; let him be placed in a large field and encouraged.' Evidently that large field should be somewhere other than Malacca. Medhurst's departure from Malacca, Milne commented, was 'an ill-advised, imprudent, precipitate step, and one very badly executed; . . . I did not know of his intention until the Captain of a ship told me'. 'I do not know why he left Malacca', Milne added, 'unless it was that he had been taught to call me arbitrary, reserved, stiff, and fond of dominion.' Then when Medhurst reached Penang he set up a separate mission there on his own to the intense annoyance of Ince and Beighton, who declared themselves 'greatly imposed upon and deceived by Mr. Medhurst', urging the Missionary Society to 'put a stop to one missionary going to the stations of others and immediately interfering with them in their work'. However, Medhurst stayed on in Penang until the end of 1821 when he transferred to Batavia in Java—'a field very much suited to his active turn', as Milne observed.[1]

Thomsen apparently had also intended to cut loose from Milne and follow Medhurst to Penang, but he was severely warned off by Beighton, who wrote: 'I beg of you not to come here without the Society's approbation. . . . I left Malacca with hope of finding peace and quietude at my own station, but you and Medhurst seem determined to overturn all rule whatever. You know this island is too small for two distinct missions from one Society. . . . Though you found fault with Mr. Milne for aiming at power, yet you encouraged Medhurst to come here and act more the part of a Pope than anyone I ever met with'. Taking the point, Thomsen, whom Milne now distrusted though retaining 'a high opinion of his usefulness as a missionary', decided to abandon the idea of joining Medhurst in Penang and to move instead to the new settlement of Singapore, founded by Stamford Raffles early in 1819. Samuel Milton, a Chinese specialist, had already moved from Malacca to the new settlement and started a mission school there in October 1819. Thomsen made a preliminary visit to assess the situation in Singapore in November 1821, reporting later to the Missionary Society: 'The field there is immense; it is the rendezvous of all the Malays in the Archipelago, and if we do not immediately get a Malay mission on foot there, other Societies will.' With his Malay tutor-assistant Abdullah bin Abdul Kadir, Thomsen finally moved to Singapore in May 1822, joining up with Milton to form a new Chinese-Malay missionary pairing.[2]

'Milne was completely deserted by all the missionaries', Morrison later commented bitterly. However, the gaps created by the departures to Penang, Singapore and Batavia were partially filled by new arrivals at Malacca. G. H. Huttman, the printer, and Robert Fleming, on the Chinese side, both arrived in 1820, though the latter was to last less than a year before being suspended by Milne 'for acknowledged adultery and for derangement of mind'. A young Scot, James Humphreys, arrived in September 1821 to join the Chinese side of the mission and to become for a time Milne's main support in the College.[3]

Of the non-missionary teaching staff, at least three Chinese instructors were supplied by Morrison from Canton during these early years. Milne employed Abdullah bin Abdul Kadir as Malay tutor and translator, and there were also Siamese and Vietnamese instructors on the staff. Milne wrote to Morrison in June 1821: 'I am quite happy at present, having Chinese, Siamese, Cochin-chinese and Malay teachers all about me—Japanese alone is wanted.' Clearly Milne had followed the advice given by the directors of the Missionary Society in 1819 that the scope of language studies at the College should be widened.[4]

Despite failing health, Milne drove himself on relentlessly. His wife had died in March 1819. He himself survived a cholera epidemic that swept through Malacca in 1819 and 1820, carrying off many of his friends including the merchant Tamby Ahmad Sahib. But in September 1821 he was laid up for a week 'with a bad cough, pain in the head, and tightness and pain at the pit of the stomach and in the region of the liver'. He feared he must have 'either a chronic liver complaint or an affection of the lungs'. He consulted George Finlayson, who had been in army medical service in India and was passing through Malacca to Singapore with John Crawfurd's embassy to Siam and Cochin-china in January 1822. Crawfurd himself called at the College at that time, noting that Milne seemed an 'industrious and highly respectable character'.[5]

Milne was advised to take a sea voyage, but he asked: 'Who would carry on the work?' In January 1822 he was starting a new series of lectures on geography at the College. However he decided to take a short coastal voyage to Singapore and Penang. Sailing from Malacca on 20 February, he arrived two days later at Singapore—'this charming settlement', he noted in his diary—where he stayed with his 'fond and constant friend' Colonel Farquhar, formerly in charge of Malacca and now Resident of Singapore. On 2 April Milne left to sail back up the west coast of the Malaysian peninsula and beyond Malacca to Penang, arriving there on 11 April and staying with the missionaries Ince and Beighton. A doctor whom he consulted on arrival in Penang diagnosed Milne's illness as due to a liver disorder, but by the middle of April he knew that his lungs were diseased and that he had consumption. 'There is a complication in my disorder', Milne wrote in a poignant letter to the secretary of the Missionary Society; 'I believe that a long sea voyage would be useful, and yet I am so tied at Malacca that I cannot take it. I *must* hang on till I see persons able to carry on the work. . . . I am, your now really useless and unprofitable servant, W. Milne.'[6]

At last Milne came to accept that his only hope was to take the long sea voyage to South Africa and ultimately to England. He decided to return to Malacca to settle his affairs before leaving, and Beighton accompanied him in the ship. But Milne became much worse during the voyage along the coast, and his condition steadily deteriorated after his arrival at Malacca on 24 May. Humphreys and Huttman helped him to arrange his affairs and to make the necessary provision for the management of the mission and the College. As Humphreys was a comparative newcomer, Huttman tried to persuade Milne to send for Medhurst, Milton or Slater to take over charge of Chinese studies at the College, but he refused to have any of them back. 'His mind clear and calm to the last', Milne died at 2 a.m. on Sunday 2 June. At four o'clock in the afternoon of the same day his body was carried from the Anglo-Chinese College and laid in a vault in the Dutch cemetery of St. Anthony on the side of St. Paul's hill. 'His works praise him', wrote Morrison on hearing of the death of his friend and colleague; 'he lived much in little time.'[7]

The mural plaque commemorating Milne in the former Dutch church at Malacca (now named Christ Church), in which he regularly preached, reads as follows:

'Sacred to the memory of the Revd. William Milne, D. D., Protestant missionary to China under the auspices of the London Missionary Society. For seven years he resided at this settlement as Principal of the Anglo-Chinese College, superintending the education of Chinese and Malay youths, composing useful and religious tracts in their respective languages, and officiating in this church as a faithful minister of the gospel of Christ; but the chief object of his labours in co-operation with the Revd. Robert Morrison, D. D., was the translation of the earliest Protestant version of the Holy Scriptures in Chinese, in which he rendered most valuable and efficient service. He was born in the year 1785 in Kennethmont, Aberdeenshire, left England as a missionary 1812, and he died in Malacca, June 2nd 1822, at the age of thirty-seven.'

According to Morrison, who was probably better qualified than anyone to judge, Milne combined great strength of will with a gentleness of manner. On meeting him for the first time Abdullah bin Abdul Kadir thought Milne 'a good-natured man, courteous in speech', and later described him as 'a man of fine character', adding that 'he said anything he had to say in a gentle voice'. But as Morrison commented, 'a man so intent on great objects, so severe with himself, might not always attend to the convenience of others and might jostle some in passing onward to gain his end.' The directors of the London Missionary Society were greatly impressed by 'the firmness and decision' of Milne's character, as well as by 'his intellectual energy, his enlarged views, his habits of application. . . .' Lovett, the historian of the Society, judged Milne to be 'a man of unusual gifts, of great force of character, and of an intense spirituality'. But however his character might be judged, Milne's real achievement was perhaps most suitably acknowledged by Morrison when he wrote: 'In the Anglo-Chinese College at Malacca there is now collected in one point every assistance, consisting in books and teachers, and perfect freedom and leisure, to acquire speedily a knowledge of the Chinese language, literature, religion and philosophy.'[8]

With the death of Milne both the *Chinese Magazine* and the *Indo-Chinese Gleaner,* his special publishing projects, came to an end. Morrison alleged that some of the missionaries who had left Malacca hoped that the College itself might also come to an end. He himself was certainly worried about the future of the College, now bereft of Milne's leadership and drive. James Humphreys, who had arrived in Malacca only nine months before, seemed the only possible choice for acting Principal, with the printer Huttman as his coadjutor for general mission affairs. Morrison wrote confidentially to the treasurer of the London Society: 'I am at a loss what to do for a successor to Milne at the College. Humphreys has made little or no progress in Chinese. Milton seems wild and extravagant. . . . I fear Slater's Chinese knowledge is not much.

Medhurst is well spoken of for his skill in the language by the
Chinese who have heard him speak in the Fokien dialect; but he
too went off with the Anti-College faction. . . .' Soon Morrison
had decided that the only thing for it was to go down to Malacca
so as to assess the situation there for himself. Now for the first time
the founder and president of the College would see it as it was.[9]

But the whole question of the College's future was to be raised
at a new level even before Morrison had begun his visitation. On
the way from Canton to Malacca in January 1823 he spent four
days (29 January–1 February) in Singapore, staying at the home
of a leading English merchant, A. L. Johnston. On the evening of
his arrival Morrison was taken by the harbour master, Captain
Flint, to meet Sir Stamford Raffles at Government House on
Bukit Larangan or Forbidden Hill (later to be named Fort
Canning).[10] As soon as they met, Raffles began to describe the
plan for a 'Malayan College' in Singapore which had been in his
mind since 1819 and for which he had already selected a site. It
would be similar to the Anglo-Chinese College at Malacca, he
explained, 'entirely of a secular nature, as far as tuition was to be
communicated directly', though dependent on missionaries for its
teaching staff. The reasoning behind Raffles' plan was described
in a later Missionary Society report. The original design of the
Anglo-Chinese College at Malacca, the report explained, was for
the cultivation of Chinese and English literature. But the College
also wanted to encourage 'the study of Malayan, Javanese, Siamese
and other languages and dialects of the Indian Archipelago'.
However, 'the great dissimilarity of the languages, prejudices and
habits of the islanders of the Archipelago from those of the Chinese
suggested the expediency of promoting the intellectual and moral
improvement of the former by modes more direct and specific than
those which the Anglo-Chinese College affords. Hence originated
the idea of establishing a Malayan College.'[11]

Having gained Morrison's interest in the idea, Raffles then
proposed that the Malacca College should be moved to Singapore

and there join with his Malayan College to form an academically balanced institution catering equally to Malay and Chinese students. To add force to his proposal Raffles pointed out the material advantages likely to follow when the Anglo-Chinese College moved from a territory under Dutch government, as Malacca now was, to a British settlement. 'For two days we conversed', wrote Morrison; but 'nothing was decided on with Sir Stamford concerning his projected Institution.' However Morrison promised that after seeing how things stood at Malacca he would return to Singapore for further talks with Raffles. Details would have to be worked out; other opinions would need to be consulted. To Morrison at the time, the whole idea must have seemed at first like a providential answer to the problem of how the Anglo-Chinese College was to survive the loss of Milne. But then, if Morrison decided to fall in with the Singapore plan, how would that be likely to affect the already delicate relationship between the Malacca College and the Missionary Society? Would not an amalgamation with Raffles' college in Singapore amount to a complete and final break with the parent Society?[12]

CHAPTER NINE

Morrison's Visit:
Malacca or Singapore?

THE interlude in Singapore and the discussions with
Raffles had revived the whole question of the relationship
between the College and the Missionary Society. But for
the moment Morrison's main concern was to carry out his visitation
to the College itself. Arriving by ship at Malacca from Singapore
on 4 February 1823 he was greeted by James Humphreys and
taken straight to the College. There he met Huttman the printer,
and also a newcomer, David Collie, who had arrived to join the
Chinese side of the mission in June 1822. Morrison was greatly
pleased with all he saw. 'I cannot express . . . the great satisfaction
afforded me by this House, the Libraries, the Chinese printers
(unawed by any Mandarins) printing the Book of God, and the
Chinese youths singing in their own language', he wrote. There
was only one source of dissatisfaction: 'the small degree of knowledge in the Chinese language' possessed by the missionary staff.
Morrison immediately began giving tuition in the language to
Humphreys and Collie. Finding that Huttman was 'totally
ignorant of Chinese' he placed Collie in charge of the Chinese
press, leaving Huttman with the secondary work of printing in
Malay and English.[1]

Morrison threw himself into the work of the College with great
zest. He began instructing a class of senior students. He taught

English to the 'munshi' Abdullah, now returned from Singapore, and gave him 'much good advice'. He commenced a translation of 'Joyce's *Scientific Dialogues*' into Chinese for use in College classes. He engaged a young Chinese who had studied Latin for three years in Penang to translate 'Stockius' *Hebrew Lexicon*' into Chinese.[2] He compiled *Memoirs of the Reverend William Milne*, based largely on Milne's own letters and papers. In honour of Milne he had a memorial tablet erected on the sea-wall opposite the College, and a Chinese style triple gateway *(pae-fang)* with 'suitable inscriptions in Hebrew and Chinese' constructed at the entrance to the College grounds. He ordered the old mission house, in which Huttman had been living, to be pulled down because it blocked the view from the College building, and arranged for three substantial stores to be built in the grounds out of the old materials.[3]

During intervals between work, Morrison held discussions with Humphreys and Collie in which the three missionaries took stock of the College's general situation and reviewed the basic problems involved in its relationship with the Society. They then composed a vigorously worded joint statement to the Society summarizing their position. In it they recalled that the Anglo-Chinese College had been founded 'with a view to prepare for entering the Chinese Empire as soon as an opening was afforded'. They went on to consider the value of education in relation to missionary aims. As evangelical missionaries they believed in the prime importance of preaching the Gospel, but since European preachers could not be provided in sufficient numbers to preach to the Chinese in their own language, Chinese preachers would have to be trained. At the same time European missionaries needed instruction 'not only in the ordinary language of the people, but also in their opinions, modes of reasoning, and that particular cast of mind which is formed by their superstitions, history and customs'. Equally, before Chinese trainees could become fitted to teach and preach they would require 'careful instruction in Christian theology and ethics'. But above and beyond these practical arguments for missionary education there lay the undisputed truth 'that Philosophy is an useful handmaid to Religion; that knowledge is intellectual power. . . .' Finally, they urged, there should be no conflict between the aims of the College and those of the Missionary Society. 'We disclaim all intention of self-aggrandizement or the setting up of a cause opposed to the cause of Missions', the three declared. 'We trust the Missionary Society will give us credit for sincerity . . . and confide in our prudence.'[4]

With reassurance thus offered to the Society, Morrison then prepared a separate statement 'To the Public, Concerning the Anglo-Chinese College'. This was the first public report on the College since Milne's pamphlet of September 1820 announcing the completion of the building. It included details of staff appointments, student numbers, fields of study, the library and museum, Morrison's deed of trust, laws and statutes, and donations and subscriptions. The statement noted that while the declared object of the College was 'the cultivation of Chinese and English literature' as well as 'the diffusion of Christianity', at the same time 'Malayan and Ultra-Ganges literature' had not been overlooked. A considerable number of Malay manuscripts had been collected. For nearly two years a Siamese writer had been employed in collecting and transcribing manuscripts in that language; and a translation of a Christian catechism had been nearly completed by 'a native of Cochin-china who resided for some time at the College'.

Then, turning to the basic principles on which the College was founded, Morrison's statement continued: 'The principles of the Anglo-Chinese College recognize no party, nor does it seek to aggrandize any country. The founder of the College and the builder of the edifice loved their own country, and they also loved the rest of the nations. China, that object of wonder and of pity to Christendom, excited in their minds a deep interest . . . China, one of the fairest portions of the globe; the most ancient, the most populous, the best skilled in the management of human nature of any country under heaven.' And the statement concluded with a challenging declaration of Morrison's educational philosophy: 'The fundamental principle acted on by the founder of the College is that all the various tribes of men have equal rights, and every system has a right to be heard. When this shall be the case, mighty Truth will prevail.'[5]

During this time Morrison naturally discussed with his colleagues at Malacca the talks he had held with Raffles, and in particular the proposal that their educational efforts should be combined and concentrated in a single institution to be located in Singapore. While no mention was made of the proposal in the body of Morrison's report *To the public* completed on 21 February 1823, the decision to fall in with Raffles' plans must have been made soon afterwards, for Humphreys wrote to the directors of the Missionary Society on 8 March: 'It is now fixed that the College moves to Singapore'; and in a postscript added to the statement *To the public* on 15 March, Morrison himself announced that 'agreeably to the wishes of a majority of the friends and supporters of the College, it has been determined to remove it to Singapore, under the auspices of the British Government. . . .' About the same time word came from C. H. Thomsen, now in the Singapore mission, that Raffles had appropriated a hill of a hundred acres for the new 'Singapore Institution', and had also made a grant of a neighbouring hill containing fifty acres to Morrison himself. Morrison also accepted a grant of land in the Chinese quarter of Singapore at this time. He wrote in confidence to the treasurer of the Missionary Society: 'Most of the friends of the College wish it removed, and I acquiesce. . . .'[6]

Morrison visited Singapore again to attend a meeting of 'the principal inhabitants', held on 1 April 1823, at which the plan for a Singapore Institution was publicly announced by Stamford Raffles. Raffles had the imaginative vision to see the proposed institution within a broad Southeast Asian framework. It would have for its object 'the cultivation of the languages of China, Siam,

and the Malayan Archipelago, and the improvement of the moral
and intellectual condition of the inhabitants of those countries'.
The threefold structure of the institution would comprise a Malayan
college, a Chinese college (provided for by the transfer of the
Anglo-Chinese College from Malacca), and a college of science.
In further discussions between Morrison, Raffles and Colonel
Farquhar, the Resident in charge of Singapore, it was agreed that
David Collie would come from Malacca to the Singapore Institution as professor of Chinese (James Humphreys remaining at
Malacca in charge of the mission), while C. H. Thomsen would be
offered the post of professor of Malay, and Samuel Milton that of
professor of Siamese. Farquhar was to be president of the Institution, and Morrison vice-president.[7]

Morrison then returned to Malacca and to his College duties
for a while longer. The foundation stone of the Singapore Institution was laid by Raffles on 5 June 1823, a few days before he was
to leave Singapore for the last time. Morrison attended a meeting
of the trustees of the Institution on 23 July during a short stay in
Singapore on his way back to China, and the whole project was
still very much alive when he went on leave to England in 1824.
Indeed one of the main purposes of Morrison's visit to Britain,
besides the general one of promoting the cause of the Anglo-
Chinese College at home, was to convince the London Missionary
Society that when the College moved to Singapore the Society
should retain and even reinforce its mission at Malacca, taking
over the College building there for its mission house. Malacca,
Morrison maintained, if less prosperous than Singapore, was a
much more suitable place for a mission. 'Commerce and missions
have no immediate relation to each other', he declared, con-
veniently ignoring for the moment his own relationship with the
East India Company at Canton. 'Indeed', he went on to generalize,
'a prosperous commercial population have generally their hearts
too much set on this world's goods, or are too busy in the enjoyment
of riches to listen to instruction; and our own merchants in distant

colonies are so often in a haste to become rich and go home, they do not generally feel much interest in any plans for the enlightening and improving of the people.'[8]

On his arrival in England in April 1824 Morrison was presented at Court as the first Protestant missionary to China. He laid before King George IV a copy of his and Milne's Chinese translation of the Bible which had been published at Malacca in the previous year, with an account of the progress of the Anglo-Chinese College, and the plan for the Singapore Institution. At a meeting held in London on 28 April at which he addressed the directors of the Missionary Society on the Chinese mission, Morrison spoke directly of the transfer of the College to Singapore and referred to the College building at Malacca as 'now the mission house'. And in a fund-raising appeal *To the British public* on behalf of the College, published in London in 1825, he again announced its removal to Singapore.

Meanwhile however in Singapore itself, with neither Raffles nor Morrison there to hold the new project together, the whole scheme had begun to fall apart. John Crawfurd, the new Resident of Singapore, regarded it as impractical and extravagant, refusing to authorize the allocation of the four thousand dollars promised to the Institution by Raffles on behalf of the East India Company. The building programme had been held up for want of money. At the same time the final transfer of Malacca from Dutch rule to the English East India Company (agreed under the Anglo-Dutch Treaty of March 1824 and made effective a year later) removed any possibility that the Malacca College might suffer political disadvantage by remaining where it was. By late in the year 1825 Morrison feared that the Singapore Institution plan would 'fall to the ground'. He alleged that Crawfurd had 'used all his influence against it'. 'Crawfurd (I think he spells his name), the infidel doctor-civilian, did all the mischief he could to Singapore and overturned the Institution', Morrison wrote with some venom. By April 1826 he had informed the Missionary Society that the move to Singapore would be cancelled. Raffles, the prime begetter of the scheme, died in England in July 1826. Morrison announced that he considered the Anglo-Chinese College completely absolved from any obligations in the matter, and that the removal of the College from Malacca was therefore 'now quite out of the question'.[9]

While in England, Morrison took the opportunity of giving the Missionary Society his views on the vexed question of the connection between missionary and educational aims. The Anglo-Chinese College had a few friends, he observed tersely in his address to the directors, but to most people who knew of its existence it was 'a literary institution totally unconnected with religion'. 'True', he went on, 'it is not solely religious'; but, he asked, 'how can the moral and spiritual truths of divine revelation be made known to, or be illustrated and enforced on, the consciences of men, without a knowledge of the language and literature of the various nations to whom your missionaries are sent?' And the directors should realize, he added, that the mission to China was a very different matter from missions to the South Seas or to Africa, for 'China is an anciently civilized state . . .; her literature both ancient and modern is as extensive as that of Greece and Rome and Modern Europe collectively.'[10]

On such matters Morrison could speak with authority. But when it came to more practical questions concerning 'the Chinese mission' he found himself on weaker ground. Rather awkwardly for him, the virtual collapse of the Singapore Institution scheme and the consequent reversal of the decision to move the College from Malacca had raised once again the sensitive issue of the relationship between the College and the mission there. The College building, on Morrison's own statement, had now been transferred to the mission. The old mission house had already been pulled down on his orders. Now, with the College remaining at Malacca after all, were it and the mission to share the one available building? In view of the frequent assertions of the College's independence, the Missionary Society's treasurer blandly enquired, 'would not Dr. Morrison consider it inexpedient that the whole plan of the Anglo-Chinese College (considering it as an Institution to a certain extent under a separate control and with secular objects in view) should be carried on in a house which belongs to the Society?' That was a delicate point. 'The mission and the College at Malacca are in fact now united by the Society's missionaries being officers in the College', Morrison retorted; 'let it alone and it will greatly subserve the cause of the Kingdom.' 'By attempting to legislate too minutely or define very exactly between the College and the Mission', he went on, 'we shall, I apprehend, do harm to both. . . . I am sorry to see the question of the old house so much mooted. Affairs had better be left alone at present. The College will be *hospitable* to all missionaries to the utmost extent of its means, but they cannot *by rights* occupy its rooms.'

Morrison had the last word on this occasion; but in effect the whole question of the relationship between College and mission at Malacca remained inconclusive, a subject for continuing debate.[11]

CHAPTER TEN

Successors to Milne

AT Malacca itself, meanwhile, James Humphreys and David Collie—both by now 'very promising Chinese scholars'—had been left in dual charge of the mission and the College. During Morrison's visit in 1823 the staff establishment of the College had been announced as consisting of a President (Morrison), a resident Principal (Humphreys), a professor of Chinese (Collie), a treasurer, a librarian and keeper of the museum, with instructors in Chinese (Lee Seën-sang), Siamese (Nunsid), Malay and Javanese (vacant). The president nominated the Principal; together they appointed the professor of Chinese, while the remaining appointments could be made by the Principal on his own.[1]

With Milne gone, it was more than ever Morrison's college. From Canton he maintained a watchful if remote control over its affairs, keeping a sharp eye also over the 'Ultra-Ganges Mission' in general. He wrote candid reports on the conduct of missionaries at the various stations. Of Milton in Singapore, for example, he reported to London: 'I have reason to fear that he is extravagant, wild, and unstable as water; incoherent, audacious and uncivil; . . . he has a great fancy to join the Established Church and was much disappointed that the College was not put under his care.' Of Slater in Batavia, too, Morrison regretted that 'nothing very encouraging' could be said. 'These two, I have heard, were audacious, extravagant, eccentric men even when at Gosport', he wrote. 'Meekness and humility do not seem to be esteemed as virtue by some Christians.' Of Thomsen in Singapore it could be said that he was 'respected and a prudent industrious missionary', but even he sometimes showed 'a little bitterness of spirit to his brethren which is very unmissionarylike. . . .' And some time later Morrison wrote critically of Thomsen's 'peculiar views of religion and his hostility to the Anglo-Chinese College'.[2]

With the arrival of a new missionary, Samuel Kidd, from London to reinforce the Chinese side of the mission at Malacca in November 1824, James Humphreys moved from the headship of the College to the general management of the mission, at the same time switching his language interest from Chinese to Malay. David Collie, 'studious and retired', took over the office of Principal of the College, with Kidd, a Hokkien specialist, as professor of Chinese. Collie and Kidd seem to have worked very well together. Some months after his arrival Kidd wrote home that he had been greatly helped by Collie in 'getting the sense of Chinese authors'; Collie himself had made excellent progress in the language and could preach fluently in Mandarin.[3]

With two such scholars as Collie and Kidd on the staff, the College was particularly strong at this time (1825-28) on the Chinese side. Instructors in Mandarin were listed as Lee, Yaou— the latter being the first student to graduate from the College—and Yim. The Chinese press was active and efficient; many tracts were being printed and distributed to Chinese centres in Southeast Asia; tracts written by Collie were produced, as Morrison reported, 'in the first style of Chinese printing'. But the Malay side of the College's work was comparatively weak at this time. Humphreys manfully tried to fill the breach caused by Thomsen's departure to Singapore. The 'munshi' Abdullah was persuaded to return once more from Singapore to run the Malay press, help as a cataloguer in the library, and give tuition in Malay to Humphreys and others.[4]

Abdullah also played a key part at this time in negotiations leading to the acquisition of a site for a mission chapel in Malacca town. The ground obtained for the purpose adjoined Abdullah's house in what was then known as Goldsmith's Street. It belonged to an Arab *khatib*[5] named Sheikh Ali, and Abdullah helped Humphreys to put the deal through. As the plot of ground for the chapel lay directly opposite the main Chinese temple across the street, there was great consternation for a time among the Chinese community about the possible ill effects of this confrontation on the *feng shui*[6] of their temple; but a friendly letter from Humphreys to the head of the community, the *Kapitan China*,[7] seems to have smoothed matters over. The foundation stone of the new chapel was laid by two visiting commissioners from the London Missionary Society on 28 January 1826, and the building was first opened for public worship on 14 April 1827.[8]

The commissioners from London, visiting Malacca in January 1826 in the course of an extended world tour of inspection, thought the town 'a poor place', but reported that the College and its ancillary buildings were 'all in satisfactory repair', adding without much enthusiasm: 'The business appears to be ably conducted.' David Collie was 'sorry to observe the minds of the deputation seemed strongly prejudiced against Drs. Morrison and Milne'; and the tone of the commissioners' report does suggest that they shared the Society's uneasy feeling that the College was a largely unnecessary adjunct to the Malacca mission, created by Morrison and Milne primarily to serve their own educational and cultural interests. Morrison himself was still in England at this time; he left at the end of April 1826, reaching Macao in September. But he had earlier put the Society in no doubt about his views on visits of inspection by itinerant commissioners. 'I think the money spent in carrying Commissioners backwards and forwards very ill spent,' he wrote, 'and indeed the principle pernicious, because it keeps up the old error that Ministers at home are a superior order of men to Missionaries abroad.' There spoke the missionary 'man on the spot'.[9]

At the College itself, Collie and Kidd continued to work in close co-operation. Kidd learned to speak well in both Hokkien and Mandarin. Collie, according to one of the Chinese instructors, spoke Mandarin like a native, and another colleague praised his 'perfect Chinese composition'. But Collie was not to last. He completed a translation of the *Four books* of Chinese classics in 1827 but towards the end of that year his health broke down rapidly, and he died at sea, en route to Singapore and the Cape, in February 1828.[10]

The loss of David Collie—'a faithful, devoted and persevering worker'—was a severe blow to the College, but it was fortunate in having at hand a worthy successor as Principal in Samuel Kidd. By this time James Humphreys had almost entirely severed his connection with the College in order to work more widely among the Malay population, retaining only a general supervision of the College press. Later, however, his health broke down and he eventually returned to England in 1829. Jacob Tomlin, who had arrived from London to join the Malacca mission in February 1827, and had studied Mandarin and Hokkien at the College for a short time before going on to Singapore, then returned to Malacca to assist Kidd. But Tomlin was temperamentally unsuited to College work and he was relieved in April 1828 by John Smith, another new missionary who had been sent out from England in 1826, studied Chinese with Tomlin at Malacca and then moved on with him to Singapore. But Smith too found work at the College uncongenial. Like Tomlin he was more inclined towards the life of an itinerant preacher, and again his health was poor. Smith remained at the College for less than a year, returning to Singapore in March 1829. Then, his health continuing to deteriorate, he decided to quit the East and sailed for England in September 1829. Morrison commented, with characteristic frankness and severity: 'Smith has been persuaded to embark for Europe, without doing any work to speak of. Kidd is now alone. . . . Had Smith, with a disease of the lungs, been content to learn and write

Chinese books, which he might have done merely by whispering, he would have been a most useful missionary. But no, he must preach or do nothing!'[11]

Samuel Kidd was thus left to carry the burden of responsibility for the College on his own. Unfortunately for him, it was at this time that the College became involved in a clash between the East India Company's government at Penang and the editor of a local journal, *The Malacca Observer*. The editor, John Henry Moor, born in Macao and educated at Trinity College, Dublin, had come out to Malacca in 1825. He joined the College in September of that year, teaching English classes in return for tuition in Chinese under Collie. In the following year Moor started publication of *The Malacca Observer,* which he arranged to have printed at the College press. In its issue of 30 June 1829 *The Observer* made what the government regarded as objectionable comment on its policy towards the small Malay state of Naning, lying inland from Malacca.[12] The governor, Robert Fullerton, 'a man of vigorous and determined character', fulminated against the journal and the College, deploring the 'scurrility and abuse' which they had published; and on a visit to Malacca in October 1829 he sent for Kidd and demanded an explanation. Kidd answered that he was not responsible for the views expressed in the journal and could not be expected to act as a censor. The governor seemed satisfied that Kidd had been 'unaware of the mischief', but added: 'I presume the paper will now cease.' *The Observer* did in fact close down, and Moor moved from Malacca to Singapore where he was to resume his publishing activities in somewhat greater freedom.[13]

But for Kidd and the College there was a serions aspect of this whole affair which remained a source of some anxiety. The College had been receiving a regular annual subsidy of 1,200 Spanish dollars from the East India Company, through the Penang government, since 1827. During the discussion of the *Observer* affair, Governor Fullerton had ominously drawn attention to this fact, and the clearly implied threat of the withdrawal of the subsidy was left hanging over the College for some time. Fullerton indeed advised the Company in November 1830 that the subsidy should be discontinued, though largely for reasons of economy, and the Penang government ceased to support the College from that time. However, the committee in charge of the Company's Canton factory, doubtless with some prompting from Morrison, stepped into the breach and restored the subsidy. Explaining its action in supporting the College, the Canton committee declared its belief that 'by means of liberal education so readily afforded to the natives of England as well as China in the learning and language of either country, we consider the intercourse between the subjects of the two empires will be materially facilitated.'[14]

But Kidd by this time was almost worn out with work and anxiety, and his health began to suffer. He wrote informing the Missionary Society in October 1831 that he had decided to leave the East on account of his health, and he was back in England by July 1832. He made a partial recovery, and five years later became the first professor of Chinese at the new University of London (founded in 1836); but he was to die in 1843 at the early age of thirty-nine.[15]

For the moment, the College was left without a Chinese scholar as its head. The only remaining missionary on the staff when Kidd left was a Malay language specialist, Josiah Hughes, who had arrived from London in November 1830 to fill the gap caused by the departure of Humphreys. When Hughes arrived, 'Munshi' Abdullah was again duly summoned from Singapore—whither he had gone when Humphreys withdrew from the College—to give language tuition and to help generally with the Malay side of the work as before. Hughes—a bluff, hearty, unmissionarylike character, according to Abdullah—took temporary charge of the College for a short period between Kidd's departure and the arrival early in 1832 of the nearest approach to a Chinese scholar available among the missionaries at the time—Jacob Tomlin.[16]

Tomlin, it will be remembered, had already put in a short

spell of service at the College in March-April 1828 when he came
from Singapore to assist Kidd soon after Collie's death. A man of
immense physical energy and remarkable enterprise, he had since
then given free rein to his talent for 'gadding about', as Morrison
caustically put it. As soon as he was freed from his duties at the
College in April 1828 Tomlin had gone off with Humphreys to
visit Chinese-owned pepper plantations inland from Malacca and
the tin mines at Lukut and Sungei Ujong to the north-west.[17] In
following years he travelled widely in Southeast Asia, visiting Siam,
Java and Bali and distributing boxes of bibles and religious tracts
in Chinese and Malay. Morrison commented drily: 'I am sorry
Tomlin does not choose to become a Chinese writer. . . . If tract
writers had not preceded him, his peregrinations would have been
of little use.'[18]

   Whatever his merits, Tomlin was clearly not cut out for a
position so static as the headship of a college. But he was a practical
man. He relied on common sense in his approach to the administrative and academic problems with which he had to deal. For
example, Tomlin himself was a Hokkien speaker; Hokkien was of
much greater value than Mandarin as a medium of communication
in the everyday life of the Chinese in Southeast Asia; therefore, he
concluded, Hokkien should replace Mandarin as the language of
instruction in all College classes. The idea was not a new one.
Milton, the Singapore missionary, had strongly advocated the
general use of Hokkien in the College in 1824. Morrison fully
admitted its practical value, and had encouraged both Medhurst
and Kidd to make a special study of it. Writing in explanation to
the Society in London, he had said: 'The Fuhkien dialect is very
dissimilar from the general language of the Empire commonly
called the Mandarin tongue. It is perhaps as dissimilar as the
Welsh or the Erse are from the general language of England. From
this you will see at once the importance to your missionaries of
Mr. Medhurst's work, for most of the settlers of the Archipelago

are from the province of Fuhkien.[19] The written language is, however, the same throughout the rest of China.'

James Humphreys on his return to England in 1829 expressed the viewpoint of the advocates of Hokkien in the College with some force. 'The study of Mandarin', he wrote, 'can be of no manner of use until China proper is open to missionaries, for there is not one in a hundred (I may say in a thousand) of those with whom the missionaries come in contact who understands it; and it is a question with me as to the utility of teaching in the College a dialect which can be of no manner of use to the students except in causing them to be considered more learned than their neighbours, and this dialect is the only one taught in the College.' And John Smith, also reporting on the College to the Society on his return to England in 1830, argued that it was absurd that Malacca Chinese students, the vast majority of whom learned Hokkien in school, should have to unlearn their own dialect and take up Mandarin if they entered the College.

Sharing these views, Tomlin proudly announced in the draft annual report of the College for 1833 what he termed his 'radical reform' in substituting the use of Hokkien for Mandarin in courses of instruction. But Morrison, hearing of this, moved swiftly; publication of the report was immediately suppressed. To Morrison there could be no question that for a full education in Chinese literature and culture a knowledge of the Mandarin dialect was a basic requirement and must come first. 'As to the Chinese Mandarin tongue', he wrote, it was his firm conviction 'that no Chinese missionary but a lazy one or an incompetent one, or one who devotes himself exclusively to teaching orally a particular class of Chinese, will ever be ignorant of it.'[20]

CHAPTER ELEVEN

Missionary Excursions

THE Mandarin-Hokkien debate reflected in part a fundamental difference of viewpoint with regard to missionary
purposes, even within the definition of evangelicalism.
That difference, which had already become apparent years earlier
between Milne and some of his younger colleagues at Malacca,
was essentially one between the viewpoint of the sedentary
missionary and that of the itinerant preacher, a difference between
the scholarly or intellectual approach and a more popular or
utilitarian attitude to missionary ends.

Morrison—partly by choice, partly by the force of circumstances
at Canton—had become the sedentary scholar devoted primarily
to a sustained study of the Chinese literary language. He was of
course a preacher as well; he was also a servant of the East India
Company; he had joined an official embassy to Peking and
performed other extra-curricular duties; but still his major role
had remained that of the scholar-missionary. Milne too had shown
himself to be of the same missionary type, even though he had
managed at first to combine itinerant preaching with his main
interests in language study, teaching and publishing. Collie and
Kidd had both also clearly belonged to the sedentary scholar-
missionary type.

Medhurst, in his strongly individual way, seems to have been
remarkably successful in bridging the gap between scholar-

missionary and itinerant preacher. But Humphreys, Hughes and Tomlin—and probably also most of the other Malacca missionaries—were by preference itinerant preachers, devoted to the more purely evangelical and immediate purpose of going among the people and 'spreading the word'. They were especially concerned to build popular support rather than an élitist base for Christianity among the Chinese. Believing in the supreme importance of personal contact and verbal communication as necessary forerunners of the printed word, they were generally interested in language study only for its practical use in direct personal communication with the ordinary man. Accordingly, they were inclined to stress the value of locally relevant language forms such as Hokkien in preference to the more universal literary form of Mandarin.

Jacob Tomlin, an ardent advocate of the study and use of Hokkien at the Anglo-Chinese College, as we have seen, was one of the special targets of Morrison's criticism. 'Tomlin's talent seems to be gadding about', was how Morrison expressed his view of the itinerant preacher. Yet some at least of Tomlin's 'peregrinations'—Morrison's word—are of considerable interest within the general context of the College record. The excursions which he undertook into interior regions of the Malaysian peninsula serve to illustrate an extramural side of the work of some of the College members while they waited at Malacca for the opening up of the interior of China itself.

Tomlin, it will be remembered, had come from Singapore to help out at the College as assistant to Samuel Kidd—on the death of David Collie—in February 1828. After only about seven weeks' work at the College he was relieved by John Smith, also from Singapore. Thus freed from 'sedentary occupations', as he wrote, Tomlin had immediately gone off in company with James Humphreys to visit the tin mining areas of Lukut and Sungei Ujong, penetrating into parts of the country which had almost certainly never before been seen by Europeans. Tomlin's reports of these journeys, in his *Missionary journal and letters* (1844), throw a most interesting and valuable light on conditions in some of the earliest Chinese tin mining settlements within the Malay States.[1]

Lukut (at that time a coastal district of the State of Selangor) and Sungei Ujong (in the present-day State of Negri Sembilan) were two of the tin-producing areas in which miners from South China, pioneers of the modern tin industry of peninsular Malaysia, first began to concentrate in the early part of the nineteenth century. Both were within comparatively easy reach of Malacca, which indeed served a key function as port of entry and supply base of Chinese labour for the mines, as well as being the main source of capital equipment and consumer goods for the miners and also of exchange commodities for the tin they produced. The Lukut mines, which Tomlin and Humphreys visited first, were some forty miles along the coast to the north-west of Malacca and about eight miles inland.[2]

Leaving Malacca on the evening of 24 April 1828 in an eight-oared Malay *prau*, the missionaries and their party reached the mouth of the Lukut river next morning about dawn. Four or five miles up river they landed and then started off along a path through the jungle. An hour or so later they suddenly came to a clearing from which they could see before them an open valley about half a mile across, 'like a garden in the wilderness', surrounded by gently sloping, thickly forested hills. In the foreground, where the soil seemed very rich, were gardens of 'plantain, sugar-cane, taro, and sireh'.[3] In the middle of the valley was a straggling village of about twenty houses, 'surrounded by the mines, much resembling white sand-pits, . . . the tin being found from six to twelve feet below the surface in dark grey sandy layers'.

On introducing themselves, the missionaries were made very welcome by the mining community of about two hundred Chinese. 'From the first moment of our arrival,' wrote Tomlin, 'we were received with the most frank generosity, and treated with unsparing hospitality during our stay; we took up lodgings with one of the headmen, who kindly gave up the only two bedrooms he had in his house for our use.' The first evening was spent in conversation with the miners, and on the following morning the missionaries went around visiting every house in the village. They found that three of the larger buildings housed the members of the three *kongsis* or gangs into which the miners were divided, each under its own headman and working in a different part of the valley. The smaller buildings were mostly the workshops of various artisans and craftsmen who serviced the mining community— carpenters, tailors, barbers and so on. The whole settlement formed a typical frontier-type community, self-contained and egalitarian, yet tightly organized under the jurisdiction of five headmen who, as Tomlin noted, took the law into their own hands and exercised the most prompt and summary justice. The visitors were struck by the 'harmony, peace and good order' which prevailed, 'though the most free and familiar intercourse is kept up between the lowest and the highest of them'. 'We are told they are remarkably honest; a spirit of sobriety and industry pervades the whole body.'

These mines at Lukut, Tomlin was told, had been worked by Chinese entrepreneurs for thirteen years (i.e. since 1815), and a tenth of the tin produced went to the Malay ruler of Selangor, the state in which the mines were situated. The miners, whose monthly wages ranged between two and ten dollars, started their labours early in the morning, working and resting alternately for an hour at a time throughout the day. 'The men are very industrious and cheerful over their work', Tomlin noted; 'it was delightful to observe with what glee they returned to their labours, and to hear the cheering shout which is generally given by all on commencing them.' Altogether the Malacca missionaries were most favourably impressed by this pioneer tin-mining community. 'We returned with joyful hearts, . . . with cheerful spirits and hearts filled with gratitude for all the kindness and hospitality we had met with', Tomlin concluded.

Fired with enthusiasm by the success of their excursion to

Lukut, Tomlin and Humphreys decided to follow it up with an early visit to the more extensive tin mining area of Sungei Ujong.[4] Leaving Malacca at nine o'clock on the evening of 5 May 1828 in the same Malay *prau* as before, they sailed again along the coast to the north-west for about twenty-five miles until, next morning about sunrise, they reached the estuary of the river Linggi. Then making their way upstream for about six miles as far as Simpang, where the river forked into two branches, they followed the lefthand branch towards the north for another seven or eight miles until about 10 a.m. when they arrived at the riverine village of Linggi, 'agreeable surprised at the bustling, commercial-like appearance of this little Malay port'. Linggi, as Tomlin noted, served as an entrepot where the consignments of tin carried down in small boats from collecting points higher up the river were exchanged for a variety of goods from Malacca (rice, opium, salt, etc.), and then transhipped in larger craft—Tomlin observed 'ten or a dozen good-sized *praus* waiting for the tin'—to Malacca or Singapore.[5]

To reach the tin areas further upriver the missionaries and their party now continued their journey inland on foot. After a friendly meeting with the *penghulu* or headman of Linggi village, they started off at about three o'clock in the afternoon through 'the tedious, dreary jungle', reaching the small village of Kundor about sunset, where they spent the night on the verandah of the headman's house. An early start next morning brought them to the village of Jemampong about mid-morning, and then to Sala village, 'where the tin mines commence', towards evening; here the Chinese *towkay* or manager gave up his bedroom to the missionaries.[6]

On the following day a two hour walk through jungle brought them to a newly cleared mining area known as Cheung-Ko; then, turning towards the Linggi river again, to the Malay village of Jeboy, a major riverside collecting centre for the tin from the various mines of the whole region, and headquarters of an important Malay official, the *shahbandar* or port officer with sole authority over river transport and 'marine affairs'. About an hour's walk further on, at Temeong, there were five tin mines. From Jeboy the missionaries returned by small boat down the narrow waters of the upper river as far as the village of Linggi, and thence by *prau* back to Malacca.

Tomlin remarked that 'it was pleasing to observe the amicable spirit subsisting between the Malays and Chinese' in Sungei Ujong.[7] The total number of Chinese connected with mining in the whole area Tomlin estimated at 'probably six hundred, divided into ten *kongsis*' or groups. He thought 'they appeared more respectable, and have a greater command of capital, than those at Lukut.' Here too, he noted, the miners had the technical advantage of 'the Chinese chain pump, used for raising the water out of the mine pit', and in his report Tomlin provides what is most probably the earliest detailed description in English of this machine, described more recently as 'a direct borrowing from the rice fields of China'.[8]

Describing the chain pump, Tomlin writes:

' The apparatus is simple, consisting of a common water-wheel, a circular wooden chain about forty feet in circumference, and a long square box or trough through which it runs in ascending. The wheel and chain, I think, revolve on a common axis, so that the motion of the former necessarily puts the latter into action. The chain consists of square wooden floats, a foot distant from each other and strung as it were upon a continuous flexible axis, having a moveable joint between each pair.

As the float-boards of the chain successively enter the lower part of the box or trough (immersed in water), a portion of water is constantly forced up by each and discharged at the top. At one of the mines we were much struck with the simple but efficient mode of its application. There were three distinct planes or terraces rising above each other. On the middle one was the wheel; the lower was the pit of the mine; from the higher a stream of water fell and turned the wheel which, putting the whole machine into motion, brought up

*another stream from the pit; these two streams from above and below, uniting
on the middle plane, ran off in a sluice by which the ore was washed.*'[9]

The chain pump, known to the Chinese miners of the Malaysian
Peninsula as *chin-chia* and to the Malays as *putaran ayer,* was to
remain a prime accessory for alluvial tin mining in the Malay
States until the introduction of the steam engine in the eighteen-
seventies.[10]

One of the motives of missionary excursions such as those
undertaken by Tomlin and Humphreys to the tin mines of the
interior of the Malaysian Peninsula was of course the distribution
of Christian literature printed in both Chinese and Malay. The
personal contact and spoken word of the evangelist needed
reinforcement and extension by means of the printed word. A
simple faith in the power of 'the Book' was shared equally by both
sedentary and itinerant missionaries, the former regarding their
work of translation and publication as an essential prerequisite for
the success of the latters' visitations. One of the main functions of
the College press at Malacca was to produce basic material in the
vernacular languages suitable for dissemination throughout the
region, and especially among the overseas Chinese of Southeast
Asia.

Other missionary journeys associated in one way or another
with the Malacca College were being made at this time among
overseas Chinese in the Malaysian Peninsula and further afield.
Walter Medhurst, whose move from the College to Penang in 1820
and thence to Batavia (Jakarta) late in the following year has
already been described, was an extremely active evangelist as well
as a remarkably gifted scholar. His ambitious travel plans for 1828
included 'a missionary tour amongst the islands of the Indian
Archipelago, hoping also to reach Siam or Cochin-china, in order
to scatter tracts and scriptures amongst the numerous settlements
of Chinese emigrants'. Having arranged to make a visit to Siam
along with Jacob Tomlin, Medhurst arrived in Singapore from

Batavia on 7 August of the same year, only to find that Tomlin
and the roving German missionary Charles Gützlaff had already
left in a Chinese junk for Siam three days earlier. After various
unsuccessful attempts to obtain a similar passage, Medhurst later
in the month boarded a vessel bound for Pahang and other ports
on the east coast of the Malaysian peninsula; he found himself in
'nothing better than an open boat or rather large barge, carrying
about fifteen tons, without any covering by night or by day except
a little *kadjang* when it rains'.[11]

On arrival at the river port of Pahang, Medhurst, suspected of
being a spy, was refused permission to visit the mines in the
interior and so had to be content with distributing tracts among
the Chinese of the port. Then continuing northward, he came to
the smaller port of Kemaman which, Medhurst noted, 'had been
established about eleven years, and at first yielded a good profit to
the Rajah of Tringano, but latterly the tin mines seem to have
failed and many of the inhabitants have dispersed, leaving only
about twenty Chinese at the settlement and one hundred at the
mines, about two days' journey in the interior'.

Further along the coast at the port town of Trengganu, where
Medhurst arrived on the last day of August, he found in this
'Malay town, large and populous . . . some hundreds of Chinese,
dwelling principally in strong brick-built houses which have every
appearance of being erected many years ago'. Continuing his
voyage northward, Medhurst next called at the southern Siamese
ports of Patani and Singora. The latter town, he noted, was
'divided into three parts in which Chinese, Siamese and Malays
severally dwell.' The Chinese part of the town, containing upwards
of one thousand inhabitants, seemed to be the centre of trade
'principally confined to junks and native vessels which pass up and
down between Siam and Singapore'. The Governor of Singora,
Medhurst observed, was 'a Chinese by extraction but a Siamese
in manners and appearance'.

Returning southward along the coast to Singapore, Medhurst

arrived there on 6 October, having distributed in the course of his voyage 'three boxes of books and tracts'. He remained in Singapore for some time 'for his health', and then returned by way of Borneo to Batavia. But neither Medhurst nor Tomlin was likely to remain at rest for long, and soon they were off together on an extended tour of the north coast of Java and the island of Bali (November 1829–January 1830).[12] Soon afterwards Tomlin was to make a return visit to Java on his own (March–April 1830). Then in June 1831 Tomlin left Singapore on a second visit to Siam, primarily in order to work with Charles Gützlaff on 'a close and final revision to the Siamese translation of the New Testament'. Sailing in 'an Arab ship' in company with the American missionary David Abeel,[13] Tomlin reached the mouth of the Menam river on 31 July only to find that the elusive Gützlaff had embarked on a junk for China ten or twelve days previously.[14]

The trend of international relations in East Asia was now beginning to draw the main thrust of Protestant missionary effort away from Southeast Asian countries to concentrate before long on China itself. Gützlaff, the itinerant missionary-scholar, would range widely along the China coast in one corner of which Morrison, the sedentary scholar, had been labouring on his own for so many years.

Meanwhile other representatives of the Anglo-Chinese College were already moving tentatively into China itself. Leang Ah Fah and Kew Ah Gung, printers at the College press and joint producers of the Bible in the Chinese version of Morrison and Milne, journeyed from Canton for 250 miles into the interior in 1830. Following in the train of one of the public examiners for the imperial civil service, they were able to mingle with candidates for the mandarinate and to distribute thousands of Christian tracts among them. A copy of one of Leang's tracts entitled 'Good words to admonish the age' (Canton, 1832) is known to have reached Hung Hsiu-ch'üan—later to become titular head of the Taiping Rebellion, 1851–1864—when he came to Canton to sit for the civil service examinations in 1833 or 1834.[15]

CHAPTER TWELVE

Death of the Founder

THE old problem of the relationship between College and mission at Malacca remained unsolved, for it involved an organizational overlap and a conjunction of authority that could not be easily clarified or defined. It was a problem which greatly vexed Morrison during the later years of his life. Or rather, being unwilling to admit that it was a real problem at all, he was greatly vexed whenever the matter was raised as such by others. The last thing Morrison ever wanted was too clear a definition of the boundaries of jurisdiction between mission and College at Malacca, as long as he was there to supervise both. Yet as he grew older he was to become more and more concerned about the future of the College, increasingly anxious that the Missionary Society should be in some way committed to its support after he was gone. The basic problem for the College would then be, as always, how to balance the desire for independence against the need for support. As the inevitable day came nearer when his guiding hand would be removed, there were times when survival seemed to Morrison even more important than independence.

The Society on its side had no wish to undertake full responsibility for the College without possessing adequate control over its organization, and it well knew that as long as Morrison lived it could not hope to obtain full control. Financial responsibility lay at the heart of the matter as far as the directors of the Society were concerned. Some of its missionaries could be highly individualistic, not to say irresponsible, in their business methods. The Society had bitter experience of having its funds or credit heavily committed by missionaries overseas without authority or even consultation. Even Morrison himself was not entirely blameless in this respect. Returning from England to China in 1826 he had taken with him the funds obtained during his leave from subscriptions and donations to the College on the ground that they were separate from the funds of the Society and under his personal control. Yet not long after his return to Canton he received a rap over the knuckles from the Society's treasurer for having so soon drawn a bill of exchange for £300 on the Society—'rather sharply, as you could not but be rich from what you took out with you'. Moreover about the same time Morrison had drawn another bill for £300 on the Religious Tract Society, which 'was still more unfortunate', as 'they were obliged to refuse acceptance to your bill, and that has thrown a further unexpected weight on us'. The treasurer went on to appeal to Morrison 'to admonish the brethren at Malacca not to incur any extraordinary outlays whatever before the Directors have been apprized and given sanction'; and he concluded sternly: 'The brethren at Malacca have drawn considerably upon us on account of the College, from the weight of whose expenses we naturally look to be relieved by the contributions made to it by the public and taken out by you.' Later, in reply to a letter of explanation from Morrison about these and other items, the treasurer wrote: 'I observe what you say about the bill of £500 by Collie on behalf of the Anglo-Chinese College. The misfortune is that they draw without proper advices and accounts. . . .'[1]

If the relationship between the College and the Society was an extremely loose one on the financial side, the same still remained true of the functional relationship between College and mission at Malacca. Even at the end of discussions held between Morrison and officials of the Missionary Society during his leave in 1824–26 the matter had not been straightened out. W. A. Hankey, the

treasurer, wrote to Morrison afterwards: 'I regret we did not arrive
at some clear understanding on the whole subject when you were
in England, but this was not for want of the subject being before
us, but from want of complacency, viz., to come to some arrangement for the future conduct of the institution and for its support.'
Hankey went on to request that Morrison should now 'bend his
mind to a more *practical* constitution' for the College. 'I do not see
how it can remain a self-dependent institution', he went on, 'for it
will be cared for by no one, and they will grudge to support it who
have no real control over it. In my humble opinion it will be best
to let the Society be its real and only trustees after your own life.'
But Hankey knew well from experience that Morrison could be
highly sensitive and at times even explosive on this whole question.
'From no individual are we, I am persuaded, more ready to
receive advice than from yourself,' he wrote soothingly to Morrison,
'especially (forgive this feeling, which I only utter as from *myself
personally*) if you will give it calmly and deliberately, in connexion
with the grounds and reasons on which you found your recom-
mendations.'[2]

But Morrison could not easily be pinned down to specifics. He
wanted the Society to accept responsibility for the College while
at the same time leaving it independent in practice under its own
board of trustees; but the exact details of any such arrangement
were always missing. 'The College will gradually become exclusively the Soci ty's institution, as indeed it has been as to any
efficiency heretofore,' Morrison wrote to Hankey. Then, moving
swiftly to the attack, he added: 'And had the College not been
there as a central point your missionaries would have been
scattered and the Chinese press neglected. You had much better
do the handsome thing and call the press the Anglo-Chinese Press,
at the same time that you give to it the whole piece of ground that
my late beloved William Milne obtained from the Penang government.' Here Morrison had put his finger on a crucial issue in this
whole problem, the fact that the College building stood on ground

belonging not to itself but to the Missionary Society. He went on:
'Poor Collie wished very much, to prevent the annoyance of envy
and carping, that the premises and the press should revert to the
College. Milne wished it and I wish it. . . . Consolidate the
institution. Singapore Institution is now totally out of the question.'
And later, alluding to 'some suggestion of the Directors to blend
the College and Mission at Malacca', Morrison declared: 'I wish
they were one concern, always having two labourers there. It is
impossible for one missionary to superintend the printing, the
schools, the preaching, and the College.'[3]

There was general agreement among the missionaries with
experience in the region that the college-mission relationship at
Malacca remained unsatisfactory as it stood and that it ought to
be more precisely defined. There should either be a clear separation between the two, or else a complete union of both. John
Smith, reporting to the directors of the Society on his return from
the East in 1830, considered that 'either the College house should
belong to the Mission, or the whole property should belong to the
College'. James Humphreys, in a report submitted on his return to
England a little earlier, had written that 'the mission should be
separated from the College'. But if separation between mission and
College were to take place, would the latter be able to stand
entirely alone? Morrison, though he would never openly admit it,
did not really believe it could. If he were pushed to a final choice
between separation and union he would rather choose union—
though still hoping to retain some of the advantages of separation.
Meanwhile he would go on fighting for independence. There was
no need, he told Hankey, for any change in the original constitution of the College; it 'would not indeed suit my views of what
I think right', he wrote unanswerably. 'All that is required may
be done by the nomination of more trustees from the Directors of
the Missionary Society', he declared, while maintaining that the
officers of the College must also be trustees. 'A great deal of
discretionary power must in my judgment be left to the officers of

the institution', Morrison continued; 'minute legislation would do more harm than good.' He would really prefer the present system, loosely structured as it was, to remain unchanged. He thought his son John, who had been a student at the College, should become President after him, and meanwhile be nominated a trustee.[4]

The directors of the Society, welcoming Morrison's suggestions, decided on a compromise. They agreed to increase the number of trustees, including John Morrison as one of them, but resolved at the same time that no official residing in the College might be a trustee. As for the wider issues involved, the newly appointed secretary of the Society, William Ellis, noted in October 1832 that consideration of the whole question of the College's future would have to be postponed, adding in explanation: 'It is a subject of a comparatively complex and difficult kind, and embraces so many important points, as to require a more patient and extended investigation and consideration.' The new secretary seems generally to have adopted a policy of by-passing Morrison in matters concerning the College and mission at Malacca, and a year later Morrison was complaining that he had heard nothing more on the subject, apart from indirect information that the funds of the College and mission were to be amalgamated. 'Against this I protest . . .', he wrote indignantly, 'for the donors gave their money to the College alone, and it would not be just to appropriate their money to an object, however good, which they did not intend.' And soon afterwards Morrison wrote in further protest to the secretary of the Society: 'You should let me have copies of instructions given to the officers of the College. I have done nothing to justify my being set aside or ousted from my situation of President. . . .' In a further letter written in January 1834 Morrison complained, with some bitterness: 'There is in some quarters a want of co-operation conducted under a specious profession of general goodwill to the cause. There is not an honest, frank-hearted opposition, but an evasion of the subject or a silence respecting it.' And he added sadly: 'Since poor Milne died, I have

never had a hearty fellow-labourer either at home or abroad.'
Some gentle reassurance was forthcoming from Hankey, who wrote
in June 1834 that 'the case of the Anglo-Chinese College was now
under the attention of a special committee . . ., and that the
utmost would be done to put it on a satisfactory basis, which at
present was far from being the case.' But before the letter could
reach him, Morrison was beyond caring about special committees.
He had passed away peacefully in Canton on 1 August 1834.[5]

At the College meanwhile, Jacob Tomlin—essentially a stopgap
Principal—had been succeeded by John Evans. Aged about thirty
when selected by the Missionary Society for the Chinese side of the
Malacca mission, Evans was considered to have 'a superior talent
for the acquisition of languages'. Sailing from London in March
1833, he arrived at Malacca in the following August. There he met
with a cool reception from Tomlin and Josiah Hughes—the latter
still in charge of the Malay side of the mission—who together
occupied the upper floor of the College building. Hughes later
agreed to move out for Evans, but Tomlin not only stayed on but
continued to perform the duties of Principal for another seven
months until Morrison, writing from Canton, finally insisted that
he quit the post and hand over to Evans. The latter meanwhile
had been making good use of his time in language study; he took
Malay lessons from Munshi Abdullah and was ready to preach his
first sermon in Chinese only nine months after arrival.[6]

Tomlin now cut himself off completely from the College, but
Hughes remained with Evans until October 1835 when he in turn
left to give place to a new arrival, Samuel Dyer. Dyer was to prove
a loyal assistant to Evans and a valuable asset to the College.
Appointed originally to Singapore in 1827 he had been retained
instead at the Society's mission in Penang, where he took up the
study of Hokkien and developed a keen interest in printing. By
1833 he had made great progress in devising new methods of
preparing moveable metal type for printing in Chinese. Morrison,
who at this time was setting up a family press with his son John in

Macao, had noted enthusiastically in a letter home: 'P. S. Concerning Chinese cast types Dyer has exceeded himself, and has given us in China a hint by which I think we shall soon exceed Dyer. . . . The great object, cheap Chinese types.' Dyer now joined Evans at the College, 'with special charge of the press'.[7]

Evans was a vigorous and effective Principal. A visitor to the College in 1837 pointedly remarked that he was not only an experienced teacher but also a skilled financier. The year 1837 was described by one of the missionaries as the most active and successful in the life of the College to date. Student enrolment, always restricted, reached a peak of over seventy. Two new wings were added to the College building by special subscription without calling on the funds of the College or the Society. Dyer's work at the press greatly enhanced the College's reputation. The junior schools in Malacca under the mission's care were flourishing. Evans could proudly claim: 'I have advanced the institution to that position of usefulness which the founders originally anticipated, and which none of my predecessors were able to accomplish.' 'Gloom was passing away and the light was springing up', wrote the enthusiastic Dyer.[8]

But there were dark clouds on the horizon. The old plan for a Singapore Institution had recently been revived by a new committee formed there in 1834. As in the earlier scheme originated by Raffles and Morrison, it was again proposed that the Anglo-Chinese College should move from Malacca to Singapore to form a component part of the new Institution. Morrison's son John, a former student of the College and now Chinese Secretary to the British merchant community at Canton, who appears to have assumed the status of patron of the College on his father's death, put his weight behind the plan. 'I am most anxious to see the College established on a firm basis in Singapore', he wrote in 1836, 'Singapore is a place of great consequence; Malacca has very much changed since Singapore was founded; its trade is utterly insignificant.' The secretary of the Missionary Society wrote in reply that while the directors regarded 'the ultimate purpose of the College as a matter of far greater importance than the precise locality of its operations'—that purpose being to furnish 'the means of introduction into China proper'—they had to admit that the Malacca mission as a whole had never been able to exert much influence on China itself. Therefore, they concluded, 'we have been led to a general concurrence in your proposal for removing the College.' But Evans and Dyer at Malacca, when informed of the proposal, protested vigorously. Singapore, they pointed out, was essentially a trading city with a comparatively small population of young people and with little interest in education, whereas 'here we have a firm and established footing'. In face of these protests and in view of the very favourable reports of the College's progress received from Malacca and from John Morrison himself, the Society decided to backtrack. 'Our views have been considerably modified since we last wrote to you on the subject', the secretary now informed John Morrison. 'Many of the advantages already gained might be lost by the transfer of the College to Singapore.' It would therefore be better 'to allow it to continue its present pleasing operations rather than risk its dissolution by an attempted removal'. Thus, for the second time, the threat to the College's independent existence by removing it from Malacca had passed. But there was yet another to come.[9]

End and Beginning

'WE are still deprived of the privilege of entering the gates of China', reported the directors of the London Missionary Society in 1833. But by the end of the 1830s it seemed very likely that this privilege could not be denied for much longer. The tensions and pressures that had been building up around the opium trade in the Canton-Macao area over the previous years had reached bursting point. The East India Company's monopoly control of British trade with China had been withdrawn by parliament in 1833, and the British government itself then took over the supervision of the Canton trade and the responsibility for Anglo-Chinese relations. In a new free-for-all atmosphere, the opium trade and the smuggling associated with it in the Canton river area boomed even more mightily than before. By about 1840 the sales of opium to Cantonese merchants had become the main source of exchange with which foreign traders at Canton paid for purchases of Chinese tea and silk.

Over sixty British merchants trading in and around Canton, with the backing of Chambers of Commerce in Britain itself, made an appeal to the British government to bring pressure to bear on China to set up 'normal' trade and diplomatic relations. But the official Chinese attitude of closed-door self-sufficiency only stiffened in response. Peking sent a prominent official to Canton in March 1839 with orders to clamp down on the opium trade. The stern measures which he adopted soon brought about the surrender of all opium contained in foreign ships lying in and outside the Canton river and the withdrawal of British subjects from Macao to Hong Kong island, then a virtually uninhabited 'barren rock'.

When news of these developments reached Britain, the Foreign Secretary, Lord Palmerston, known to history as the arch-exponent of gunboat diplomacy, ordered a naval expedition to proceed to north China waters and present a set of demands to the Peking government. These were to include the opening of five ports to British trade and consular representation, and the cession of an island off the Chinese coast. But although the expedition carried out its mission and negotiations were begun, no agreement could be reached. The British therefore resorted to force and the 'Opium War' began. Chinese forts protecting the mouth of the Canton river were attacked and captured in January 1841. A local compromise agreement then followed which allowed for the cession of Hong Kong to Britain, but this was soon repudiated by the governments of both sides.

The final stage in this protracted crisis began when in August 1841 Sir Henry Pottinger arrived from England to take charge of the situation on the China coast. Under his command an expedition moved north again, this time striking at the vital internal communications of China itself. Taking Shanghai in June 1842, the whole British naval force sailed up the Yangtze river. When it reached Nanking in August the Chinese imperial government gave in, accepting the terms of the Treaty of Nanking by which five ports were opened to British trade and residence, and Hong Kong was ceded to Britain.

The war clouds were already gathering over the China coast when James Legge arrived at Malacca to join the Anglo-Chinese College in January 1840. He had been selected by the London Missionary Society as 'a young man very well qualified' to serve as an assistant to the Principal, John Evans. Born at Huntly in Aberdeenshire in 1815, Legge had joined the Missionary Society in 1839 after training at Aberdeen University and Highbury Theological College.[1] He received his first tuition in Chinese from a former Principal of the Anglo-Chinese College, Samuel Kidd, then professor of Chinese at University College, London. On arrival at Malacca, Legge was received kindly by Evans and arrangements were soon made for him to begin an intensive study of the Hokkien dialect. But Legge seems to have started his work at too hard a pace; it was later said of him that he never in his whole life took more than four hours' sleep out of twenty-four. Not long after his arrival at the College he had to admit: 'I have been studying hard, too hard for the climate; I was obliged to call in the doctor . . .; my illness has thrown me somewhat back with the language.'[2]

Now, due perhaps in part to a temporary psychological imbalance resulting from overwork and illness, and in part to the somewhat brash impatience of an ambitious young man of twenty-four, Legge became at times moody and depressed, and at other times aggressively critical of his surroundings, his colleagues and the College itself. He wrote to the Missionary Society of his 'depressing sense of loneliness'. He complained that conditions at Malacca were 'not so encouraging as he had reason to expect'; the town itself was 'daily dwindling' as a European settlement, and the College was really not much more than 'an elementary school'. Evans on his side seems to have had much to put up with from Legge at this time, as he wrote to the Society's directors in November 1840:

'*It has been for some time a matter of much grief to me to see a young person who has so recently joined me as a colleague, entirely ignorant of the manners and customs of the natives and quite inexperienced, not only desirous of introducing and setting up his own plans, but insisting on having them carried into effect. . . . It is grievous, very grievous, for me to inform you that in consequence of Mr. Legge acting as above stated, both Mr. Werth[3] and myself feel it to be our conscientious duty to separate ourselves from him. Indeed, to speak quite correctly, he cut us first. Mr. Legge kept aloof. . . .*

We cannot any longer unite, but we will endeavour to continue discharging
our duties as heretofore, until you send out others to succeed us in the work.
It will be exceedingly unpleasant to carry on even for five or six months;
however we will endeavour to do so. . . .'

But, as it happened, Evans did not have to carry on much longer.
Less than a month later a cholera epidemic, sweeping through
Malacca, had claimed both him and Josiah Hughes among its
victims.[4]

Meanwhile, however, Legge had continued to denounce the
College and to disparage the work of his predecessors in a torrent
of complaint and criticism. The College, he observed, had been
praised by many in the past, but 'never was praise more unde-
served; never had Institution more of pretence and less of reality'.
'It was altogether uncalled for,' he went on; 'the founding of it
was unwise and inexpedient.' The intentions of Morrison were
sincere, but the College had been an imposition on the public
because of mismanagement and dishonesty. There had been 'a lack
of moral courage to lay the real position before the Directors'.[5]

Whatever element of truth there may have been in Legge's
accusations, it seems difficult at first to understand the purpose
behind his shrill denunciation of the College and the serious if
unspecific charges which he brought against his predecessors at this
time. But an explanation suggests itself at once in the conclusion
which he went on to draw. 'The programme of Dr. Morrison
cannot be effected in Malacca, nor *out of China,*' Legge wrote.
'May it not be possible to transfer it there? The providence of
God is doing great things in China. . . .' For Legge had not been
slow to realize which way the wind of change was blowing. By
August 1840 the British were hammering at the doors of China.
If those doors were opened and remained open, the great day
would have arrived for the Missionary Society to advance from
its stations in Southeast Asia to new forward bases on the coast of
China itself. Legge was determined that he should be included in

the great forward march rather than be left behind to soldier on at Malacca. He must therefore completely disassociate himself in spirit from the College's past and from Malacca itself, repudiating the whole concept of an Anglo-Chinese College outside of China as being essentially unsound and doomed to failure from the start. He felt the need to condemn the past regime at the College in order to establish his own image in the minds of the Society's directors as a man of the future, one who, as a prime mover, would unquestionably be included in any plan to transfer the mission from Malacca and make a fresh start in China. Hence the part which it seems Legge had chosen to play, that of the pure knight in shining armour, condemning the wrongs of the past and pointing the way ahead to a noble future. 'This institution will probably remain my care', he wrote to his brother, 'not here, but established in Hong Kong on a noble basis. . . .'[6]

Even after the death of Evans, when Legge took over charge of the College, he continued to denounce the abuses, real or imagined, of the past. He complained about the state of the College library, the incomplete or missing copies of books, the lack of a catalogue.[7] The College, he asserted, had never been successful in its aim of promoting the study of Chinese and English literature. In the task of spreading the Gospel it had been more of a hindrance than a help, for it had absorbed the time and energies of the missionaries and prevented them from mixing with the people. 'You have been imposed upon, as well as the public in general', Legge reiterated to the directors of the Missionary Society. And on the long-debated question of the College-Mission relationship his verdict was pointed and brief. 'The College and the Mission here are in truth but one thing—to their mutual injury. So close is their connection that they have nearly stifled each other.' The remedy was simple, and consisted of two clear steps. First, a chosen individual (could it be Legge himself?) should be placed in sole charge of the College with the combined salaries and living allowances of the Principal and the professor of Chinese; and that individual 'should be enjoined to perfect himself especially in the Chinese language'. Second, the College should be moved to China as soon as possible. 'It is impossible that the institution can ever realize the wishes of its founder or yourselves out of China', Legge declared. 'It will be of little use to transfer it to Singapore or any other such station; for there are the same radical objections to the establishment of a great institution everywhere but in China itself or on its immediate borders.'[8]

Other interested voices besides that of Legge were being raised at this time in support of the idea of moving the College to China. John Morrison, son of the founder, who as we have seen had advocated the amalgamation of the College with the revived Singapore Institution in 1836, now began to recommend the removal of the College to Hong Kong island (on which British subjects had collected after July 1839), there to combine with the Morrison Education Society which had been formed in 1836 at Canton in memory of his father. Writing from Hong Kong, John Morrison put forward a practical point of view in his letter to the directors of the Missionary Society: 'On the settlement of commercial and political affairs here', he wrote, 'the funds will readily take a new start, and there is no object that will so much open men's purses here as the Anglo-Chinese College, can we but give a fair ground of assurance that it is to take new life.' Morrison urged that 'the College be removed to China as a school of higher education in connection with the Morrison Education Society and under its trustees as the local managing committee'. Legge, writing in March 1842, observed that many substantial houses had already been erected in Hong Kong, but now his ideas had further expanded and he had begun to visualize himself and the College located somewhere nearer than Hong Kong to the heart of China: 'I should prefer seeing the College established in some place further north than Hong Kong', he wrote.[9]

The London Missionary Society noted these various suggestions about the future of the College, while keeping the current context of affairs in East Asia under constant review. It expressed its general attitude to the China situation in March 1841 in cautiously optimistic terms:

'With the great public question in agitation between our own Government and that of China we, as a religious body, have no direct concern; but while we cannot but feel, with every friend of humanity, the most earnest desire that all the causes of difference may be adjusted without recourse to the arbitration of war, we further anticipate that the Divine purposes of mercy on behalf of China are ripening fast and that whatever may be the issue of the present commotions, in a political or commercial point of view, a way is gradually opening, by means of these events, for the unfettered diffusion of Gospel light through the length and breadth of that vast Empire.'

The underlying community of political, commercial and religious interests in the British approach to China could hardly have been more elegantly expressed.[10]

By the end of the year 1841 the Missionary Society had arrived at the decision to close down the College at Malacca. Legge was informed in November that according to legal advice the College trustees had never been properly appointed and that the trust had thus devolved on the Society's directors; he was now therefore authorized to wind up the affairs of the College. At the same time John Morrison was informed that 'in all probability' his suggestion to remove the College from Malacca to China would be adopted. By February 1842 the Society felt able to assure Legge that it agreed with his view that 'no permanent institution in the nature of an Anglo-Chinese College can be conducted with effect out of China Proper'. Then events on the China coast, as already described, began to move into their final phase. The Chinese government bowed at last to the inevitable. The Treaty of Nanking, with its provision for the opening of the 'treaty ports' and the cession of Hong Kong to Britain, was signed on 29 August 1842. 'The establishment of peaceful relations between England and China forms a new and most important era in the history of missions', observed the directors of the Missionary Society on hearing the news. 'How important an event is the throwing open of China to European intercourse and enterprise', Legge exclaimed; 'this treaty is the lighting up of the scene for a mighty drama.'[11]

'China is open. . . . What are we to do?' asked Samuel Dyer in October 1842; and he went on as if in reply: 'We are decidedly of opinion that the reasons which led to the establishment of Chinese missions in the Archipelago exist no longer, and that the time is come when every Chinese missionary must feel that he ought to be in China.' The Missionary Society was of the same mind. Considering 'the gratifying and important intelligence' of the peace treaty with China at a meeting in London at the end of December 1842, the directors resolved that all the Society's missionaries in the East Asian field should assemble at Hong Kong to draw up detailed proposals for future operations in China. With regard to the Anglo-Chinese College, application should be made to the Hong Kong government for a grant of a suitable site for a new building on the island, and if the application were unsuccessful a site should be purchased out of the proceeds of sale of the Society's property at Malacca.[12]

James Legge was then instructed to arrange for the sale of the Malacca property, which took place on 28 April 1843. The College building, outhouses and grounds went to J. B. Westerhout, assistant Resident of Malacca at this time, for 2,120 Spanish dollars. The total amount realized by the sale of the property, which included two dwelling houses acquired by John Evans, was 3,650 dollars. The mission chapel built in 1826–27 was left in trust for the use of the people of Malacca. Legge had already sent the Malay and English printing equipment to Singapore; the Chinese press and the library were now packed up and sent to Hong Kong. Finally Legge himself, happy to have presided over the dissolution of the Anglo-Chinese College in its original home, left Malacca on 6 May 1843 for Singapore, reaching Hong Kong eventually on 10 August.[13]

With Legge's arrival, seven missionaries[14] were assembled in Hong Kong, forming a general committee of the London Society's China Mission. They included William C. Milne, a son of the builder of the Malacca College; also taking part in the early discussions was John Morrison, son of the founder. The latter had a footing in both missionary and governmental camps, since he represented the family interest and the Morrison Education Society on the one hand, and—unofficially—the government of Hong Kong as acting Colonial Secretary on the other. Only three of the seven missionaries present had direct experience of work at the College—Samuel Dyer, James Legge and Walter Medhurst. Dyer had always been a loyal supporter of the College, but Legge had roundly condemned it from within, while Medhurst had left it years before in a mood of anger and resentment.

Following the instructions of the Society in London, the missionaries duly submitted a formal request to the government of Hong Kong for a grant of land for a new College building. In his reply the Governor, Sir Henry Pottinger, revealed that John Morrison and the Morrison Education Society had already moved ahead of the missionaries in obtaining 'an extensive and valuable piece of land' on Hong Kong island in the previous year, 'with the idea that the [Education] Society was to supersede the Anglo-Chinese College'. Not only that, but the annual official subsidy of 1,200 dollars allocated to the College for many years had been transferred to the Morrison Education Society at the same time. Pottinger, it also appeared, had been particularly nettled by the fact that his invitation in early 1842 for applications from Malacca, Penang and Singapore for posts of Chinese interpreter in Hong Kong 'during the late war with China' had evoked not a single response. So much, the Governor must have concluded, for the results of subsidizing the education of overseas Chinese in those centres. In any case, he announced, the home government's instructions precluded any further grants of land in Hong Kong. This was an unexpected rebuff for the missionaries. Samuel Dyer,

acting as secretary of the missionary conference, wrote to London
of the 'serious and unexpected difficulties' which had arisen.
Legge commented: 'The fact is that Sir Henry Pottinger has
evidently got a very unfavourable opinion regarding the College ...,
but though the College was for many years an imposition on the
Government and the public, he ought to do what the rules of
honour would require him to do, without respect to the deserts of
the institution. I do not blame him for stopping the grant, but
only for stopping it without warning or notice.'[15]

An immediate result of this setback to the plans of the missionary conference was that its attitude was now completely changed
into one of disillusionment with the idea of an Anglo-Chinese
College as originally conceived by Morrison and Milne—that is,
as an institution of higher education. As such, the missionaries told
themselves, the College had failed to produce the goods. What
practical results could it show? Where were the Chinese graduates,
so carefully trained in English as well as in their own language and
literature, when they were wanted? Where were the interpreters
when they were called for? Legge himself had dutifully exclaimed:
'The Anglo-Chinese College has not yet furnished so much as a
common interpreter'—which was in fact quite untrue, as we shall
see. Now, reacting strongly against Robert Morrison's earlier
vision, the missionaries would be content to see the future of the
College in a much more subdued light, in narrower and more
functional terms, as indeed little more than a training school for
gospel preachers. Legge had already anticipated this narrowing
down of Morrison's purpose when he wrote of his future students:
'It will be my task more to train them in theology and Biblical
science.'

On 26 August 1843 the missionary conference in Hong Kong
passed the following resolutions:

*As the confidence and support of the Government has been withdrawn from
the Anglo-Chinese College it seems desirable that the institution should be*

devoted principally, if not exclusively, to the training of converts and candidates for the Ministry, especially as it seems unadvisable to combine secular with religious objects in one institution when they are in danger of coming into collision.

That the name of the Anglo-Chinese College be dropped, and that the institution be henceforth denominated The Theological Seminary of the London Missionary Society's Missions in China.[16]

A year later the directors of the London Missionary Society reported that in accordance with the recommendation of the Hong Kong conference held in August 1843 they had resolved on converting the Anglo-Chinese College into a Theological Seminary.

Thus the Malacca 'liberal arts' college of 1818 was to become the Hong Kong theological seminary of 1843. Robert Morrison would undoubtedly have deplored this decision; he would surely have poured scorn on those who thus denied the wider educational vision by which both he and Milne, the founder and the builder, had been inspired. But the Missionary Society had got what it had always really wanted in the end.

James Legge soon became reconciled to the location of the new theological seminary in Hong Kong rather than somewhere further to the north. 'I like the aspect of Hong Kong', he wrote in August 1843. 'It is a congeries of hills. The only level ground is in the intervening valleys. No people living here could fall into the mistake that the Earth was a vast plain. The Chinese population is not yet very large, but as soon as the mercantile houses come over from Macao there will be an increase of several thousands. Ultimately the island will become a hive. . . .' Prophetic words![17]

Apart from a handful of students, only Legge, Medhurst and three Chinese printers—Leang Ah Fah, Kew Ah Gung and Ho Ah Sun—remained to represent the Anglo-Chinese College of the past. James Legge was to carry on his work in Hong Kong until 1873, with return visits to England and Scotland in the years 1845 to 1848, 1858, and 1867 to 1870. In Hong Kong he devoted his

time to church affairs—serving as minister of the independent
Union Church and managing the theological seminary (never
very successful and finally closed down in 1856)—as well as to the
study of Chinese language and literature. His great work of
scholarship was to be the edition of *The Chinese classics*, with
Chinese text, translation and notes, which was published in five
volumes between 1861 and 1872.[18] Returning finally to England
in 1873, Legge was appointed in 1875 professor of Chinese at
Oxford University, a position which he held with distinction until
his death in 1897. 'Next to Hong Kong,' he once wrote to a friend,
'Oxford is the most delightful place in the world.' His considered
judgment on the whole matter of the missionary approach to
China was one that would have been accepted by Morrison and
Milne. 'Missionaries have not merely to reform,' Legge wrote,
'they have to revolutionize. . . . Confucianism is not antagonistic
to Christianity. It is, however, a system whose issues are bounded
by the East and by time. . . . Let no one think any labour too great
to make himself familiar with Confucian books. So shall missionaries in China come fully to understand the work they have to do.'[19]

Walter Medhurst, whose earlier career in Malacca and Penang
we have already traced, was not likely to remain in Hong Kong—or
indeed in any one place—for long. Always adventurous and a
compulsive traveller, he was naturally eager to move on to some
point nearer to the heart of China. Mention has already been made
of his earlier travels in Southeast Asia—his voyage along the east
coast of the Malaysian peninsula in 1828; his journeys in Java and
Bali in company with a fellow missionary, Jacob Tomlin, in
1829–30. Then in 1835 he voyaged along the coast of China from
Canton to Tientsin and back in an American ship, the brig *Huron,*
distributing tracts at a number of ports on the way. Returning to
England in 1836, Medhurst there wrote *China, its state and prospects*
(London, 1838), a useful survey of the Protestant missions in East
Asia up to that time, with a discussion of the broad cultural
framework within which missionaries would have to operate. By

1. Robert Morrison, D. D. as President of the Anglo-Chinese College. Drawn by J. Wildman, engraved by T. Blood. *Reproduced by permission of the Urban Council of Hong Kong from the collection of historical paintings of the Hong Kong Museum of Art.*

2. Dr & Mrs Milne. Drawn by G. Baxter. From Robert Philip, *The life and opinions of Rev. William Milne, D. D., missionary to China,* London, John Snow, 1840.

Between pages 114 and 115

3. Malacca. From *Missionary Sketches*, no. LIV, July 1831. *With the permission of the London Missionary Society.*

4. The Anglo-Chinese College at Malacca. Drawing by Capt. P. J. Begbie, water-colour by J. Gantz. From Capt. P. J. Begbie, *The Malayan Peninsula*, Madras, 1834.

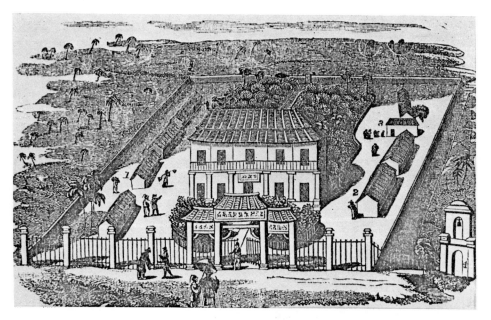

1. Chinese Printing Office   2. English Printing Office   3. Chinese School   4. Western Gate of Malacca

5. Bird's-eye view of the Anglo-Chinese College-House at Malacca. From *Missionary Sketches,* no. XXVIII, January 1825. *With the permission of the London Missionary Society.*

6. Claudius Henry Thomsen, member of the College staff, 1818–22. *With the permission of the London Missionary Society.*

7. Walter Henry Medhurst, member of the College staff, 1818–20. Drawn by W. T. Strutt. *With the permission of the London Missionary Society.*

8. Rev. William Milne, D. D.
From *The Indo-Chinese Gleaner.*
no. 1, May 1817.

9. Rev. Robert Morrison, D. D.
and his assistants in the translation of the Bible into Chinese.
Engraved by Jenkins from a
painting by George Chinnery.
From E. Morrison, *Memoirs of
the life and labours of Robert
Morrison, D. D.,* London, Longman, Orme, Brown, Green and
Longmans, 1839.

THE

INDO-CHINESE GLEANER.

No. II. August, 1817.

CONTAINING

EXTRACTS OF THE OCCASIONAL CORRESPONDENCE

OF THOSE

MISSIONARIES IN THE EAST,

WHO LABOUR

Under the Direction of the Missionary Society;

TOGETHER WITH

MISCELLANEOUS NOTICES RELATIVE TO THE PHILOSOPHY
MYTHOLOGY, LITERATURE, AND HISTORY OF THE INDO-
CHINESE NATIONS; DRAWN CHIEFLY FROM THE NATIVE
LANGUAGES.

PUBLISHED QUARTERLY,

OR AS OFTEN AS MATTER CAN BE FURNISHED.

MALACCA:

Printed at the Mission Press.

1817.

10. Title page of *The Indo-Chinese Gleaner,*
no. 2, August 1817.

A

RETROSPECT

OF

THE FIRST TEN YEARS

OF THE

PROTESTANT MISSION

TO

CHINA,

(NOW, IN CONNECTION WITH THE MALAY, DENOMINATED,
THE ULTRA-GANGES MISSIONS.)

*Accompanied with Miscellaneous Remarks on the Li-
terature, History, and Mythology of China, &c.*

BY

WILLIAM MILNE.

MALACCA:

PRINTED AT THE ANGLO-CHINESE PRESS.

1820.

11. Title page of William Milne, *A retrospect of the first ten years of the Protestant
mission to China,* Malacca, 1820. From
Robert Morrison's library, now in the
University of Hong Kong Library.

12.   The Dutch Church and Stadthuis at Malacca, 2 January 1807. Drawn by E. H. Locker, engraved by George Cooke. From John Pinkerton, *A general collection of the best and most interesting voyages and travels in all parts of the world,* London, Longman, Hurst, Rees, Orme and Brown, 1808–14, vol. 8.

13.   Mr Medhurst with Choo-Tih-Lang, attended by a Malay boy. Painted by G. Baxter. From W. H. Medhurst, *China, its state and prospects*, London, John Snow, 1838.

14. James Humphries, member of the College staff, 1821–29. *With the permission of the London Missionary Society.*

15. Josiah Hughes, member of the College staff, 1830–35. *With the permission of the London Missionary Society.*

16. John Evans, member of the College staff, 1833–40. *With the permission of the London Missionary Society.*

17. Samuel Dyer, member of the College staff, 1835–42. *With the permission of the London Missionary Society.*

18.　Drawbridge at Malacca, 2 January 1807. Drawn by E. H. Locker, engraved by George Cooke. From John Pinkerton, *A general collection of the best and most interesting voyages and travels in all parts of the world*, London, Longman, Hurst, Rees, Orme and Brown, 1808–14, vol. 8.

19.　Dr Legge and his three Chinese students. From a painting by H. Room. From Helen E. Legge, *James Legge, missionary and scholar*, London, The Religious Tract Society, 1905.

1838 he was back in Batavia (Jakarta), which had been his main base since leaving Penang in 1821. Then with the opening of the 'treaty ports' to British residents in accordance with the Nanking Treaty of August 1842, Medhurst quickly moved to Shanghai and opened a mission for the London Missionary Society there. He attended the missionary conference in Hong Kong in August 1843 when, as we have seen, the future of the Anglo-Chinese College was settled. Back in Shanghai, Medhurst was soon making new travel plans, and in the spring of 1845, in defiance of existing regulations, he journeyed from Shanghai into the interior of China for seven weeks, visiting 'the silk and green tea districts'. Wearing Chinese dress, a false pigtail or queue, and dark glasses, he was in 'constant danger of detection, especially from his habit of talking Malay in his sleep'. However he survived the perils of the journey, returned safely to Shanghai, and wrote an excellent account of his experiences.[20]

An intrepid traveller, Medhurst was also a gifted linguist and an accomplished scholar. He took a prominent part in the Chinese translation of the Bible known as the Delegates' version (1855). Towards the end of his career in China he established himself as a pioneer in Taiping studies, translating official documents of the Taiping rebels and publishing a 'Critical review of the books of the insurgents' in 1853. Leaving Shanghai for the last time in September 1856 Medhurst reached England in January 1857, but died in London only a few days after his arrival.

CHAPTER FOURTEEN

College Teachers

WITH the closing of the Anglo-Chinese College at Malacca and its removal in a changed form to Hong Kong, the past activities and achievements of its members could now be viewed in some perspective. The aim of this and the next chapter is to present a general impression of the internal organization of the College as a working institution, and of the day-to-day activities of its teachers and students.

In practice the College and the mission at Malacca, as Morrison himself had to admit, were in fact one and the same in terms of personnel, 'the Society's missionaries being officers in the College'. From the time of Milne to that of Legge, the senior member of the mission had normally been the College Principal, and other members of the mission had regularly taught in the College. But if all the missionaries taught at the College, not all who taught were missionaries. Language instructors and assistants in Chinese, Malay, Siamese and Vietnamese were recruited from time to time as non-missionary teachers. Usually, however, their names went altogether unrecorded or, if they did appear in the record, would often be reproduced in a crude form of romanized spelling that gave only a rough approximation to the original sounds.

The first of the Chinese instructors to join the College staff was named simply as Lee. Like other Chinese instructors he was regularly referred to by the title *Seën-sang* (i.e. teacher) following his name, viz., Lee Seën-sang. Lee came with Milne from Canton to Malacca in 1815 as tutor-assistant in the mission and joined the College when it opened in 1819, remaining on the staff until at least 1830. Another Chinese instructor who came from Canton to join the College in its early days was Chu Tsing (Chu Seën-sang). He taught at Malacca until 1832, when he returned to Canton, was baptized by Morrison, and served as the latter's personal assistant during the last nine months of his life. Names of other Chinese teachers recorded on the staff lists from time to time included Yaou (who had been the first student to enter the College, presumably Malacca-born) in 1824, 1826 and 1834; Yim (1827); K'o (1834, 1835), and Chuy Gwan (1835).[1]

Besides such teachers, there were of course Chinese printers and typecutters in the Anglo-Chinese press which was very closely linked to the work of the College. Leang Ah Fah, the best known of the Cantonese printers, came to Malacca with Milne in 1815, and his chief assistant, Kew Ah Gung, arrived not long afterwards. Leang, then aged about twenty-three, was baptized by Milne in November 1816 and later was ordained by Morrison before the latter sailed for England in 1824. Leang and Kew worked closely together at Malacca for years on the printing of the Chinese translation of the Bible by Morrison and Milne which was completed in May 1823. Kew Ah Gung was also baptized at some stage, and was said to have visited England several times before 1816. He seems to have worked at the College press at Malacca from beginning to end, moving with Legge to Hong Kong in 1843. Other Cantonese printers mentioned as having trained at the College press were Ah Chaou and Ah Tsieh. The former was back in Canton early in 1824, working with Morrison as 'writer or copyist'.[2]

Other teachers even more generally nameless than the Chinese were the instructors in 'Siamese, Cochin-chinese and Malay' occasionally referred to in the records. A Siamese teacher named

Nunsid was listed in 1823, and 'a native of Cochin-china' was said
to be engaged in translation work at the College in the same year.
We are left with only the sketchiest of information about such
individuals. The only non-missionary teacher and general assistant
at the College who has spoken for himself was the Malay scholar
Abdullah bin Abdul Kadir, author of the autobiographical *Hikayat
Abdullah,* first published in 1849.[3]

Abdullah was an alert and sympathetic observer of the world
around him. His *Hikayat* or 'story' interestingly reflects a perhaps
untypical Malay response to change at that time. Tolerant,
humane and progressive in outlook, he was always ready—perhaps
too ready—to accept and admire the Western ideas and innova-
tions that were rapidly entering his world. He was a man of
considerable talent if of no great depth of understanding, and he
possessed the great qualities of charity and humility.

Born in Malacca in 1797 of mixed Arab, South Indian (Tamil)
and Malay parentage, Abdullah soon showed an enquiring mind
and a gift for languages. He had already studied Tamil and
Hindustani as well as Arabic and Malay when, at the age of
fourteen, he was employed as a writer and copyist on the staff
of Stamford Raffles during the latter's visit to Malacca in 1810–11
as special agent in connection with the British-Indian expeditionary force against Java. Then when William Milne came to
Malacca to start the London Society's mission in 1815, Abdullah
attended the first mission school to learn English. Thus began his
association with the missionaries and the College at Malacca which
was to last on and off until 1840. Abdullah was Malay tutor to
Milne, Thomsen and many of the later missionaries; he worked in
the College library and on translation, printing and publishing for
the Malay press. He went with Thomsen to Singapore in 1822 and
thereafter moved frequently between that city and Malacca until
1840, when he settled permanently in Singapore and started
writing his *Hikayat.* He died on a pilgrimage to Mecca in 1854.

Abdullah provides a lively and most valuable witness of the

events of his day, even though he could be thoroughly unsystematic, vague and muddled in his treatment of facts and the sequence of events, including those relating to his work at the Anglo-Chinese College. He left vivid pen-pictures of many of the people he met and worked with—Milne, 'a good-natured man, courteous in speech . . .; a man of fine character . . .; very persevering in his studies'; Morrison, 'an upright man, clever at gaining people's confidence . . ., in his behaviour, speech, habits and mannerisms, and the things in his room, he was just like a Chinese man'; John Slater, with 'white hair and pale eyes'; John Ince, 'good-looking and very clever'; and Walter Medhurst, 'a most enthusiastic teacher' with 'a logical mind and a clever head; anything that was taught him he learnt quickly'.

Abdullah himself, as he appeared to an observer in Singapore in the 1840s, was described as follows: 'In physiognomy he was a Tamilian of southern Hindustan; slightly bent forward, spare, energetic, bronze in complexion, oval-faced, high-nosed, one eye squinting outwards a little. He dressed in the usual style of Malacca Tamils; Acheen *seluar*, check *sarong*, printed *baju*, square skull cap, and sandals.[4] He had the vigour and pride of the Arab, the perseverence and subtlety of the Hindoo—in language and national sympathy only was he a Malay.'[5]

The reference to dress in the above description of Abdullah's appearance suggests the question—How did the 'Ultra-Ganges' missionaries dress? Morrison supplies a clue to the answer in the final lines of a revealing self-portrait penned in Macao in September 1817, which is perhaps worth quoting at length for the personal details it provides:

I hasten to notice that subject which is of most importance in the letter before me, viz., the opinion of a gentleman who had been in Canton that I had become quite a convivial man, quite a bon vivant. It is difficult for me to speak of myself. If I am now what he means by the language he uses, I was always so, for I am not different now from what I have been the last twenty

*years. If he says that I am fond of society, of joining convivial parties, of being
at the tables of the rich or luxurious, he says what is not true. I am expected
to be at the Company's table, and might be there every day of the week, but I am
seldom there more than once a week. And at home I have seldom more than
one dish; I eat my solitary meal without any luxuries and sometimes for months
together the same dish every day—a little Irish stew. I visit little and never
long. I am seldom invited to private parties. I should have thought that what
has emanated from my study during the last ten years incompatible with being
a very convivial man. I never was a great talker, and I rarely talk at table.
I am more disposed to melancholy than to conviviality. I sometimes defend in
company what I consider moral and religious truth, and I may occasionally
take part in what I consider innocent cheerfulness. I am stout, and he perhaps
thinks it necessary that a missionary should be emaciated. I walk out in a
white jacket and a white straw hat, which has given offence to some visitors
from England. . . .*[6]

For other details concerning missionary wear we are again
indebted to Morrison. While he was on leave in England in 1825
the Missionary Society received a letter from Samuel Milton, the
Singapore missionary, sharply criticizing the teaching staff of the
Anglo-Chinese College, whom he described as giving themselves
great airs and decking themselves out in 'gorgeous robes and
mandarin caps'. The letter was referred by the secretary of the
Society to Morrison, whose first comment was that Milton had
been bitterly disappointed that he was not made Principal of the
College when Milne died. He then went on:

*As to the 'gorgeous robes and mandarin caps', the fact is this: the
Principal and Professor and Missionaries at Malacca wear usually a white
sailor's jacket and trousers—which short jacket is not deemed by Asiatics a
very decent dress for grave persons, nor would English think it a becoming
dress for leading divine worship in public. Humphreys and Collie therefore
had sent them from China a black gown in the fashion of those at Glasgow,
which they throw over their shoulders when they conduct the devotions of the*

congregation of workmen and students in the College Hall. And they have a Chinese trencher cap, not worn by any mandarins but an old-fashioned chieftain's cap resembling the trencher caps in Europe, and this is the innocent badge of the Anglo-Chinese College.[7]

A further footnote on dress comes from the pen of the missionary John Smith, writing home from Singapore in April 1827, six months after his arrival in the East. The plaintive note of his remarks must have been re-echoed many times during the nineteenth century by newcomers from Britain experiencing for the first time the oppressive tropical heat of the Malaysian region. 'My European clothes are here scarcely of any use', Smith wrote to the treasurer of the Missionary Society; 'for a part of them might be substituted calico, which is here universally worn. No one who has not endured on a ship's deck or on a sandy soil the burning rays of a vertical sun can have any idea of the comfort which you would administer by substituting thin white cotton for heavy woollen cloth, which is enough to melt one away.'[8]

Despite such difficulties the first courses of instruction commenced at the College in the autumn of 1819. They reflected the teaching aims and 'the declared object of the institution, . . . the cultivation of Chinese and English literature'. Students would read and discuss 'the books of Confucius, the Gospel of St. Matthew, the Epistle to the Hebrews, and the Chinese classic Shoo-King'. They would be required to read and memorize 'Morrison's Dialogues in Chinese and English, and a similar production by Dr. Milne; a Christian catechism called the Yew-heo, and two Chinese moral compilations called Ming-sin-poou-keen, and Seaou-heo'. They were also taught essay-writing in Chinese and English, and the outlines of geography. Milne strongly favoured a course in geography on the ground that 'what tends to enlarge the mind is friendly to the Gospel'.[9]

The general course structure introduced by Milne was retained with little variation until after his death in 1822. Then Morrison, with a larger staff at his disposal, appears to have widened the scope of studies as a result of his visitation of 1823. In his report *To the public* (1823) he announced under the heading of tuition that 'the Chinese students shall be taught to read and understand the Chinese classics and the Christian scriptures, and to read and write the English language; also History, Geography, the Use of the Globes, Logic, Moral Philosophy and Theology.' Lectures would be given three times a day, at 9 a.m., 4 p.m. and 8 p.m. It was recorded in July 1823 that students in the senior class were being taught 'English Grammar and Sacred Theology by a perusal of the Holy Bible both in Chinese and English', and that they had also 'lately copied and read in English and Chinese a part of Joyce's Scientific Dialogues and various papers in English and Chinese' prepared by Morrison.[10]

The main lines of instruction thus laid down seem to have been followed, with interesting variations but without any basic deviation, through the 1820s and into the 1830s. Senior students in 1826 were being taught 'Sacred history, English grammar, Chinese and English composition, astronomy, geography, and beginning geometry'. The senior class of 1827 studied 'arithmetic, geography, Christian theology, Euclid, mechanics, and astronomy (a reprint, with some alterations, of Joyce's first and second volumes of Scientific Dialogues)'. Senior courses in 1829 included 'philosophy, astronomy, geography, history of Greece, arithmetic. etc. . . .'[11]

If the senior courses thus listed for the years approaching the middle period of the College's life be taken as a fair sample, one cannot but be impressed by the variety and breadth of scope of the courses offered in what was after all a distinctly small-scale institution, working always within very narrow limits of finance and manpower. There was nothing narrow about the vision that lay behind the devising of such a curriculum, even if—as surely must have been the case—performance fell short of promise. This was no 'elementary school', as Legge chose to describe it. And it was something very much more, of much broader human purpose, than a 'theological seminary'. For Milne and Morrison, the introduction of Christianity into a country as civilized as China could only hope to succeed if it were visualized as part of a process of acculturation, a gradual integration into the pattern of traditional Chinese culture. Christianity could not simply be sold to the Chinese as a kind of export commodity. Its introduction must somehow form part of a meeting of the two cultures, European and Chinese. European culture was a single whole; the Christian religion was but one expression—though no doubt the supreme one—of that culture. For Morrison and Milne therefore the great aim of the Anglo-Chinese College should be to contribute in some way to the introduction of Christianity into the Chinese world, not as a system of belief in itself, but as a moral and cultural force deriving from the totality of the European tradition. Their students would be helped and encouraged—though never compelled—to absorb the Christian outlook not simply as a vocational training but rather as part of a broad and rich intellectual experience.

CHAPTER FIFTEEN

College Students

IN terms of student numbers the original proposals for a College at Malacca as drawn up by Morrison in October 1815 had been extremely modest. They provided for no more than twelve students—six Chinese and six European. There were in fact only seven students enrolled in the College in its first year, 1819–20. However, each of the following years saw a steady though slow expansion: ten or eleven students in 1821, and fifteen or sixteen in 1822, the year that Milne died. Morrison's visitation to the College in 1823, when he joined with Humphreys and Collie in teaching for about five months, must have given a boost to student enrolment. Numbers rose to around twenty-six in 1824–26, then to around thirty in 1827–29, in a period during most of which Humphreys, Collie and Kidd were working together as a powerful team. Then followed a three-year period of contraction (1830–32) when Kidd was on his own on the Chinese side, student numbers falling away to around twenty-five.

Enrolment began to take an upward turn again during the interim period of Tomlin's headship in 1832–33, but the arrival of John Evans in 1833 really put new life into the College. Student numbers more than doubled during his regime as Principal, rising from thirty-two in 1833 to seventy and over in the years 1835–39. A right wing was added to the main College building to provide additional student accommodation early in 1837; Evans wrote to the Missionary Society that he hoped to defray the construction cost of $400 from the proceeds of a 'Malay Vocabulary and Dialogues' which he was then publishing. He reported later in the year that a second wing had to be erected to provide further accommodation, the final cost of construction of both wings amounting to $1,200, for which he had 'solicited no aid from the Society nor drawn on College funds', having apparently made a successful local appeal for public donations. In November 1839 Evans wrote to the secretary of the Society: 'The number of youths in the College has increased; we are now quite full.'[1]

When the College was founded it was announced that 'native Chinese, whether born in China itself or in any of the outside countries, whether professing Christianity or not', would be admitted as students, as would 'Europeans and Americans, whether born in India or not'. An official of the East India Company who visited the College in 1828 later wrote: 'The object of the Anglo-Chinese College is the instruction of Chinese boys who would otherwise receive no instruction at all; they are taught their own and the English language and elements of useful science. No profession of religious belief is required on entering the institution, nor are compulsory means in any way employed with a view to conversion. . . . Thus does the son of a Malacca peasant derive an enlightened education denied to the son of the Emperor of China.'[2]

If not all sons of peasants—more likely indeed to be sons of merchants or shopkeepers—the College students were almost all Malacca-born Chinese. As such, from their earliest years they would have spoken a form of Malay—the language of the country and the *lingua franca* of Malacca's plural society—and through the medium of Malay they would later have learnt the Hokkien or Cantonese form of speech and the universal Chinese form of writing. Then on entering the College these students would have commenced, virtually from scratch, the study of the Mandarin form of speech, English speech and writing, and other various 'arts and science' subjects in the curriculum. In such a system the

levels of instruction and learning must have been 'elementary' in
some fields, but the standards ultimately reached were clearly far
above the primary and well into the secondary stage of education
and higher. That students would have considerable leeway to make
up in some fields was acknowledged in the fact that the normal
period of study laid down for those who were supported by College
funds was six years. Students accepted for full admission on the
foundation after an initial probationary period of three months
were required to sign a form of agreement in Chinese which read
in part: 'A. B. of the province of Fuh-keën in China now enters
the Anglo-Chinese College to study the language and literature
of China according to the correct pronunciation of the Mandarin
tongue, also to study the English language and literature . . .; it is
agreed that he shall remain six whole years . . .; during the first
year he may return to his home to eat and sleep. . . .' This six year
curriculum remained in effect until at least 1823 but was reduced
to five years by about 1830 and apparently to four years by 1837.
A system of financial support for students admitted 'on the foundation' was continued until 1833, when Tomlin decided to abolish
it as no longer necessary to attract candidates for admission. At the
close of 1833 there were twenty students on the foundation out of
a total of thirty-two.[3]

Not all the students were local-born Chinese. Writing of the
College in 1826 Walter Medhurst noted that at least one of the
students, born in China itself, 'had in little more than a year
acquired such a knowledge of English as to enable him to translate
Keith's *Treatise on the Globes* into Chinese'.[4] This was almost
certainly the 'young man, a native of China' who came to Malacca
in 1823 after studying Latin for three years in a Catholic college
in Penang;[5] named Shaou Tih, he had been born in the Chinese
province of Szechuan. While a student at the Anglo-Chinese
College he also translated 'Stockius' *Hebrew Lexicon*' into Chinese.[6]
A fellow student, J. H. Moor, wrote in September 1825: 'The
Roman Catholic Chinese in the College who translated *Stockii*

Clavis from the Latin is learning Euclid with me out of an old Latin Euclid which I had when in College [Trinity College, Dublin]; but as I have no compasses he has requested me to write to England for a case of mathematical instruments . . .; a cheap one would answer him very well . . .; we also read Grotius and the Latin Bible together often.'

This student, Shaou Tih, also collaborated with David Collie in the preparation of an *English and Chinese students' assistant, or colloquial phrases,* printed at Malacca in 1826. But in the following year, to the dismay of Collie, he suddenly left the College and went to Canton. A reason for his sudden departure is suggested in the annual report of the College for 1829. 'The student Shaou Tih', it reads, 'who translated *Stockii Clavis* into Chinese, and who left the College from fear of the Triad [secret] Society, has been employed since his return to China as Imperial Interpreter of Western Languages at the Court of Peking. He set off for the capital in July 1829.'[7] Shaou Tih was to be seen again in Canton from time to time; indeed he was said to have been a member of the staff of the famous Imperial Commissioner Lin Tse Tzu who came to Canton in 1839 with orders to suppress the opium trade. According to a contemporary witness, Shaou Tih was employed to provide an English translation for some of the Commissioner's public pronouncements. Legge should have thought of Shaou Tih when he declared in 1842: 'The Anglo-Chinese College has not yet furnished so much as a common interpreter.'[8]

J. H. Moor, mentioned previously, was one of a handful of non-local students who attended courses at the College for shorter or longer periods. He took tuition in Chinese in exchange for giving lessons in English and other arts subjects between 1825 and 1827. He was to become headmaster of the Malacca Free School and founder-editor of the *Malacca Observer* (1826), then school-master and editor in Singapore (from 1830), and later author of the valuable *Notices of the Indian archipelago and adjacent countries* (Singapore, 1837). Also contemporary with Moor and Shaou Tih as a student at the College (1825–27) was a young American, William C. Hunter, later to become a member of an American trading firm at Canton (Russell & Co.) and author of *The 'Fan Kwae'* [Foreign devils] *at Canton before Treaty days 1825–1844,* an entertaining volume of reminiscences. Another non-local student was John Robert Morrison, son of the founder, who resided at the College from early 1827 until May 1830 when, following in his father's footsteps, he became Chinese Translator to the English East India Company at Canton. On his father's death in 1834 the young Morrison became Chinese secretary and interpreter to the British merchant community of Canton. He acted as official interpreter during the Anglo-Chinese confrontation which led eventually to war in 1839, and also in the post-war negotiations at Nanking in 1842. Later, in 1843, he became acting Colonial Secretary in the new settlement of Hong Kong but died the same year.[9]

The first student admitted to the College by Milne in October 1819 was listed simply as 'Yaou . . ., to study Mandarin'. He would normally have graduated in 1825 and is probably the same person who appears in the list of teaching staff as Yaou Seën-sang in 1824 and again in 1826 and 1834. It was College policy to employ its graduates as teaching assistants whenever possible. Morrison wrote in 1823: 'The College is pledged to employ some of the best qualified of these students . . . to act hereafter as undermasters in the College or readers of the Scriptures or catechists among the Chinese . . .', though 'the missionaries do not press them to become baptized.' Morrison in the same year published the first list of seventeen students at the College (not including four student missionaries—Medhurst, Slater, Ince and Milton—who had studied Chinese under Milne before the College building was actually completed), with dates of admission.

These first seventeen students were listed as follows:

Yaou, October 1819, to study Mandarin.

Loo, January 1820, to study Mandarin.

Rev. R. Fleming from Scotland, January 1820 to 1821; left on account of disease.

Mr James Bone, aged 16, of Malacca, February 1820 to May 1821, on the foundation.

Leang A Fah, Cantonese, aged 35, January 1820 to May 1821; made good progress in theological studies, partly on the funds.

Chang-Chun, aged 16, of Malacca, March 1820 to present; has learnt Mandarin; studying Chinese classics and Christian books in Chinese; learning to read English; on the funds.

Tsze-Hea, aged 13, of Malacca, same course as previous; on the funds.

Ma-King-Tseuen, of Malacca, August 1820 to present; same course.

Woo-Tuy-Pe, aged 25, of Malacca.

Tsang-Kow-Gan, aged 16, September 1821 to May 1822; left to go to Singapore.

Woo-Heun-Chan, September 1821. Was on the foundation; dismissed for bad conduct; readmitted.

Kow-Kwang-Tih, September 1821; on the foundation.

Rev. James Humphreys from Scotland; entered September 1821.

Soo-Yuen-tseuen, aged 15, February 1822 to present; on the funds.

Teen-Sang, April 1822, and Mang-Teen-Yin, both on the funds.

Rev. D. Collie from Scotland, June 24th 1822.[10]

One student in the above list, Tsang-Kow-Gan, is noted as having left Malacca for the new settlement of Singapore, founded in the same year that the Anglo-Chinese College opened, 1819. It seems likely that a fair proportion of those who had studied at the College followed his example, putting their college education and particularly their knowledge of English to good use in the expanding commercial world of Singapore. 'Most of the old students are engaged in trade at Singapore, several filling respectable situations under English merchants', the College reported in 1834. Indeed Morrison's College, as it turned out, seems to have been a training school and supplier of workers for the commercial field of Singapore rather than for the missionary field of China.[11]

The 1834 annual report of the College gave the names of forty students who had been educated at the College, with an indication of their later careers. One had become a government interpreter, another a writer in the custom-house, in Singapore. One student had remained at Malacca as a government interpreter. Among the remainder, four were described as merchants, six as merchant's clerks, and seven as shopkeepers. There were also two ship's captains, a Chinese doctor, and a medical assistant.[12]

Inevitably there were some students who found the College curriculum too demanding and failed to stay the course. 'James Bone, aged 16, of Malacca', a student in 1820–21, was an early example.[13] Milne wrote of him in January 1822: 'Bone's removal from the College and betaking himself to a seafaring life . . .; his reasons for this are dissatisfaction with the mode of instruction, thinking it too strict and rigorous; the ill conduct of Mr. F[leming]; the narrowness of the allowances; a change in his views with respect to the line of life he should adopt; and, as he conceives, an incapacity to apply with that closeness and constancy which are necessary to the successful prosecution of Chinese.' After this frank and sympathetic assessment of a student's difficulties, Milne consoled himself with the thought: 'We shall be able to support three Chinese lads with Bone's allowances.'[14]

A handful of students and others connected with the College went with Legge to Hong Kong in 1843 or followed him there not long afterwards. Besides the printers Leang Ah Fah, Kew Ah Gung, and Ho Ah Sun, at least four students seem to have joined Legge in Hong Kong. One, named Ho Tsun-cheen, was the son of a printer at the College press. As a youth he had gone off to

Calcutta where he learnt English, worked in a druggist's shop, and for a time attended classes at Bishop's College. Returning to Malacca he entered the Anglo-Chinese College as a student in 1840. Legge's daughter recalled years later how her father had taken Ho under his wing, 'educated him in Western knowledge, especially in history, general and ecclesiastical . . ., and also taught him both Greek and Hebrew, being astonished at his progress in those languages. . . . His enthusiasm was boundless; he would travel, he would see the world, he would intermeddle with all science. But filial obedience obliged him, after much hesitation, to return to China in 1843 and marry a girl to whom he had been bethrothed as a child. With her he lived happily in Hong Kong until his death, taking great pains in teaching her.' But such individual case histories are unfortunately rare.[15]

Three other students of the Anglo-Chinese College who joined Legge in Hong Kong for a time were named as 'Ah Sou, Kim-lin, and Hoot-kien'. The last-mentioned was Song Hoot-kien (or -kiam), who was later to join a British shipping company in Singapore.[16] These three young men accompanied Legge when he went on home leave in November 1845. For two years they lived in his father's house in the town of Huntly in Aberdeenshire, attending the parish school there. It was from the Congregational church at Huntly that William Milne had originally gone out to become a China missionary in 1810. Now, thirty-seven years later, on 15 October 1847, the three young Malacca Chinese were baptized in the same church. The spirit of William Milne had come home at last.[17]

CHAPTER SIXTEEN

Mission Schools

QUITE distinct from the Anglo-Chinese College, which contrived to remain a quasi-independent institution down to the end of 1841, there were a number of junior schools under the direct control and supervision of the London Society's mission at Malacca. These schools, as Morrison himself pointed out, were not specially designed as preparatory schools or feeders for the College, but rather formed a self-contained educational system in themselves. However, it was only to be expected that many of the students selected for admission to the College would come from the senior classes of such schools. These therefore need to be taken into account, to some extent at least, in any assessment of the role of the College in higher education—as well as, more broadly, the contribution of the missionaries to general education —in Malacca at this time.[1]

The formal education of Malay children had for long consisted almost exclusively of the study of the Koran, and that mostly by rote learning. Abdullah bin Abdul Kadir describes in his *Hikayat* a school in the Malacca district of Kampong Pali, where he was born, in which some two hundred boys and girls learnt the Koran. 'From early morning until six o'clock in the evening no sound was heard but the chanting of the Koran.' Some but by no means all pupils learnt to write the Arabic script by transcribing parts of the holy book. Thus all reading and writing at school was in Arabic, the language used by Malays in worship and prayer. Education for the Malays was strictly non-utilitarian. 'What is the good of learning our own language?' the Malays asked, according to Abdullah. 'It was right to learn Arabic because of its value for purposes of religion and theology, and this language alone was regarded as important by Muslims . . .; nobody had ever started a school for teaching the Malay language.'[2]

Several points should be made here by way of qualification. The Malay written language had adapted a modified form of Arabic script, and a basic reading ability was in fact fairly widespread among Malays. Even if comparatively few Malay children were sent regularly if at all to school, most were taught to read at home. Also there was a small professional class of letter-writers available for those occasions when the ordinary non-commercial Malay really needed to have something written down. Again, the serious study of Malay language and literature did exist, though only as a highly specialized interest among a handful of devoted scholars detached from and elevated above the mainstream of Malay education.[3]

An article in Milne's *Indo-Chinese Gleaner* for October 1819 summarized the state of Malay education in Malacca at the time, and provides some interesting detail. The main curriculum, it explains, consisted in learning to recite the Koran in Arabic, and sometimes learning to write as well. There were then two Malay schools, one in Malacca town and the other in the suburb of Tranquerah. Five years previously there had been altogether between 160 and 170 children in the two schools, but now, owing to the increase of poverty among the inhabitants, the total had dropped to fifty. The regular age for entering school was seven, and the average length of schooling was seven years. School hours were from six to ten o'clock in the morning, 11.30 a.m. to 2 p.m., and three to five o'clock in the afternoon. School fees were fixed at four *pice* a week and were called *duit Khamis* (Thursday money), being payable on Thursday, the last day of the Moslem week.[4]

But it was with Chinese rather than Malay school education in Malacca that the London Society's mission, in view of its ultimate objectives, was primarily concerned. Malacca Chinese children, the product of many generations of Chinese-Malay intermarriage, spoke a maternal patois as their first language, and later—at home and at school—would learn to speak their paternal Chinese dialect and to read Chinese script or characters. In 1815, before Milne started the mission, Malacca had eight schools for Hokkien-speaking Chinese boys with about 150 pupils, and one Cantonese school with only ten or twelve. Such small unit schools must have been single owner-teacher enterprises. By 1820, apart from those started by the mission, the Chinese schools had been reduced to five in number with not more than a hundred pupils—a reduction possibly due as much to worsening economic conditions in Malacca as to competition from the newly opened mission schools.[5]

The mission's first aim was to open free or 'charity' schools for Chinese, introducing modern teaching methods from the West, more comprehensive and practical curricula, and where possible the teaching of Christianity. Milne made a start in 1815 with a free Hokkien school in his back garden in which the pupils were taught 'the elementary books common in China, writing and arithmetic'; and the next year he opened a similar Cantonese school. By the middle of 1816 he had a total of about eighty pupils in the two schools, each under a Chinese teacher paid by the mission. C. H. Thomsen opened a school for Malays in 1816. From then on the story of the mission schools at Malacca is one of slow but steady expansion and continual experiment, until twenty years later, in 1836, there were 220 boys and 120 girls in the mission's Chinese schools, and 120 boys and 60 girls in its Malay schools; while a few years later, in 1838 and 1839, two remarkable new experiments were begun with the opening of an adult school for Chinese women and a boarding school for Chinese girls.[6]

Milne and his successors were naturally inclined to introduce the latest Western teaching methods known to them into the mission schools. One of the most influential systems of primary education in England in the first quarter of the nineteenth century was that developed by Joseph Lancaster, a Quaker, in his school in Borough Road, Southwark, from 1801 onwards. It was especially popular with Dissenters—there was something democratic and anti-establishment about it—though a similar system was introduced by Andrew Bell for Anglican schools. The main method involved was the monitorial system, the use of abler and senior pupils as monitors to teach the rest. This was done with the aid of a carefully planned and graded series of lessons and textbooks which could be followed in routine fashion by the monitors and the pupils under them, divided into classes. With something like military precision Lancaster also devised 'elaborate rules for keeping hats, slates and pencils in their proper places; the alphabet and spelling were learnt from placards hung on the walls of the schoolroom'. When Milne opened his first school in Malacca in 1815 he decided to adopt what was known as the Lancasterian system, introducing 'writing in sand, and monitors, and division into classes'.[7]

In 1818 there were three Chinese schools under the mission, and Thomsen opened a new one for Malabari Indians. W. H. Medhurst took charge of the Chinese schools, developing a great enthusiasm for this side of the mission's work. He soon learnt to speak Hokkien well enough to converse with the children, and he published 'a school book in the form of a Chinese Primer called San Tsze-king.'[8] By the middle of the year 1818 Milne could report that there were six 'charity' schools under the mission's care: 'three Chinese day schools, one Chinese evening school, one Malabari day school, and one day and evening school for Malay and English.'[9]

With the restoration of Dutch government over Malacca in September 1818 there must have been a falling off in demand for English language instruction in favour of Dutch. A public school was opened in January 1819, supported partly by the new government and partly by public subscription, for 'the cultivation of the Dutch and Malay languages' and to provide a general education (in reading, writing and arithmetic) in both. This school was placed under the superintendence of C. H. Thomsen, with a managing committee of prominent citizens. It was an international school open to children of all races and creeds, and to all classes of the community 'even to the meanest slave', providing free education for the poor student and charging a fixed scale of fees to those who could afford to pay.[10]

The mission's first Malay school, started by Thomsen, disappears from the record at this point. It may have succumbed to the competition of the new public school or, more likely, have become merged with it. But James Humphreys' wife, who had learnt to read and write as well as speak in Malay, branched out in a new direction for the mission in 1822 by opening a Malay girl's school, 'a new thing at Malacca' as her husband explained, indeed 'a new thing in this part of the world, the people seldom giving their daughters any education.' Meanwhile the Chinese mission schools, now under the superintendence of James Humphreys himself, continued to flourish. There were four free schools at the beginning of 1823—one in the College grounds, one in Malacca town, one in the old fort, and one in the village of Kantung (Kandang) about four miles outside the town, containing altogether about 120 pupils. Another Chinese school was started in the town in the same year, bringing the pupil total up to nearly 140. The mission also ran a school for South Indian (Madrasi or Tamil) children with upwards of twenty pupils at this time.[11]

With the final transfer of Malacca from Dutch government back to the British in March 1825 the demand for tuition in English naturally revived among the inhabitants. The Dutch-Malay public school inevitably closed down with the ending of the Dutch regime. J. H. Moor, already referred to as an enterprising young teaching assistant at the Anglo-Chinese College in 1825, decided to start an English free school. He proposed to follow 'the Lancasterian plan', sending to England for 'another set of . . . cards, with a few slates and pencils, which are rarities here but essential in the system.' 'I am anxious to form an English School in Malacca for poor Dutch and English and Portuguese children,' he wrote in January 1826. 'They are in a deplorable state and there is no school for them. They cannot speak English, or indeed any language, properly. . . . I shall shortly make an open attempt. Of course it will be on the Borough Road plan.' With Moor as headmaster, the Malacca Free School opened towards the end of 1826 'for the instruction of the male children of the Indo-Portuguese and Natives, and of such other individuals as might be esteemed fit objects of the institution.' Encouraged by a government annual subsidy of 1,200 Spanish dollars and by public subscriptions, the school managing committee decided to open a section for girls, and by April 1828 the school contained 156 boys and 65 girls. Although it was described as 'strictly a Christian school', the pupils were said to consist of 'Malays, Chinese and Portuguese'.[12]

The story of the early years of the Malacca Free School lies strictly outside the scope of the London mission's educational activities, yet the mission, the College and the Free School were all closely interrelated through the person of the versatile J. H. Moor who, it will be recalled, was not only a college instructor and schoolmaster but also a newspaper editor, whose paper, *The Malacca Observer*, was printed at the mission or college press. Besides, the Free School deserves more than a passing mention at this point because it represented so well the aim which the mission schools also held before them, that of applying Western educational ideas and techniques to Eastern conditions. The school managing committee's report of November 1829 describes in interesting detail the Lancasterian plan in operation through the eight classes of the boys' school; from the first—'learning the alphabet and words of one syllable; writing small and capital letters and figures on sand'—through the seventh—in which the pupils worked as

apprentices to the printing, shoemaking or tailoring trade from
8 to 11 a.m., wrote on paper, cyphered in multiplication and
division, and read and spelled from the New Testament from
11 a.m. to 2 p.m.; to the eighth or head class 'composed of the
monitors', who studied 'English Grammar, Abridgment of
Geography, and Carpenter's Spelling with explanations', reciting
prose once a week from 'Murray's English Reader'. At noon each
day the whole boys' school would be assembled and interrogated
by the headmaster 'from a Malay and English Vocabulary, on
stated periods in the church from Walls' Catechism, and in single
exercises in the four first rules of arithmetic.'[13]

Moor's headship of the Free School came to an end, it will be
remembered, as a result of an offending paragraph in *The Malacca
Observer* of 30 June 1829 critical of the government's policy towards
the state of Naning, which incurred the wrath of Governor
Fullerton. The school managing committee reported tactfully in
November that 'Mr. Moor . . ., having particular calls elsewhere,
has expressed his desire to resign', also that they had written to
England inviting out another master; and eventually a Mr. Collard
arrived to take up the post in December 1830. The school managed
to survive these vicissitudes. Fullerton advised in November 1830
that the government annual subsidy should be continued, and in
1835 the managing committee was able to add two branch schools,
one Portuguese and one Malay, containing upwards of one
hundred children, 'all of whom, after they had made a tolerable
proficiency in their own language, are transplanted to the Free
School to be instructed in English Literature.'[14]

Meanwhile the Society's mission was going ahead with its own
schools programme. Reporting to the new British administration
in September 1826, James Humphreys and his colleagues stressed
the 'importance and beneficial influence' of their Chinese schools,
and urged 'the claims of the Chinese on an European Government
arising out of their industrious character and the benefits which
their exertions produce wherever they reside.' There were, they

stated, 'at present five schools in the Town of Malacca and one in the Country, taught by native masters under our superintendence, and supported at the sole expense of the London Missionary Society.' These schools contained about two hundred boys who were taught 'to read and write their own language, and to understand some of the best native and Christian books.' At the same time, the missionaries added, they would be happy to superintend Malay schools 'could children be procured to attend', though they would not feel justified in incurring any expense on account of such schools without authorization from their Society, because 'their main attention is required to be bestowed on the Chinese.' This diplomatic approach had at least some of the desired effect. The government agreed to subsidize a Malay and a Tamil school under the supervision of the mission. It was proposed to start a Malay school at 'Kampong Melayu', where the 'Malay Captain' had allotted a small space on his own ground and 'a number of children, including female' might be attracted. 'A fairer field for the exertion of Benevolence in respect of Schools could not probably present itself,' commented Samuel Garling, the British Resident Councillor of Malacca, adding judiciously: 'As the principles of the Lancasterian system of tuition may with the greatest facility be introduced, much benefit may be effected at a comparatively trifling expense.' In the event, the Malay school was opened in 1826 in 'a small bungalow, the property of Government, on the side of St. Paul's Hill', but in the early months of 1827 there were less than a dozen pupils, and the 'female department' had already been written off as 'a failure'. The Tamil school, more successful with about twenty-five pupils, occupied a room in the premises of the Free School.[15]

James Humphreys, who announced his resignation from the headship of the Anglo-Chinese College on 1 January 1827 in order to devote himself mainly to educational work among Malacca's Malay population, explained that the purpose of the Malay and Tamil schools was 'to teach the children to read and write their own language.' 'The method pursued,' he wrote, 'is as near as possible that of the British and Foreign School Society. Both schools are under the care of a native master and superintended by me. The books used in Cling [Tamil] schools are printed at the Church Mission Press in Madras, together with some of their own books. The books used in the Malay school must for some time be elementary; after a time books, strictly moral, of their own, and extracts from the Scriptures, may be used, without making any mention of those points which come in conflict with their religious opinions.' By April 1828 the Tamil school had forty boys, but the Malay school still no more than a dozen. Humphrey's guiding influence was lost when he returned to England in 1829 but the arrival of Josiah Hughes in 1830 brought new life into the Malay school programme. In 1831 three new Malay schools were opened under the mission with an average attendance of upwards of eighty boys and girls. The American missionary David Abeel, commenting that Malacca was 'highly and justly celebrated for the number of its native schools,' reported in March 1832 that there were between 250 and 300 Malay children under the care of Hughes, as well as about two hundred more, principally Tamil and Portuguese, 'in charge of the ladies belonging to the Resident's household.'[16]

The Chinese schools under the mission in 1831 were reported to be 'in a very flourishing state', containing some 200 pupils. The overall picture of school organization in Malacca in 1831 showed a total of twenty-five schools containing upwards of 620 children. Of these schools, fifteen were Chinese, four Malay, two Tamil, three Portuguese, and one English (the Free School). Thirteen out of the total number of schools (Chinese and Malay) were supported by the London Society.[17]

A particularly interesting side of the mission's pioneer work at this time consisted of experiments in the field of education for girls. Mrs Humphreys, as we have seen, had made a start for the mission with a Malay girls' school in 1822, but she died in 1827. By that time, however, the London Society had decided to send out an experienced female teacher to join the mission. Maria Newell arrived at Malacca in August 1827, having suffered a great deal on her voyage 'from seasickness and a wet cabin', but somewhat flattered to find herself received by the British Resident, Samuel Garling, 'with all the hospitality, politeness and dignity of an elegant English gentleman.' She opened an English school for girls in January 1828 and announced that she intended to start 'a native girls' school' as soon as she could 'find a place and learn enough Malay to make myself understood.' 'Malay and Portuguese are most wanting', she wrote home; 'I am studying both with all my might.' 'Send whatever you can in the school way,' she requested; 'elementary books of *all* kinds, stationery, needles, thread, thimbles, pictures, infant school paraphernalia, British and Foreign school ditto, we can turn it all to account.'[18] And she ended her letter plaintively: 'Write soon . . ., and in whatever you write remember I am alone, and have none to prop up my spirits.' Before long Miss Newell had started a 'native school' of twenty girls as well as her English school, she was assisting in the female section of the Free School which contained between sixty and seventy girls, and she had published from the mission press 'an *Abstract of Geography* for the use of children.' 'Female education is a new thing in Malacca', she wrote. 'Taking all together I have not less than a hundred looking to me for instruction. I wish to teach knitting in my native school; . . . send cotton and needles.'[19]

By the end of 1829, however, Miss Newell was reported to have 'removed' from Malacca; she had in fact married the roving German missionary Charles Gützlaff.[20] But by good fortune another female teacher appeared to fill her place, though she was not at first formally connected with the mission nor on its pay-roll. Mary Christie Wallace left England in August 1828 and arrived at Malacca via Calcutta at the beginning of May 1829. She was described by one of her colleagues as 'a remarkably timid, modest, retiring character among English people; but bold, undaunted and active among the natives.' On the departure of Miss Newell, Miss Wallace took over the superintendence of girls' schools under the mission, and did so 'very diligently.' There were ten such schools in 1831: eight of them Chinese, one Malay and one Tamil. By October 1832, however, the number of Chinese girls' schools had fallen to five. And before long another break occurred in the continuity of supervision of the girls' schools when Miss Wallace joined the 'American Missionary Society' in 1834 to superintend its schools in Canton or Macao.[21]

All the mission schools—as indeed the College itself—had suffered from lack of continuity in supervision for many years. With the arrival of John Evans to head the mission in 1833 the schools as well as the College soon entered a new phase of vigorous growth. In 1834 there were five Chinese boys' schools with two hundred pupils, two Chinese girls' schools with sixty pupils, and five Malay schools with some two hundred pupils, all under the care of the mission. Two more Chinese girls' schools were opened in 1835, and in 1836 there were six altogether (with 130 pupils), as well as four Chinese boys' schools (160 pupils) and now as many as six Malay schools. Towards the end of 1836 Evans reported attendance figures of 220 boys and 120 girls in Chinese schools, and 120 boys and 60 girls in Malay schools, adding the comment: 'The number of Malay girls is much greater than at any former period.' There was a slight falling off in attendance figures for the year 1838—205 boys and 115 girls in Chinese schools; 70 boys and 20 girls in Malay schools—but Evans explained: 'In the Malay department we could treble the number of children had we time to visit the schools and attend to the education of the children.' Finally, as noted earlier, two bold new ventures were undertaken by the mission in 1838 and 1839—a school for adult Chinese women, and a boarding school for Chinese girls.[22] However, all the mission's educational activities in Malacca, from school level to the Anglo-Chinese College itself, were to close down when in 1843 the

London Society decided to transfer its operations from Southeast Asia to Hong Kong and China.

Even in such a brief account, enough has been written to suggest that the contribution of the London Missionary Society to general education in Malacca during this early period, not only for the Chinese but also for the Malay, Indian and Portuguese (or Eurasian) communities, was quite considerable. While waiting for China, the mission thus served the people of Malacca well. And in doing so it set new directions for school and college education which were to be followed by future generations not only in Malacca itself but also in Singapore and Malaysia.

CHAPTER SEVENTEEN

Retrospect

W ITH the possible exception of David Livingstone, the nineteenth century missionary is seldom found among the heroic figures of modern literature. When he does make an occasional appearance a note of derision almost invariably creeps in. He tends to be regarded as an object of quiet amusement, if not of cynical contempt or even outright opprobrium. He may be portrayed as a simpleton, a bigot or a sham. Or he is exhibited as the pliant tool of Western cultural empire-building, a mere stooge of imperialism. Generally, the missionary is liable to come in for the roughest critical treatment.

For we are all social psychologists now; with the aid of finer critical perception as well as the advantage of hindsight we can easily see through the naive assumptions and the self-deceptions of the missionaries. We almost take it for granted that those who went out to preach the Gospel were merely attempting to compensate for a sense of inadequacy and frustration at home by seeking to gain power over the souls and bodies of defenceless 'natives' overseas. The whole missionary movement, we conclude, was a regrettable and even a shameful business, a crude projection of the ethnocentricity and the cultural arrogance of the European. Who did we think we were, trying to foist our own peculiar set of religious ideas on all and sundry?

There is of course an element of truth in all this. But it is also probably true that the current image of the missionary represents an over-reaction from that of an earlier age when he was readily accepted at his own high evaluation. We have tended to replace the nineteenth century image of the missionary—that of the dedicated, selfless apostle to the heathen, enduring every hardship in order to bring the light of truth into the dark and ignorant corners of the world—by an equally synthetic image of our own—that of a narrow-minded, presumptuous fraud—thus merely substituting one set of stereotypes for another.

The members of the London Society's mission at Malacca in the early nineteenth century certainly did not conform to any particular type but were a decidedly mixed lot in every way—in social and educational background, in temperament and disposition, in attitude to their calling, in approach to their objectives. It can be seen that many of them were rugged individualists, full of determination, impatient of interference, sensitive to criticism, inclined to self-dramatization—yet there were some who appear as modest, gentle and patient. Some were men of broad vision and of considerable intellect; most were men of a simple faith, an unquestioning religious conviction—though a few, such as Morrison, could feel that mere piety was not enough. In general, the characteristics and motivations of the Malacca missionaries were probably no less varied and complex than those of all who were involved in the great missionary movement of the nineteenth century—itself a complex historical process forming an integral part of the wider world process of 'Europeanization'.

In historical perspective, Christian missions in East Asia formed part of this process of European expansion in more senses than one. Firstly, in a general sense, missionary activities in India, Southeast Asia, China and Japan grew and developed (with notable setbacks, as in Japan) during the first and comparatively limited phase of European expansion lasting from the early sixteenth to the late eighteenth century. And thereafter, in the nineteenth and early twentieth centuries, a more organized missionary movement developed at a greatly accelerated pace within the framework of a second and much more dynamic phase of European expansion, the colonial-imperial phase. Inevitably, although some individuals—Morrison and Milne, for example—might achieve a remarkable degree of detachment, the outlook of the missionary during both phases of expansion tended to be a 'metropolitan' or imperial one, offering general loyalty and support to the supposed interests of Europe (or, more narrowly, those of his mother country) in Asia. So much may be granted without necessarily accepting either a general theory of permanent and complete identification of missionary and imperialist interests, or any such particular assumption as that of an unholy alliance between opium, gunboats and bibles in the English approach to China in the early nineteenth century.

Secondly, in a more particular sense the European missionary outlook always tended to mirror the attitudes and modes of thought that were peculiar to the movement of expansion, colonialism or imperialism at each different historical phase. In this respect, Morrison and Milne stood between two worlds, between the two main phases of European expansion in Asia. They belonged in outlook partly to the earlier 'trading company' phase which lasted down to about the end of the eighteenth century, when colonialism was still tentative and limited, when Europe had not yet established a position of decisive superiority either in trade or in technology, and so had to make some effort to adapt itself to Asian conditions and attitudes. For although the British had made some impact on the political and social structure of India by the end of the eighteenth century, as had the Dutch on that of Java and the Spanish in the Philippines, Europeans were still largely confined to the fringes of the Asian world—to seaports, forts and settlements. They could not yet hope to lay down their own terms in their dealings with Asians; rather they had to come to terms with Asia as they found it. Within the context of such a relationship we may imagine that an educated European in Asia would not find it difficult to accept as valid—even to respect and admire—the forms and expressions of the indigenous cultures around him. And so it had been with the earlier Catholic mission-aries to China—the Italian Matteo Ricci in the sixteenth century and his Jesuit successors in Peking in the two centuries following—who had developed a warm admiration for Chinese culture. Such too had been the attitudes of Warren Hastings and Sir William Jones in Bengal in the latter part of the eighteenth century, with their active support for the study of the languages and cultures of India. This approach may be seen as generally typical of the earlier phase of European expansion in Asia, a phase to which Morrison and Milne largely belonged in spirit.

For the Jesuits in seventeenth and eighteenth century Peking, as for these early nineteenth century Protestant missionaries in Canton and Malacca, the ideal to strive for was a meeting and mixing of the two cultures, Western and Eastern; certainly not a superimposition of one on the other. It was in line with this approach that the Jesuits had even been prepared to allow a certain amount of accommodation or assimilation between Christian and Confucian concepts, a coming to terms between two somewhat kindred systems of thought. It is true that such readiness to compromise might be regarded as not so much an indication of respect for Chinese ideas and institutions as a tactical manoeuvre in the grand strategy for the conversion of the Chinese people—a tactic similar in essence to the wearing of the Confucian scholar-official's gown or the Manchu hair-queue by missionaries (includ-ing Morrison in his early days at Canton) even down to the latter part of the nineteenth century. However, it must be granted that the approach in each case was based to some extent at any rate on respect for Chinese institutions and ideas—respect for their strength and powers of resistance if not always for their merit or validity.

But if Morrison and Milne belonged in part to that earlier phase of European expansion, with its respectful regard—at times even enthusiasm—for Chinese culture, they also belonged to the beginning of a new age, an age in which a more dynamic and aggressive colonialism was to break out of previous limitations and restrictions, and to take up a commanding position in Asia. The European sense of superiority, fed by a growing industrial and technological pre-eminence, was to become dominant; attitudes of compromise, conciliation or cultural sympathy were to become correspondingly more difficult to maintain. In a way, the decision in 1843 to transform Morrison's liberal college of Malacca into the theological seminary of Hong Kong was symptomatic of the mood of the new colonial-imperial age, more direct in the pursuit of its interests, concerned less with cultural reconciliation or adaptation than with command and control, less with the means than with the end. Similarly, the decision made in India in the spirit of the Macaulay Minute of 1835 in favour of English rather than the classical languages of India as the medium of higher education in that country might be regarded as an indicator of the same trend in a different context.

Morrison and Milne undoubtedly shared to some extent that sense of superiority—cultural and religious as well as scientific and technical superiority—which was to characterize the general European attitude to Asia in the nineteenth century. This, it is true, could at times be an enlightened superiority, graciously conferring some of the benefits of a higher culture upon those unfortunate enough to have been born outside it. But that the influence of Europe should expand and that Europeans should ultimately inherit the earth seemed (to most Europeans at that time) only natural, a kind of natural law that could not be questioned. Equally, missionaries such as Morrison and Milne assumed as inevitable the ultimate triumph of Christianity along with that of European science and reason, even when faced with a powerfully self-contained culture such as that of China. Progress was assumed to be inevitable, and progress would unquestionably mean Westernization and Christianization.

This was the great age of European self-confidence, a mood that could easily slide into an arrogant self-complacency—especially perhaps among the British, acknowledged leaders of nineteenth century overseas expansion. In such a mood of supreme self-satisfaction the author of an essay on Asian trade could write in 1813: 'It is to British manners and customs that all nations now conform themselves. . . . It appears that there is something in our national character and condition which fits us for this exalted station. . . . It was the privilege of Britain to receive first the purest beams of reformed religion.'[1]

Yet even this European sense of superiority did not necessarily preclude a measure of genuine interest in Asian culture. As a Southeast Asian administrator Stamford Raffles, for example, certainly possessed the outlook of an 'empire-builder', yet in some respects he was a man of wide and generous views, and he undoubtedly displayed an active interest in the culture of the Malaysian world around him. As missionaries, Morrison and Milne too could combine a feeling of innate spiritual superiority with a deep interest in and respect for the Chinese people and their culture. In this sense all three men stood between two worlds, between two phases of European expansionism.

An assumption of spiritual and cultural superiority was after all one of the original sources of the missionary urge. And as the sense of overall superiority grew with time, so the missionary urge became all the more compelling. Morrison and Milne shared something of that spirit of crusade which was to form part of the British world outlook in the later nineteenth century. At the same time they displayed a considerable measure of the spirit of dedication, the self-discipline, determination and endurance which— imponderable and unquantifiable as such qualities must be—were as decisive as technical or military superiority in creating and shaping nineteenth century imperialism. Indeed it was largely from the missionary idea, from the example of men such as Morrison and Milne, that imperialism was to derive much of its fervour; the imperialist, one might say, borrowed the missionary's clothes. For the deep missionary conviction of having been chosen to serve a higher cause among the heathen was closely related, both intellectually and emotionally, to that wider sense of imperial mission—whether described as *mission civilisatrice,* 'the white man's burden', or 'manifest destiny'—which increasingly became one of the most powerful driving forces of modern imperialism. Thus in its heyday—particularly between about 1880 and 1914—imperialism was to become very much a kind of evangelical religion. Missionary and imperial fervour acted as mutually sustaining emotional forces.

Within the British context, we can perhaps see a more specific ideological link between the nineteenth century missionary and the imperialist in the principle of Free Trade. For just as 'the imperialism of free trade' was based upon a confident belief in the superiority of one's own national product over that of any competitor in a free and open market, so the missionary went out into the world fully confident in the superiority of his religious beliefs over those of all others, asking only the opportunity to proclaim his faith freely and openly. All that he, like the free trader, asked for was an 'open door'. For both Morrison in Canton and Milne at Malacca, as also for the cotton-goods exporter in Manchester, there could be no question that each possessed a superior product and that freedom to promote it must inevitably lead to its wider acceptance. For the missionary, freedom to preach and teach could only result in the vindication of the 'ultimate truth' of Christianity. 'Every system . . . has a right to be heard', Morrison asserted, but he added: 'mighty Truth shall prevail'. Truth, needless to say, would be on the side of the missionary; mighty truth would in the end drive out 'superstition'; freedom of competition would ultimately favour the better product. It was a kind of commercial-ideological version of the Darwinian 'survival of the fittest'.

Apart from sharing such attitudes and aims, the London

Missionary Society itself was virtually a type of imperial authority —in its organization, in its need to maintain the direction and remote control of its overseas agents, and in the multiplicity of problems arising from the wide variety of local circumstances with which it had to deal. Morrison had made the point with some effect in a letter to the Society's treasurer in 1819 when he observed that the relationship of the Society to its missionaries overseas was similar to that of 'a home government' to its colonial officials and their problems.

The Malacca College was of course only one of the Missionary Society's many perplexing problems. But it was one which it was inclined especially to resent because it could never quite get rid of the uncomfortable feeling that the whole College plan had been cleverly foisted on it by Morrison and Milne. And in any case, if it had to have such an institution on its hands, the Society would have much preferred something rather narrower in scope and more strictly missionary in concept; something, in fact, more like a theological seminary.

In this respect as well as in several others, we may observe a number of interesting parallels between the London Missionary Society's College at Malacca and a contemporary Baptist Missionary Society College at Serampore, near Calcutta in India, though the Serampore College was not intended for a wider field than India. How far one may have been influenced by the other in its origins and development is largely a matter for conjecture. Morrison was careful to point out that 'the Anglo-Chinese College plan preceded the Serampore College'. The truth seems to be that while the Serampore College was earlier in conception it was some time later in realization.[2]

Both colleges were almost entirely a result of individual enterprise. The guiding influence at Serampore was William Carey, ex-shoemaker and Baptist missionary, who arrived at Calcutta from Britain in 1793—without a licence from the East India Company. Not long afterwards he and two friends—Joshua

Marshman, Baptist schoolteacher, and William Ward, ex-printer
—set up a mission in Serampore, a Danish trading settlement some
sixteen miles north of Calcutta, where they started schools and
a printing press. Carey, like Morrison, was 'a linguistic genius and
a diligent orientalist as well as a great missionary'. As early as
1795 he produced a plan for one or two colleges of higher education
in which a selected group of Indian youths would study oriental
literature and the Bible along with such general subjects as
geography or philosophy. It was not until 1818, however, that the
Serampore College was actually founded; it started classes early
in 1819, though its main building was not even roofed until July
1821. The Serampore and Malacca colleges, then, came into being
at roughly the same time.[3]

The two colleges also shared generally similar aims. The
Serampore College was to be 'no narrow, denominational affair'.
It would provide not only theological training for Christian
students but also a comprehensive higher education in 'Eastern
literature and European science' for all. Eastern literature would
be studied in the classical languages of Sanskrit, Arabic and
Persian, while the 'common languages', Bengali and Hindi, would
be used both in study and instruction. Like the Malacca missionaries, the Serampore group were convinced 'Orientalists', believing
that the best approach by Eastern students to a comparative
appreciation of the civilizations and cultures of both East and West
would be through the medium of the indigenous languages. That
however was a point of view which had ultimately to yield to an
official policy of higher education for Indians through the medium
of English, a policy recommended in the famous Macaulay Minute
of 1835 and thereafter adopted with momentous consequences for
India's future history.[4]

Both the Malacca and Serampore colleges were based upon
the conviction that Asian societies must be reformed and regene-
rated; that this could only be accomplished through a dual process
by which both the Christian faith and Western science were

communicated to and adopted by those societies; and that this in turn could be achieved only through a process of education in which an essential element would be the training of new generations of native or local-born Christian religious and social leaders. Moreover, such a process of education should involve much more than merely turning out a task force of home-made missionaries from local theological seminaries. It must constitute a broad intellectual education in both Eastern and Western religion and science, literature and philosophy, if the new leaders were to hope to gain the respect of their own people and win over their allegiance.

The reaction of the Baptist Missionary Society to such ideas was very similar to that of the London Missionary Society. Both felt that their limited funds might be better spent on such bread-and-butter purposes as preaching, printing and distributing Christian literature, and elementary school-teaching. If there must be a college of education then let it be restricted to purely missionary aims, and let there be no co-education of Christian or theological with non-Christian or lay students lest the former be corrupted by the latter. On this last point Carey and his colleagues, like Morrison and Milne, took a completely opposite view. Missionaries, they argued, must be trained for work in the world as it is. 'A strictly theological seminary for missionary students, whether native or East Indian, was calculated to produce contracted views, and to give too much of a professional bias to the character.'[5]

Again, each college became involved in a protracted jurisdictional wrangle with its parent Society over the broad issue of the relationship between college and mission. At Serampore this led to quite dramatic developments; the College took over control of the mission stations in 1825, and two years later the missionaries actually broke away from the Baptist Society. At Malacca, however, the College and the London Missionary Society managed to keep working together down to the end, despite differences of opinion and clashes of personality. Though the College remained somewhat on the defensive, it succeeded in maintaining a position

of virtual independence. A passing remark by a contemporary
observer, Captain P. J. Begbie, to the effect that the College
building was assigned to the London Missionary Society in 1834—
the year of Morrison's death—has been wrongly interpreted by
later writers to mean that the Society took over actual control of
the College itself in that year. But as we have seen, it was not in
fact until the end of 1841, when the decision had already been
made to transfer the whole of the Society's interests from Malacca
and other Southeast Asian stations to China, that the College
was taken over. By then Malacca had served its purpose. What
remained of the College's identity and of its personnel were soon
to become absorbed in that great original design, the Protestant
mission to China itself.[6]

Thus by 1841 Malacca had served its purpose as a preparatory
launching site for the Protestant mission to China. But in the
process the people of Malacca must surely have gained something
of value from the presence of those who planned and prepared for
the mission there. They had seen growth and experiment in
education at both school and college levels. There had been for
some at least the stimulus of cultural interchange, the opening up
of new horizons of thought, the excitement of intellectual discovery.
The Anglo-Chinese College had done much to foster and develop
the study of the Malay language and literature as well as the
Chinese. It had promoted important experimentation and development in translation, printing and publishing in both languages.
In a wider context, with its active interest in the neighbouring
countries of the region, it had done pioneering work in the field of
Southeast Asian as well as Malaysian linguistic and cultural studies.
Generally, the College represented a significant initiative in the
application of Western educational ideas and techniques to
Southeast Asian conditions. More specifically, Morrison's College
provided both the inspiration and the model for Stamford Raffles'
concept of a Malaysian university college, a concept only very
partially realized in the Singapore Institution revived in 1835 and

renamed Raffles Institution in 1868, but eventually to become more fully embodied in Raffles College, Singapore, which opened in 1928, and in the later University of Malaya in Singapore, founded in 1949.

In the field of Chinese studies the College was definitely ahead of its time. Morrison wrote in 1831: 'The Anglo-Chinese College is the only place, I believe, in the British dominions where Chinese is regularly taught; . . . there is no school for Chinese in England.' Writing earlier—and in more characteristic style—to a friend in Britain, he commented: 'There is indeed less encouragement in our country for the learning of Asia than on the continent of Europe. To have no wish for a few men in the United Kingdom acquainted with the language of the oldest and most extensive empire on earth, shews an indifference about general knowledge which I consider anything but reputable to Britain.' In the end Morrison's achievements and renown as a Chinese scholar and the range of studies and publications of the Anglo-Chinese College combined to form a most powerful influence for the growth of a tradition of Chinese scholarship in Britain. It is most likely that the College, along with its counterpart in Serampore, was one of the formative influences leading to the establishment of University College, London, a 'dissenting academy' to start with, in 1825–26. And when eventually University College joined with its Anglican counterpart, King's College, to form the University of London in 1836, it was a former Principal of the Anglo-Chinese College, Samuel Kidd, who became the University's first professor of Chinese. One of Kidd's pupils, as we saw, was James Legge, later to become head of the Anglo-Chinese College, Hong Kong missionary, professor of Chinese at Oxford University, and probably the greatest of early British sinologues.[7]

China, after all, was the ultimate goal of endeavour for Morrison, Milne and the Anglo-Chinese College. As Milne wrote, the Malacca mission was 'originally formed with an especial view to China, and as the best substitute for an actual residence in that country'.[8] In these pages the main interest has been directed to the educational and cultural rather than to the religious aspects of the work of the early Protestant missionaries. It could be fairly argued that such an emphasis indeed reflects what were really the primary interests of Morrison and Milne in their approach to China. For that approach was essentially based upon a deep respect for China's ancient culture. It enabled them though missionaries to see beyond immediate missionary aims, to perceive that if Chinese society were to be reformed this must involve not simply a process of religious conversion but a cultural revolution. More than that, they saw that scientific and technical modernization must accompany cultural and religious adaptation and reform.

In this respect, as we have seen, Morrison and Milne resembled the earlier Jesuit missionaries who had not only brought to China the teachings of Christianity along with European scientific knowledge in such fields as mathematics, mechanics, medicine and astronomy, but had also given Europe a new awareness of and even enthusiasm for Chinese civilization and culture through their letters and reports and more especially by their translations of the Chinese literary classics. The Jesuits in Peking had succeeded in communicating their admiration for the teachings of Confucius to influential European thinkers of the eighteenth century from Leibnitz to Quesnay. They had helped to stimulate that interest in Chinese art and architecture which created a whole European fashion in *chinoiserie*. As a result, the Western world—not for the first or last time—had built up a largely imaginary concept of China, in this case a rose-tinted picture of an almost ideal society—rational, humane, harmonious and well-ordered.[9]

Whatever the reality behind the image, Morrison and Milne helped to keep alive something of this earlier spirit of informed admiration for China and things Chinese into a new age when relations between Europe and China were to become steadily both more open and more difficult than ever before. For them China was still 'an object of wonder' if also 'of pity'; 'an object of literary and philosophical speculation'. 'One of the fairest portions of the globe', it was 'in point of territory, riches and population . . . the greatest of the nations'. Its 'ancient rulers and sages', wrote Milne, had 'formed a code of laws which, with many defects, possessed also many great excellencies'. China's great weakness lay not in any defect of human capability but in its social and intellectual rigidity and conservatism. 'For ages the arts and sciences in China', Milne observed, 'have been stationary', but 'the obstinate refusal of the Chinese to improve is rather to be viewed as the effect of principle than the want of genius. They consider the ancient sages, kings and governments as the prototypes of excellence, and a near approximation to the times in which they lived the highest display of national wisdom and virtue. They are still the blind slaves of antiquity. . . .'[10]

In terms of European thought of their time, the approach of Morrison and Milne to China may be seen as based upon that spirit of liberalism which derived from 'the triumphant, rationalist, humanist Enlightenment of the eighteenth century'. They lived in an age when it seemed reasonable to believe in the inevitability of progress and the perfectibility of human nature. In particular, they lived at a time when it was still possible for Europeans to assume with confidence that Western religion and culture, along with science and technology, marching forward together hand in hand, must inevitably rescue China from 'ignorance and super-stition' once her doors were opened. 'Literature and science', declared Morrison, were 'the auxiliaries of true religion'; together they would bring about China's transformation.[11]

But there was a wider vision behind the long hard struggle to build and to sustain the Anglo-Chinese College at Malacca, a vision that embraced not only China but the whole of East Asia. 'To aid the diffusion of literature, knowledge, and the Christian religion without respect of nation, colour or persuasion among the inhabitants of Eastern Asia, especially the Chinese-language nations, is the fundamental object of the Institution', the College's

annual report for the year 1829 declared. William Milne had put
it rather more concisely when he explained to the new Dutch
governor of Malacca in 1821 that the College had one purpose and
one alone. Its sole aim, he declared, was 'to promote the gospel of
humanity and of literature'.[12]

CHAPTER EIGHTEEN

Postscript

W HAT was the good of it all? What did the Anglo-Chinese College and all the Malacca-based missionary effort for China achieve in the end? Very little indeed, it must be admitted, if achievement is measured quantitatively in terms of the number of known Chinese conversions to Christianity.

By the end of the eighteenth century, after about two hundred years of continuing Catholic missionary labour centred mainly in Peking and Macao, the number of Christians in China had reached an estimated 150,000.[1] The efforts of the English Protestant missionaries in Canton and Malacca in the early nineteenth century can hardly have added significantly to that number. It has been estimated that Morrison's work in Canton resulted directly in no more than ten Chinese conversions. It took the American missionaries working later in Foochow nine years (1847–56) to win a single convert.[2] Subsequent foreign missions in China were to become much more highly organized and heavily financed, and correspondingly much more effective, yet after well over another century of sustained missionary endeavour the number of Chinese Christians in 1967 was estimated at possibly four million out of a total population of nearly 700 million.[3]

To attempt a satisfactory explanation of the comparative failure of the Christian missionary struggle for the soul of China would probably require not only an analysis of the components of

Chinese culture and society, with some assessment of the place of religion in the Chinese tradition, but also a consideration of the status of Christianity as a foreign import associated with the militant imperialism of the West. But whatever the real roots of failure may have been, that Christianity did ultimately fail to gain a substantial following in China is hardly in doubt.

Yet from the standpoint in time of the early Protestant missionaries there appeared reasonable grounds for optimism with regard to the prospects for Christianity in China. It was still possible to hope that a new and highly effective phase of missionary activity would commence with the opening of China's doors to foreign trade and diplomacy. After all Buddhism, although of foreign origin—having been introduced from India during the first or second century A.D.—had eventually become acceptable to the mass of the Chinese people as one of the 'three religions' of China alongside the indigenous systems of Confucianism and Taoism. Why should Christianity not achieve at least something like similar status?

It might indeed have done so had the culturally liberal approach of the earlier missionaries, that of the Jesuits in Peking as well as of Morrison and Milne at Canton and Malacca, been sustained. However, time was to show that such an approach, though never entirely lost, would become heavily outweighed and largely counteracted by the increasingly powerful commercial and military pressures of a culturally arrogant West.

But to judge the effectiveness of the missionaries by numbers of converts to Christianity would be to adopt a crude 'body count' criterion of success and to take too narrow a view of their whole achievement. A wider view would attribute greater long-term effectiveness to the work of the missionaries in the broad process of change and modernization in China. Their real contribution, after all, was not religious but cultural, and it is by this aspect of their work that Morrison and Milne stand out as pioneers in the vital process of bringing the culture of the modern West to bear

on the traditional culture of China. For such men one may
reasonably claim a significant place in that historical process of
the meeting and interaction of the European and Chinese traditions which has so greatly shaped the China of today. Their
over-confident assumptions proved indeed to be unwarranted,
their interpretation of religious 'truth' did not in the end prevail;
yet in their own way they helped to bring about a cultural revolution which was ultimately to transform China. Certainly for
Morrison and Milne in particular the main emphasis was always
on the cultural context of the religious thought of the West rather
than on religious doctrine itself. In this respect they stood somewhat apart from the branch of the missionary movement to which
they belonged, for evangelicanism was generally anti-intellectual
in tone.

But comparatively open-minded and appreciative of Chinese
culture as they may have been, Morrison and Milne tended to
underestimate the great width of the cultural gap between East
and West which they so confidently hoped would be bridged.
Perhaps Morrison came nearer than any European of his day to an
understanding of the Chinese mind, but neither of the two
missionary-teachers could really appreciate the complexity of the
problems of culture-contact, the strength of the deeply rooted
social and psychological as well as the intellectual barriers to the
acceptance by Chinese of Western ideas and attitudes, the
difficulty of reaching from outside into the hard inner structure
of Chinese society. But even so, they and those who followed after
them did help—far more than they themselves could have foreseen
—to shape the social and intellectual forces which were ultimately
to bring about revolutionary change in China.[4]

The work of the nineteenth-century China missionaries was
inevitably associated with colonialism; bibles were linked with
gunboats and opium. And because it was associated with colonialism, Christianity in China—like colonialism everywhere—contained within itself the seeds of its own destruction. For it taught

people first how to question the system itself, and ultimately how to undermine it.

But nineteenth-century colonialism, or in more general terms the impact of the modern West on relatively under-developed regions overseas, must be seen from our standpoint in time as essentially a catalyst of change, as a necessary dissolving agent, or perhaps as the ultimately intolerable irritant that was needed to provoke revolutionary change and to induce modernization within comparatively static and traditional societies. Missionaries such as Morrison and Milne, bringing their own peculiar brand of cultural colonialism to bear on China, certainly acted as irritants and agents of revolutionary change in that sense.

Today the 'right' approach to China, which Morrison and Milne tried to map out in their own way at Malacca, remains a matter of concern and of controversy. While the religious ideas which the missionaries stood for may have been largely rejected in contemporary China, the ultimate effects of the educational and cultural changes to which they contributed have yet to work themselves out.

Notes and references

Abbreviations

LMS: London Missionary Society records

SSR: Straits Settlements records (English East India Company)

JMBRAS: *Journal of the Malayan/Malaysian Branch of the Royal Asiatic Society*

(Full titles of record series and other publications are given in the Bibliography)

Preface (pages xi–xiv)

1.   See for example Donald W. Treadgold, *The West in Russia and China,* vol. 2 (China, 1582–1949), where Morrison is not only classed among the pietists but even dismissed as one of the 'unlettered soldiers of the gospel' who were 'frankly not learned and at worst aggressively anti-intellectual' (pp. 37, 180).

2.   The whole question is discussed in Chap. 17 and briefly reviewed in Chap. 18. For an interesting discussion see Jessie G. Lutz (ed.), *Christian missions in China: evangelists of what?*

CHAPTER ONE
The Indirect Approach (pages 1–9)

1.   Both the L.M.S. and the C.M.S. drew their main inspiration from John Wesley (1703–1791), particularly in his protest against the prevailing apathy of the established Church.

2. The missionary training college at Gosport was founded by the Rev. David Bogue (1750–1825); b. Berwickshire; studied theology at Edinburgh University; became independent or congregational minister at Gosport; developed a scheme for foreign missions which led to the foundation of the L.M.S.; awarded the degree of Doctor of Divinity, Yale College, Conn., 1815; his various publications included a *History of the Dissenters . . .*, 3 vols., 1809.

3. Laird, *Missionaries and education,* pp. xiii, 60, 67, 191; *Cambridge history of India,* VI, pp. 95–120.

4. Mills, *British Malaya,* pp. 44, 83; Turnbull, *Straits Settlements,* p. 1.

5. Dr W. Brown, later secretary of the Scottish Missionary Society. See Gützlaff, *Journal of three voyages,* p. lv.

6. 'A room in the factory of Messrs. Milner and Bull of New York'; see S. W. Williams, *The Middle Kingdom,* II, p. 325. The first American trading ship to sail direct for Canton was the *Empress of China* in 1784, and from then on American merchants were the strongest rivals of the English in the Canton tea trade.

7. Matteo Ricci, pioneer Jesuit missionary to China; reached Goa in India, 1578; assigned to China, 1582; established residence in Peking, 1601, and died there, 1610.

8. Ride, *Morrison,* pp. 5–10.

9. Morrison to Waugh, 27 Sep. 1807; same to Hardcastle, 4 Nov. 1807; same to Shrubsole, 20 Dec. 1807; and same to Directors, 4 Dec. 1809, Morrison, *Memoir,* I, pp. 164, 169, 186, 273; Morrison's diary, 20 Feb. 1808, and 15 Feb. 1809, LMS, Journals, S. China; Morrison, *Memoir,* I, p. 250; and Morrison letter, 21 Jan. 1809, LMS, S. China.

10. Morrison letter, 21 July 1813, Morrison, *Memoir,* I, p. 368.

CHAPTER TWO

The Road to Malacca (pages 10–18)

1. Morrison, *Memoir,* I, p. 309.

2. Milne, *Retrospect,* p. 101 *seq.;* Morrison, *Memoirs of Milne,* p. i; *The Chinese Repository,* I, 8 (Dec. 1832), pp. 316–25; Lovett, *History of L.M.S.,* II, pp. 429–30; and Neill, *Concise dictionary.*

3. Milne to Directors, 16 June 1813, LMS, S. China.

4. *Ibid.*

5. *Ibid.* and Milne's Journal, 16 June 1813, LMS, Journals, S. China.

6. Milne to Directors, 10 Sep. 1813, LMS, S. China; and Morrison, *Memoir*, I, p. 367.

7. Milne to Directors, 10 Sep. 1813 and 16 Jan. 1814; and same to Rev. Tracy, 4 Feb. 1814, LMS, S. China; and Lovett, *History of L.M.S.*, II, p. 431.

8. Morrison's diary, 7 July 1813, Morrison, *Memoir*, I, p. 367; Milne, *Retrospect*, p. 112; Morrison to Directors, 20 Sep. 1813; and Milne to same, 10 Sep. 1813 and 16 Jan. 1814, LMS, S. China.

9. Milne to Directors, 16 Jan. 1814; and Morrison letter, 7 Jan. 1814, LMS, S. China; and Milne, *Retrospect*, p. 112.

10. Milne to Directors, 16 Jan. 1814 and 23 March 1814, LMS, S. China; and Milne, *Retrospect*, pp. 112–14.

11. Tin was mined on Bangka island (under the jurisdiction of the Sultan of Palembang) from the early years of the eighteenth century, and the Dutch East India Company later secured exclusive purchasing rights. The island was brought under the English East India Company's wartime control from 1812 to 1816.

12. Milne to Directors, 23 March 1814, LMS, S. China. Major M. H. Court later published *Relations of the British government with Palembang*. London, 1821.

13. Milne to Directors, 10 May 1814 and 1–2 July 1814, LMS, S. China; and Wurtzburg, *Raffles*, p. 352.

14. Milne's Journal, 11–19 Aug. 1814, LMS, Journals, S. China.

15. Milne to Directors, 1–2 July 1814 and 24 Sep. 1814, LMS, S. China.

CHAPTER THREE

Malacca Beginnings (pages 19–27)

1. Morrison to Directors, 22 Dec. 1812, LMS, S. China; and Morrison, *Memoir*, I, p. 355.

2. Milne to Directors, 16 Jan. 1814, LMS, S. China.

3. Memoir on Malacca, partly embodied in instructions to C. H. Thomsen, Feb. 1815, LMS, Malacca.

4.   Milne, *Retrospect,* pp. 135–36.

5.   Morrison to Rev. G. Burder, 11 Jan. 1815; Morrison's diary, 21 Jan. 1815; and Morrison to Directors, 2 March 1815, LMS, S. China.

6.   Milne, *Retrospect,* pp. 137–40.

7.   Milne to Directors, 30 Dec. 1815, LMS, Malacca; Milne, *Retrospect,* p. 141; and Farquhar to Penang, 22 May 1815, SSR, vol. 49.

8.   The Cheng Hoon Teng ('Abode of the Green or Merciful Clouds') temple at Malacca, primarily dedicated to the worship of the goddess of mercy, Kwan Shih Yin, and founded according to tradition about the middle of the seventeenth century; the oldest Chinese temple on the Malaysian peninsula.

9.   Milne's Journal, 1816–17, LMS: Journals, S. China; and Milne, *Retrospect,* p. 164.

10.   'Malacca Church Records: Statement of Accounts, 31 Dec. 1815', Malacca Church Records, *Kerk Boek.*

11.   Milne, *Retrospect,* pp. 146–49, 162–64, 175; Milne to Directors, 30 Dec. 1815, LMS, Malacca; and Milne's Journal, 1816–17, LMS, Journals, S. China.

12.   Milne, *Retrospect,* pp. 138, 154–56; and Milne to Directors, 15 Dec. 1815, LMS, Malacca.

13.   *The Sacred edict* (Sheng Yü) was a series of sixteen maxims for proper conduct issued by the K'ang Hsi emperor in 1670 and intended to be read out aloud to the people in each district twice a month; see J. K. Fairbank, E. O. Reischauer and A. M. Craig, *East Asia, the modern transformation,* II, p. 85. Cf. Chapter 7, note 9.

14.   Milne, *Retrospect,* p. 139; Milne to Directors, 15 Dec. 1815, LMS, Malacca; and Milne's Journal, 1816–17, LMS, Journals, S. China.

15.   Milne, *Retrospect,* pp. 169, 174; Milne to Burder, 25 Sep. 1815; and same to Directors, 12 March 1816, LMS, Malacca.

16.   *Munshi* (Malay): tutor, language teacher.

17.   Milne to Directors, 22 June 1817, LMS, *Quarterly Journal of Transactions,* I, pp. 214–17.

CHAPTER FOUR

Planning a College (pages 28–36)

1. Milne, *Retrospect,* pp. 171–73; Milne's Journal, 1816–17, LMS, Journals, S. China; Milne's memorial discussed under Penang Council minutes of 25 Jan., and Council's reply of 26 Jan., SSR, vol. 54; and Penang Misc. Letters Out, 26 Jan. 1816, SSR, series I, p. 18.

2. Tranquerah (Portuguese): a rampart.

3. Milne, *Retrospect,* pp. 173–74, 187–89; Milne to Directors, 12 March 1816, LMS, Malacca; Milne's Journal, 17 March, 13 and 15 Aug. 1816, LMS, Journals, S. China; Macalister to Penang, 18 May 1816, SSR, vol. 55; Hill, *Hikayat Abdullah,* p. 113; *Indo-Chinese Gleaner,* 2 (Aug. 1817), p. 32; Milne to Directors, 22 June 1817, LMS, *Quarterly Journal Transactions,* I, p. 216.

4. *Ssu shu,* the Four books or Books of the four philosophers: *Lun Yu* (Digested conversations or Confucian analects), *Ta hsio* (Great learning), *Chung yung* (Doctrine of the mean), and the works of Mencius. See Legge, *Chinese classics,* Prolegomena, p. 2.

5. Milne, *Retrospect,* pp. 121, 188, 238; and Morrison to Burder, 13 Jan. 1817, LMS, S. China.

6. Morrison to Burder, 27 and 28 Nov. 1815, 1 Jan., 18 March 1816, and 23 Feb. 1817; Burder to Morrison, Dec. 1816, LMS, S. China; Milne, *Retrospect,* p. 186; and Milne's Journal, 28 Nov. 1816, LMS, Journals, S. China.

7. David Bogue (1750–1825), *Essay on the Divine authority of the New Testament.* 1801 (see Chap. 1, note 2). Philip Doddridge (1702–1751), *On the rise and progress of religion in the soul.* 1745.

8. Milne, *Retrospect,* pp. 180, 190–92; *Indo-Chinese Gleaner,* 1, Introduction; Morrison to Burder, 3 Feb. 1818, LMS, S. China; and Morrison, *Memoir,* I, p. 500.

9. Milne, *Retrospect,* p. 195; Instructions to Medhurst, 29 Aug. 1816, LMS, Malacca; Burder to Morrison, Dec. 1816; and Directors to same, Nov. 1817, LMS, S. China; and *Dictionary of national biography.*

10. *Indo-Chinese Gleaner,* 1 (May 1817), p. 13; 2 (Aug. 1817), p. 35; Milne's Journal, 11 Aug. 1816, LMS, Journals, S. China; and Medhurst, *China,* p. 311.

11. The Amherst embassy was the third in a series of unsuccessful British attempts to establish trade relations with the Chinese government (Charles Cathcart, 1787; George Macartney, 1792–94; Lord Amherst, 1816).

12. Morrison, *Memoir,* I, p. 474; and Morrison to Burder, 28 Nov. 1815, and 13 Jan. 1817, LMS, S. China.

13. Morrison to Burder, 23 Feb. 1817, LMS, S. China.

14. Morrison, *Memoir,* I, p. 475; Morrison to Burder, 14 Sep. 1817, LMS, S. China; and Milne, *Retrospect,* p. 197.

15. Morrison, *Memoir,* I, pp. 502 *seq.;* and Milne, *Retrospect,* p. 204.

16. Morrison to Directors, 22 Dec. 1812; same to Milne, 15 July 1815; and same to W. Shrubsole, 9 Jan. 1815, Morrison, *Memoir,* I, pp. 355, 377, 426.

17. Morrison, *Memoir,* I, p. 502; *Indo-Chinese Gleaner,* 3 (Feb. 1818), p. 68.

18. Morrison to Burder, 7 Dec. 1817; and same to Directors, 18 Jan., 30 Jan. 1818, LMS, S. China.

19. Morrison to Burder, 23 Feb., 14 Sep., and 7 Oct. 1817; same to Hankey, 29 Oct. 1817; and same to Langton, 7 Dec. 1817, LMS, S. China.

CHAPTER FIVE

The Foundation (pages 37–44)

1. Thomsen to Directors, 26 May 1818, LMS, *Reports of directors,* II, p. 116; *Indo-Chinese Gleaner,* 2 (Aug. 1817), p. 32; 4 (May 1818), p. 131; 9 (July 1819), p. 168; and Milne, *Retrospect,* p. 212.

2. Burder to Morrison, Dec. 1816; and Directors to same, Nov. 1817, LMS, S. China; *Indo-Chinese Gleaner,* 3 (Feb. 1818), p. 68; 5 (Aug. 1818), p. 176; 8 (April 1819), p. 116; 10 (Oct. 1819), p. 220; and Milne, *Retrospect,* pp. 211, 213.

3. Morrison to Burder, 7 Dec. 1817; and same to Hankey, 12 Nov., 9 Dec. 1818, LMS, S. China.

4. *Indo-Chinese Gleaner,* 3 (Feb. 1818), pp. 68–70.

5. Farquhar to Commissioners Woltenbeck and Thyssen, 16 Sep. 1818; and Milne to same, 18 Oct. 1818, Jakarta, *Buitenland* 29; and LMS, *Reports of directors,* 11 May 1820, II, p. 131.

6. *Indo-Chinese Gleaner,* 6 (Oct. 1818), after p. 217; LMS: *Quarterly Journal Transactions,* I, pp. 406–8, and *Reports of directors,* 11 May 1820, II, p. 145.

7. Morrison to Hankey, 28 Oct. 1818, LMS, S. China.

8. 'The Anglo-Chinese College, under the auspices and at the expense of Robert Morrison, D.D., the founder, 1818'.

9. Engelbert Kaempfer (1651–1716), German botanist and traveller; *The history of Japan, together with a description of the Kingdom of Siam, 1690–1692.* 1727. Karl Peter Thunberg (1743–1828), Swedish naturalist and traveller; *Travels in Europe, Africa and Asia, 1770–1779.* 1794. A footnote to the printed speech by Milne cites in addition Marsden's *History of Sumatra.* 1811; Leyden's 'Dissertation on the Languages and Literature of the Indo-Chinese Nations', written in Penang in 1805 and afterwards printed in *Asiatic Researches,* X; the same author's *Comparative vocabulary,* and Raffles's *History of Java.* 1817, 'which we have had the pleasure to see since the first edition of this paper'.

10. Milne, *Retrospect,* pp. 356–64; and LMS, *Quarterly Journal Transactions,* I, pp. 400–405; and *Reports of directors,* 11 May 1820, II, pp. 139–44.

CHAPTER SIX

College and Mission *(pages 45–53)*

1. Milne to Directors, 24 Jan. 1818, LMS, Malacca.

2. Burder to Steven, n.d. (? Nov. 1818), LMS, Malacca.

3. Directors to Morrison, 26 Feb. 1819, Morrison, *Memoir,* I, pp. 539–40; and *Reports of directors,* 13 May 1819.

4. Morrison to Directors, 8 Feb. 1819; and same to Hankey and Burder, 12 Feb. 1819, LMS, S. China.

5. Morrison to Directors, 21 Dec. 1819, LMS, S. China.

6. Morrison to Hankey, 22 Dec. 1819, LMS, S. China.

7. Morrison to ?, 14 Nov. 1820, LMS, S. China.

8. Morrison to Rev. C. B. Cracknell, 19 Dec. 1820; and same to Directors, Dec. 1820, LMS, S. China.

9. The 'tyranny of distance' is the phrase used by Geoffrey Blainey as the title of his survey of Australian history, *The tyranny of distance.* Melbourne, 1966.

10.   Thomsen to Directors, 5 Dec. 1821; and Beighton to Thomsen, 24 April 1821, LMS, Malacca; and Morrison to Burder, 9 March 1819, LMS, S. China.

11.   Slater to Hankey, 12 Nov. 1821, LMS, Batavia; and Morrison, *Memoir*, II, p. 156.

12.   Beighton and Ince to Directors, 1820, LMS, Penang.

13.   Morrison to Hankey, 14 Nov. 1822, LMS, S. China.

CHAPTER SEVEN

The Building (pages 54–61)

1.   Morrison to Hankey, 11 April 1826; John Smith to Directors, ? 1830, LMS, Malacca; and Morrison, Memorial of the Chinese Mission, 28 April 1824, LMS: China Personal, R. M.

2.   From the earliest days of European trading in East Asia, the Spanish or Mexican silver dollar was the standard coin in general use. In 1836 the Spanish dollar was officially (though not effectively) replaced by the Indian rupee in the Straits Settlements of Penang, Malacca and Singapore. C. M. Turnbull, *Straits Settlements*, Introduction, gives the following equivalents: rupees 220 = Spanish dollars 100 = pounds sterling 21.

3.   Morrison, *Memoir*, II, p. 52; *Anglo-Chinese College*, a four-page pamphlet, ? 1820, LMS, China personal, R. M.; *Missionary sketches*, no. 27 (Jan. 1825); *Quarterly Journal Transactions*, III, p. 309; Begbie, *Malayan Peninsula*, p. 368; and Hunter, *Bits of old China*, pp. 237–39.

4.   Louis Le Comte, *Nouveaux mémoires sur l'état présent de la Chine*, Paris, 1696; *Lettres édifiantes et curieuses écrites des Missions étrangères*. Paris, 1780–83, 'a series of volumes published periodically throughout the century; . . . they supplied the European reading public with a panoramic view of the rich and complex culture of China'. See Arnold H. Rowbotham, *Missionary and Mandarin*, p. 351; H. Cordier, *Bibliotheca Sinica*, cols. 39–43, 54–59.

5.   LMS, *Quarterly Journal Transactions*, I, p. 53; Milne to Directors, 30 Dec. 1815; and same to same, 14 April 1821, LMS, Malacca; Morrison, *To the public*, pp. 7, 21; Morrison, *Memoir*, I, p. 500; and II, p. 288. Edward King (1795–1837), member of an Irish family of Boyle, Co. Roscommon; styled Viscount Kingsborough from 1799; entered Exeter College, Oxford, June 1814; M. P. for Co. Cork,

1818–26; an antiquary of some repute, he edited Aglio's *The antiquities of Mexico*. 6 vols., 1831.

6. Morrison, *Memoir*, II, pp. 288, 317, 439. Joseph Henri Marie de Prémare (1670–1735), French Jesuit and sinologue; went to Peking, 1698; devoted his life to the study of Chinese literature and antiquities; d. Peking, 1735. The *Notitia Linguae Sinicae* was printed from his manuscript for publication by the Anglo-Chinese Press in 1831. The volume was reviewed in *The Chinese Repository*, I (4) (Aug. 1832), pp. 152–55. See also H. Cordier, *Bibliotheca Sinica*, cols. 1664–1669.

7. Morrison to Burder, 13 Jan. 1817, LMS, S. China; and Milne, *Retrospect*, p. 130.

8. Medhurst, *China*, p. 312; *Indo-Chinese Gleaner*, 7 (Jan. 1819), p. 44; 9 (July 1819), p. 168; 10 (Oct. 1819), p. 220; Milne, *Retrospect*, 220–21; LMS, *Reports of directors*, III, p. 27.

9. Milne's *Sacred edict* was reviewed in *The Chinese Repository*, I (8) (Dec. 1832), pp. 297–315. 'Among all the numerous writings published for the improvement and instruction of the people by their rulers, none has been so celebrated as the *Shing yu*, or *Sacred command*, a sort of politico-moral treatise, which has been made known to English readers by the translation of Dr. Milne.' See S. W. Williams, *The Middle Kingdom*, I, p. 553.

10. Morrison to Burder, 14 Sep. 1817; same to same, 24 Jan. 1819 and 12 Feb. 1820; Morrison to Directors, 25 Nov. 1819, LMS, S. China; Milne to Directors, 14 April 1821; same to same, 23 Aug. 1821, LMS, Malacca; Milne, *Retrospect*, pp. 156, 289; Morrison to Hankey, 5 Jan. 1823; same to Hankey and Burder, 10 Nov. 1823, LMS, S. China; and LMS, *Transactions*, II, p. ix.

11. *Indo-Chinese Gleaner*, 2 (Aug. 1817), p. 32; 4 (May 1818), p. 131; 9 (July 1819), p. 168; 10 (Oct. 1819), p. 220; 16 (April 1821), p. 107; Milne to Directors, 14 April 1821, LMS, Malacca; Hill, *Hikayat Abdullah*, pp. 123–25.

12. Hill, *Hikayat Abdullah*, pp. 115–18; and Milne, *Retrospect*, Preface.

13. Milne to Morrison, 30 Sep. 1820, Morrison, *Memoir*, II, p. 68; Milne to Directors, 16 Nov. 1821; and Morrison to Hankey, 19 Feb. 1823, LMS, Malacca.

14. *Indo-Chinese Gleaner*, 14 (Oct. 1820), p. 462; and Morrison, *To the public*, p. 22.

15.   Broomhall, *Robert Morrison,* p. 107; Slater to Hankey, 12 Nov. 1821, LMS, Batavia; and Newbold, *British settlements,* p. 183.

16.   Original deed of trust, signed and sealed by Morrison, dated 20 March 1820, LMS, China Personal, R. M.; Morrison, *Memoir,* II, pp. 47–51; Morrison, *To the public,* p. 22; and W. Ellis to J. R. Morrison, 18 June 1836, LMS, Eastern outgoing letters.

17.   Morrison, *Memoir,* II, pp. 40–47, 51, 53; *Anglo-Chinese College* (pamphlet, ? 1820), LMS: China personal, R. M.

CHAPTER EIGHT

Death of the Builder (pages 62–69)

1.   Milne to Directors, 23 Aug. 1821, and 16 Nov. 1821, LMS, Malacca; Ince and Beighton to Directors, 25 April 1821, LMS, Penang; and Medhurst, *China,* p. 326.

2.   Beighton to Thomsen, 24 April 1821; Milne to Hankey, 2 Jan. 1821; and Thomsen to Directors, 5. Dec. 1821, LMS, Malacca; Thomsen to Directors, 1 July 1822, LMS, Singapore; Milne, *Retrospect,* p. 289; Hill, *Hikayat Abdullah,* p. 160; Gibson-Hill, C. A., 'The date of Munshi Abdullah's first visit to Singapore', JMBRAS, 28 (1) (March 1955) 191–95.

3.   Morrison's notes on Milton's letter of 31 Dec. 1824, LMS, Singapore; Milne to Directors, 14 April 1821; and Humphreys to same, 30 Nov. 1821, LMS, Malacca.

4.   Milne to Directors, 14 April 1821, LMS, Malacca; LMS, *Transactions,* I, p. 297; Morrison to Hankey, 15 Feb. 1822, LMS, S. China; Milne to Morrison, 25 June 1821, Morrison, *Memoirs of Milne,* p. 227; and Hill, *Hikayat Abdullah,* pp. 103 *seq.*

5.   Medhurst, *China,* p. 314; *Indo-Chinese Gleaner,* 11, p. 247; Morrison, *Memoir,* II, pp. 124, 150; Milne to Directors, 16 Nov. 1821, LMS, Malacca; Morrison, *Memoirs of Milne,* p. 106; and Crawfurd, *Journal of an Embassy,* p. 34. John Crawfurd had served as an administrator in Java during the British occupation, 1811–16, and was to become Resident of Singapore, 1823–26. Finlayson accompanied Crawfurd to Siam as physician and naturalist, writing a journal of the mission which was published posthumously, *Mission to Siam and Hué.* London, 1826.

6. Milne to Morrison, 26 Sep. 1821; same to same, 6 March 1822, Morrison, *Memoir*, II, pp. 124, 150, 152; Milne's diary 1822, Morrison, *Memoirs of Milne*, pp. 106–9: Milne to Directors, 15 Feb. 1822; same to Burder, 7 March and 17 April 1822; and same to Phillip, 16 April 1822, LMS, Malacca.

7. Beighton to Phillip, 17 June 1822; Morrison to Hankey, 5 July 1822, LMS, S. China; Huttman to Morrison, 14 June 1822, Morrison, *Memoir*, II, p. 158; Grave-digger's report, 30 June 1822, Malacca Church Records, *Kerk Boek;* Morrison, *Memoirs of Milne*, pp. 110–11; and Morrison to Hankey, 19 Feb. 1823, LMS, Malacca.

8. Morrison, *Memoir*, II, pp. 156, 181; Hill, *Hikayat Abdullah*, pp. 104, 109; LMS, *Reports of directors*, 1823, p. 35; *The Chinese Repository*, II (5) (Sep. 1833), p. 235; and Lovett, *History of L.M.S.*, II, p. 430.

9. Morrison's notes on Milton's letter of 31 Dec. 1824, LMS, Singapore; Morrison to Hankey, 5 July 1822, 14 Nov. 1822, LMS, S. China; and Morrison to Staunton, 7 Oct. 1822, Morrison, *Memoir*, II, p. 174.

10. Captain William Flint, R. N., first Master Attendant of Singapore, who married Raffles' sister.

11. Morrison, *Memoir*, I, pp. 185–86; Morrison to Hankey, 19 Feb. 1823, LMS, Malacca; same to same, 14 Nov. 1822, LMS, S. China; LMS, *Reports of directors*, 1824, p. 43; Hough, 'Educational policy of Raffles'; and Wurtzburg, *Raffles*, pp. 618–19.

12. Morrison to Hankey, 19 Feb. 1823, LMS, Malacca.

CHAPTER NINE

Morrison's Visit: Malacca or Singapore? (pages 70–77)

1. Morrison, *Memoir*, II, p. 192; Morrison to Hankey, 19 Feb. 1823, and 29 April 1823, LMS, Malacca.

2. Jeremiah Joyce (1763–1816), educational writer 'of advanced political views, . . . an excellent scholar' (see *Dict. nat. biography*); became secretary of the Unitarian Society; *Scientific dialogues.* 1807. Christopher Stock (1672–1733), German orientalist.

3. Hill, *Hikayat Abdullah*, pp. 121–22; Morrison, *Memoir*, II, p. 193; and Humphreys and Collie to Directors, 13 June 1823, LMS, Malacca.

4. Morrison, Humphreys and Collie to Directors, 24 Feb. 1823, LMS, Malacca.

5. Morrison, *To the public,* pp. 3, 7, 25.

6. Humphreys to Directors, 8 March 1823; and Morrison to Hankey, March 1823, LMS, Malacca; and Morrison to Hankey, 7 Nov. 1826, LMS, S. China.

7. Raffles, *Minute on the Singapore Institution;* Hill, *Hikayat Abdullah,* pp. 180–81; Hough, 'Educational policy'; Wijeysingha, *History of Raffles Institution,* pp. 6–11; Morrison, *Memoir,* II, p. 193; Morrison to Directors, 3 April 1823, LMS, Singapore; Morrison, Humphreys and Collie to Directors, 18 June 1823, LMS, Malacca. The meeting of 1 April 1823 included the Sultan of Johore; the proceedings are described in C. E. Wurtzburg, *Raffles of the Eastern Isles,* pp. 626–35.

8. Morrison to Treasurer and Secretary of L.M.S., 10 Nov. 1823, Morrison, *Memoir,* II, p. 219.

9. Morrison's notes to Milton's letter of 31 Dec. 1824, LMS, Singapore; Morrison, *Memoir,* II, p. 194; Wijeysingha, *Raffles Institution,* p. 31; Morrison to Directors, 16 Aug. 1826, LMS, S. China; Morrison to Fisher, 5 Oct. 1827, LMS, China personal, R. M.; Morrison to Collie and Kidd, 17 Nov. 1827, Morrison, *Memoir,* II, p. 402; LMS, *Reports of directors,* 1824; Memorial of the Chinese Mission, 28 April 1824, LMS, China personal, R. M.; Morrison, *To the British public,* p. 9; Kidd to Arundel, 25 Aug. 1825; and Morrison to Hankey, 11 April 1826, LMS, Malacca.

10. Memorial of the Chinese Mission, 28 April 1824, LMS, China personal, R. M.

11. Morrison to Hankey, 11 April 1826, with enclosure 'Answer to queries respecting Anglo-Chinese College', LMS, Malacca.

CHAPTER TEN

Successors to Milne (pages 78–85)

1. Morrison, *Memoir,* II, pp. 219, 224; Morrison, *To the public,* p. 14; and Smith's Report, 1830, LMS, Malacca.

2. Morrison to Hankey and Burder, 10 Nov. 1823, LMS, S. China; same to Fisher, 23 Nov. 1829, LMS, China personal, R. M.

3. LMS, *Reports of directors,* 1825; Morrison, *Memoir,* II, p. 214; Kidd to Hankey, 1 July 1825; and same to Arundel, 25 Aug. 1825, LMS, Malacca.

4. LMS, *Reports of directors*, 1825–28; Medhurst, *China*, p. 316; Morrison to Clunie, 13 March 1826, *Memoir*, II, p. 341; and Hill, *Hikayat Abdullah*, pp. 228–29.

5. *Khatib* (Malay): preacher or reader in a mosque.

6. *Feng shui* (Chinese): lit. wind and water; the principles of geomancy which governed the selection of a Chinese building site or burial place.

7. *Kapitan China* (Malay): headman or chief representative of the Chinese community.

8. Hill, *Hikayat Abdullah*, pp. 230–32; Humphreys, Collie and Kidd to Burder, 6 Oct. 1825; same to Directors, 28 April 1827, LMS, Malacca; Tyerman and Bennet, *Journal of voyages*, II, p. 274.

9. Tyerman and Bennet, *Journal of voyages*, II, p. 271; Collie to Directors, 1 Feb. 1826, LMS, Malacca; Morrison, *Memoir*, II, p. 341; Medhurst, *China*, p. 270; and Morrison to Hankey, 22 Dec. 1819, LMS, S. China.

10. Kidd to Hankey, 5 April 1827; same to L.M.S., 10 March 1828; and Kidd and Humphreys to L.M.S., 25 Feb. 1828, LMS, Malacca; Morrison to Hankey, 10 Oct. 1828, LMS, S. China; same to Staunton, 11 Oct. 1828, Morrison, *Memoir*, II, p. 409. The *Four books;* see Chapter 4, note 4. Collie also published *Abridgment of the sacred history*. 1826; and *The Celestial mirror*, in Chinese, 2 vols. 1826.

11. Orme to Morrison, 27 April 1829, LMS, Eastern outgoing letters; Humphreys to Hankey, 1 Jan. 1827; same to Orme, 30 Nov. 1829; Tomlin to Hankey, 3 March 1827; Smith's Report, 1830; and Smith to Orme, 10 Feb. 1830, LMS, Malacca; Smith to Hankey, 25 April 1827; same to Orme, 12 April 1828, LMS, Singapore; LMS, *Reports of directors*, 1829; Morrison to Orme, 1 Dec. 1829, LMS, S. China.

12. The policy of bringing Naning under British jurisdiction as part of Malacca territory, and requiring a tribute of one-tenth levied on its crops, was to lead to the Naning War, 1831–32, 'an egregious blunder'; see L. A. Mills, *British Malaya*, p. 118.

13. Moor to Arundel, 20 Sep. 1825, 4 Jan. 1826; and Kidd to Orme, 9 Nov. 1829, LMS, Malacca; Anderson to Garling, 15 July 1829; and Governor Fullerton's minute, 22 Oct. 1829, SSR, vol. 169; C. A. Gibson-Hill, 'The Singapore Chronicle', JMBRAS, 26 (1) (July

1953) 175-99; C. B. Buckley, *An anecdotal history of old times in Singapore*, p. 133.

14. Fullerton to Governor-General, 13 Nov. 1830, SSR, series V, 4; Morrison, *Memoir*, II, pp. 64, 445, 447; and Newbold, *Political and statistical account*, pp. 184-85.

15. Kidd to L.M.S., 11 Oct. 1831, LMS, Malacca; LMS, *Transactions*, IV, p. xvi.

16. LMS, *Reports of directors*, 1832; Hughes to Arundel, 5 Dec. 1830, LMS, Malacca; and Hill, *Hikayat Abdullah*, p. 245.

17. See Chapter 11.

18. LMS, *Transactions*, IV, pp. 65-67, 69-82, 225-67; Abeel, *Journal of a residence*, pp. 200-273; Morrison letters, 10, 11 Oct. 1828, LMS, S. China.

19. W. H. Medhurst, *A dictionary of the Hok-këen dialect of the Chinese language*. Macao, 1832. According to F. W. Williams, *Life and letters of S. W. Williams*, p. 81, Medhurst's dictionary was printed by the American missionary Samuel Wells Williams at Canton.

20. J. R. Morrison letter, 20 July 1837, LMS, S. China; Morrison to Treasurer and Secretary of L.M.S., 10 Nov. 1823, Morrison, *Memoir*, II, p. 226; Humphreys to Directors, 15 Dec. 1829; and Smith's report, 1830, LMS; Malacca; Morrison's notes on Milton's letter of 31 Dec. 1824, LMS, Singapore.

CHAPTER ELEVEN

Missionary Excursions (pages 86-94)

1. Jacob Tomlin (1793-1880), *Missionary journal and letters written during eleven years' residence and travels among the Chinese, Siamese, Javanese, Khassias and other Eastern nations*, pp. 60-100. Begbie made extensive use of Tomlin's reports on the Malaysian tin-mining districts; see his *Malayan Peninsula*, pp. 390-427. He expressed his gratitude for 'unlimited access' to the library of the Anglo-Chinese College in the preparation of his work, see *ibid.*, Introduction, p. viii.

2. Lukut was later ceded to Negri Sembilan by a frontier adjustment of 1880.

3. Plantain: a banana-like tree; taro: plant of arum family with edible root; *sireh* (Malay): a creeper or climbing plant, the leaf of which is chewed with betel nut *(buah pinang)* and lime as a sedative.

4. Sungei Ujong, one of the provinces of present-day Negri Sembilan (Nine States) and the only one with a coastline; its people are of Minangkabau (west-central Sumatra) descent, though the people of Linggi district formed a distinct settlement of Bugis (originally from the area around Macassar in Celebes or Sulawesi).

5. According to Begbie, *Malayan Peninsula*, pp. 401–4, the 'straggling village' of Linggi, lying on the left bank of the river and consisting of about 112 houses, had three *pengkalan* (wharves or landing-places) where goods were offloaded for transhipment or storage, the main wharf having three warehouses. T. J. Newbold, who visited Linggi village in 1832, provides further information; see Moor, *Notices*, Appendix, pp. 85–86; and Newbold, *Political and statistical account*, II, p. 115.

6. Moor, *Notices*, facing p. 246, 'Map of Malacca territory' shows Salangore country to N.W. of Lingee River, with *Pangkalang Mangies* and *Pangkalang Durian* (named from the mangosteen and durian fruit trees) on the river at the village of Lingee; also Condore village to E.N.E. of Lingee.

7. But serious disturbances were to occur at Sungei Ujong two years later in which a number of Chinese were killed, resulting in the temporary abandonment of the mines; and there were similar disturbances at the Lukut mines in 1834; see Begbie, *Malayan Peninsula*, p. 408.

8. Yip Yat Hoong, *The development of the tin mining industry of Malaya*, 85 n.

9. See Joseph Needham and Wang Ling, *Science and civilization in China*, IV, part 2, p. 339, where the chain pump is described as 'the most characteristic of Chinese water-raising machines'.

10. Wong Lin Ken, *The Malayan tin industry to 1914*, p. 48; Yip Yat Hoong, *Development of tin mining*, pp. 83–84, for a diagrammatic cross-section of the *chin-chia*; and Moor, *Notices*, Appendix, p. 82.

11. W. H. Medhurst, 'Journal of a tour through the settlements on the Eastern side of the Peninsula of Malacca, 1828', in *A collection of journals of the Ultra-Ganges mission . . .*, vol. I (Aug. 1828–Jan. 1832), Singapore/Malacca, n.d.; reprinted in *The Chinese Repository*, I, 6 (Oct. 1832). Medhurst makes no mention of the Englishman Charles Gray who had performed an amazing cross country trek from Malacca to Pahang in January 1827 to barter opium for gold dust; returning by the same route to Malacca in early February, Gray died a few weeks

later of jungle fever; see Charles Gray, 'Journal of a route overland from Malacca to Pahang across the Malayan Peninsula', in *Journal of the Indian Archipelago and Eastern Asia*, VI (1852), 369–75, reprinted from the *Malacca Observer*, 27 Feb. 1827; and T. J. Newbold, 'Johole and its former dependencies . . .', in Moor, *Notices*, Appendix, p. 67. *Kajang* (Malay): matting of palm leaves used as covering for boats and carts. Karl Friedrich Gützlaff (1803–51), born in Pomerania, Prussia; after training in Berlin and Rotterdam, joined the Netherlands Missionary Society in Java, 1824, but soon decided to become an independent missionary and went with Jacob Tomlin to Siam in 1828; visited the Anglo-Chinese College at Malacca in 1829 and again in 1834; between 1831 and 1833 undertook a series of voyages along the China coast (described in his *Journal of three voyages* . . .), serving as an interpreter— he was an excellent linguist—and distributing bibles, religious tracts and medicines; served as interpreter during the Opium War with British forces in North China waters, 1840–41, also in the Nanking treaty negotiations, 1842; Chinese secretary to the Superintendent of Trade in Hong Kong, 1843; formed the Chinese Christian Union to train Chinese youths for missionary work, 1844; died in Hong Kong, 1851.

12.   *First report of the Singapore Christian Union (formerly called Singapore Committee) formed in September 1827 for extending the benefits of education and the knowledge of Christianity in Singapore and other parts of the Malayan Archipelago* . . ., pp. 30–33.

13.   David Abeel (1804–1846), born in New Brunswick, N. J., was ordained in the Dutch Reformed Church there in 1826. He and Elijah Bridgman were the first American Protestant missionaries to China, arriving in Canton in 1830. Bridgman remained in Canton where he commenced publication of *The Chinese Repository* in 1832, but Abeel left for a tour of Southeast Asia in 1831, visiting Java, Malacca and the Anglo-Chinese College, Singapore, and (with Jacob Tomlin) Siam, and developing fluency in the Hokkien (Amoy) dialect of Chinese. He returned to America via England in 1833 because of poor health, and in the following year published his *Journal of a residence in China*. However by the spring of 1839 he was back in the Far East, travelling from Canton to Southeast Asia once again and then back northward along the China coast in 1841. After the opening of Amoy as a 'treaty port' (following the Anglo-Chinese treaty settlement of 1842–43) he started a mission there, but finally returned home on account of ill health in 1845. He died in Albany, N.Y., the following year. G. R. Williamson,

Memoir of the Rev. David Abeel, D.D., late missionary to China, includes observations by Abeel on his exploratory tours of Java, Malacca, Siam, etc. Abeel's portrait forms the frontispiece to Samuel Wells Williams, *The Middle Kingdom,* vol. II. Williams and Dr Peter Parker, both of the American Board of Foreign Missions, followed Abeel and Bridgman as American missionaries to China, Williams arriving at Canton in 1833, Parker in 1834 (the year of Robert Morrison's death).

14. J. Tomlin, *Missionary journal kept at Singapore and Siam from May 1830 to January 1832.*

15. E. P. Boardman, *Christian influence,* p. 42.

CHAPTER TWELVE

Death of the Founder (pages 95–102)

1. Hankey to Morrison, 9 April 1827, and 15 April 1828, LMS, Eastern outgoing letters.

2. Hankey to Morrison, 2 May 1830, and 12 April 1831, LMS, Eastern outgoing letters.

3. Morrison to Hankey, 10 Oct. 1828, and 14 Nov. 1830, LMS, S. China.

4. Smith's report, 1830; Humphreys to Directors, 15 Dec. 1829, LMS, Malacca; and Morrison to Hankey, 26 Sep. 1831, LMS, S. China.

5. Hankey to Morrison, 5 May 1832, LMS, Eastern outgoing letters; Morrison to Hankey, 9 Oct. 1833; same to Ellis, 22 Dec. 1833; and Hankey to Morrison, 14 June 1834, LMS, S. China; and Morrison letter, 30 Jan. 1834, LMS, China personal, R. M.

6. Ellis to Morrison, 24 Oct. 1832, and 2 March 1833, LMS, Eastern outgoing letters; LMS, *Reports of directors,* 1834; Evans to L.M.S., 4 Aug. 1834, LMS, Malacca; Medhurst, *China,* p. 320; and Hill, *Hikayat Abdullah,* p. 248.

7. L.M.S. to Thomsen, 7 April 1827; and same to Dyer, 13 March 1828, LMS, Eastern outgoing letters; Medhurst, *China,* p. 327; Morrison to Ellis, 14 Oct. 1833, LMS, S. China; LMS: *Reports of directors,* 1836; and Byrd, *Early printing,* p. 5.

8. Malcom, *Travels,* p. 98; Medhurst, *China,* p. 323; Evans and Dyer to L.M.S., 14 April 1837; and Evans to L.M.S., 16 Aug. 1837,

LMS, Malacca. Publications of the Anglo-Chinese College press in
1837 included *The periodical miscellany and juvenile instructor* (in English),
edited by John Evans (1836–38 ?); *Vocabulary of the English and Malay
languages in the Roman and Arabic characters*, new edition enlarged and
improved (first edition published at Malacca in 1820); and a *Malay
reading book* (in Arabic script or Jawi); see Byrd, *Early printing*, p. 32.

9. Wijeysingha, *Raffles Institution*, pp. 47–54; J. R. Morrison to
Hankey, 14 May 1836, LMS, S. China; Ellis to J. R. Morrison, 9 Feb.
1837, 16 March 1838; and same to Evans and Dyer, 4 July 1838, LMS,
Eastern outgoing letters; and Evans and Dyer to L.M.S., 14 Aug. 1837,
LMS, Malacca.

CHAPTER THIRTEEN

End and Beginning (pages 103–115)

1. The Hoxton Academy, where Robert Morrison had trained,
became the Highbury Theological College in 1826.

2. L.M.S. to Evans and Dyer, 3 May 1839, LMS, Eastern outgoing
letters; Cook, *Sunny Singapore*, p. 16; and H. E. Legge, *James Legge*,
p. 13.

3. Heinrich Christian Werth, a German missionary sent from
Singapore in 1839 as temporary replacement for Samuel Dyer, on sick
leave in England.

4. Directors to Legge, 26 Oct. 1840, LMS, Eastern outgoing letters;
Legge to L.M.S., 1 Aug. 1840; Evans to Directors, 5 Nov. 1840, and
Legge to Directors, 2 Dec. 1840, LMS, Malacca.

5. Legge to Secretary of L.M.S., 23 Oct. 1840, LMS, Malacca.

6. H. E. Legge, *James Legge*, p. 13.

7. Yet years later Legge was to write, in *The Chinese classics*, p. vii, of
himself: 'He was favourably situated, the charge of the Anglo-Chinese
College having devolved upon him, so that he had free access to all the
treasures in its library. He had translations and dictionaries in abund-
ance, and they facilitated his progress'.

8. Legge to Rev. A. Tidman, 26 Dec. 1840; same to Trustees,
19 Jan., and 17 Aug. 1841, LMS, Malacca.

9. J. R. Morrison to Hankey, 25 Jan. 1841; same to Directors,
30 April 1842, LMS, S. China; and Legge to Tidman, 12 March 1842,
LMS, Malacca.

10. L.M.S. to W. C. Milne, Lockhart and Hobson, 30 March 1841, LMS, Eastern outgoing letters; and Legge to Trustees, 17 Aug. 1841, LMS, Malacca.

11. L.M.S. to Legge, 4 Nov. 1841; same to Morrison, 30 Dec. 1841; and same to Legge, 28 Feb. 1842, LMS, Eastern outgoing letters; LMS, *Reports of directors,* 1843; and H. E. Legge, *James Legge,* p. 24.

12. Dyer to Tidman, 15 Oct. 1842, LMS, Singapore; and L.M.S. to J. R. Morrison, n.d., LMS, Eastern outgoing letters.

13. Legge, Dyer and Stronach to L.M.S., 28 April 1843, LMS, Malacca; H. E. Legge, *James Legge,* p. 13; and LMS, *Reports of directors,* 1843.

14. Samuel Dyer, Benjamin Hobson, James Legge, W. H. Medhurst, William C. Milne, Alexander Stronach, and John Stronach.

15. L.M.S. Missionaries to Government of Hong Kong, 18 Aug. 1843; Governor's reply, 21 Aug. 1843; Legge to Tidman, 14 Dec. 1843, LMS, S. China; Bonham to Resident of Malacca, 27 Jan. 1842; and Bonham to Pottinger, 29 March 1842, SSR, series U 8, V 8.

16. Legge to Tidman, 1 Sep. 1842, LMS, Malacca; and Conference resolutions, 26 Aug. 1843, LMS, S. China.

17. Legge to Tidman, 31 Aug. 1843, LMS, Malacca.

18. James Legge, *The Chinese classics,* 5 vols., 2nd ed. Oxford, 1893; reprinted by the Hong Kong University Press with *Biographical note* by Lindsay Ride. Hong Kong, 1960.

19. Lindsay Ride, *op. cit., Biographical note,* p. 10.

20. J. K. Fairbank, *Trade and diplomacy,* I, pp. 294–95; W. H. Medhurst, *A glance at the interior of China,* quoted in Fairbank, *loc. cit.*

CHAPTER FOURTEEN

College Teachers (pages 116–123)

1. Milne's Journal, 28 Nov. 1816, LMS, Journals, S. China; Morrison to L.M.S., 10 Oct. 1828; same to Ellis, 22 Dec. 1833, LMS, S. China; Medhurst, *China,* p. 276; Hunter, *Bits of old China,* p. 259; and Anglo-Chinese College annual reports.

2. Lovett, *History of L.M.S.,* II, pp. 426, 434, 449; Medhurst, *China,* p. 274; Milne's Journal, 28 Oct. 1816, LMS, Journals, S. China; LMS, *Reports of directors,* 1844; and Morrison to Ellis, 11 March 1834, LMS, S. China.

3. Morrison, *Memoirs of Milne,* p. 227; and Morrison, *To the public,* p. 5.

4. Acheen *seluar:* three-quarter length trousers in a style ascribed to Achin in northern Sumatra; *Sarong:* skirt-like cloth tucked around the waist; *baju:* coat or jacket.

5. Hill, *Hikayat Abdullah,* Introduction and *passim.*

6. Morrison to Burder, 4 Sep. 1817, LMS, S. China.

7. Morrison's notes on Milton's letter of 31 Dec. 1824, LMS, Singapore.

8. John Smith to Hankey, 25 April 1827, LMS, Singapore.

9. Morrison, *To the public,* pp. 3, 6; Milne to L.M.S., 27 Jan. 1814, LMS, S. China. Shoo-King, The Book of History (Shu Ching), is one of the Five Classics. 'The Shu King contains the seeds of all things that are valuable in the estimation of the Chinese; it is at once the foundation of their political system, their history, and their religious rites, the basis of their tactics, music, and astronomy.' See S. Wells Williams, *The Middle Kingdom,* I, chap. XI, p. 505. *Yew-heo: a catechism for youth,* by William Milne is listed in Alexander Wylie's *Memorials of Protestant missionaries,* but the Ming-sin-poou-keen is not mentioned there. Seaou-heo: Primary learning (Hsiao hsüeh). 'Siau Hioh, by Chu Hi: Primary Lessons or Juvenile Instructor; intended as a counterpart to Ta Hioh or Superior Lessons, one of the Four Books. Siau Hioh is divided into two books, the first of which is the fountain of learning, and the latter the stream flowing from it. It is probable that the precepts of the higher classics have been more extensively diffused among the lower classes through means of the Siau Hioh than they would otherwise have been.' See S. Wells Williams, *The Middle Kingdom,* I, chap. XI, pp. 538-39.

10. Morrison, *To the public,* p. 20; To the Christian Public, 10 July 1823, LMS, China personal, R. M.; Joyce's *Scientific dialogues,* see chap. 9, note 2.

11. College annual reports.

CHAPTER FIFTEEN

College Students (pages 124–131)

1. Evans to L.M.S., 14 April, 16 Aug. 1837, and 1 Nov. 1839 LMS, Malacca; and LMS, *Reports of directors,* 1838.

2. LMS: *Transactions,* I, p. 398; Morrison, *Memoir,* II, pp. 61, 397; and Morrison to Hankey, 26 Sep. 1831, LMS, S. China.

3. Morrison, *To the public,* pp. 1, 5; Humphreys to Directors, 8 March 1823; and Smith's Reports, 1830, LMS, Malacca; LMS, *Reports of directors,* 1837; Medhurst, *China,* p. 320; and Tomlin's Report, 1833, LMS, China personal, R. M.

4. Thomas Keith (1759–1824), mathematician; became tutor in geography to Princess Charlotte of Wales in 1810; *Treatise on the use of the globes.* 1804.

5. A seminary was opened in Penang in 1808 for the training of Chinese, Siamese and Vietnamese clergy under the French *Société des Missions Etrangères.*

6. Stockius, see chap. 9, note 2.

7. Triad Society: a secret society founded in China according to tradition in 1674 and particularly strong in the southern provinces of Fukien, Kwangtung and Kwangsi. The first specific reference to a Triad society in Malaysia occurs in an article written by William Milne in 1821 and published posthumously in *Royal Asiatic Society Transactions,* I, 2 (1827) 240–50. See Wilfred Blythe, *The impact of Chinese secret societies in Malaya: a historical study,* p. 46.

8. Medhurst, *China,* pp. 317, 319; LMS, *Reports of directors,* 1827; Humphreys and Collie to Directors, 13 June 1823; Moor to Arundel, 20 Sep. 1825, LMS, Malacca; Morrison to Shaou Tih, 21 June 1827, LMS, China personal, R. M.; College annual report, 1829; and Hunter, *Bits of old China,* pp. 260–63. According to Peter W. Fay, *The Opium War, 1840–1842,* p. 160, Commissioner Lin had at least four interpreters. 'One, known to foreigners as Shau Tih (actually Yuan Te-hui), was an overseas Chinese who had studied with the English Protestants at Malacca and with the French Catholics at Penang, and had subsequently been employed at Peking as a sort of general interpreter. . . . He was considered Lin's senior interpreter.' According to another source, Chang Hsin-pao, *Commissioner Lin and the Opium War,* pp. 258–59, 'Yuan Te-hui arrived at Malacca in the fall of 1825 and studied at the Anglo-Chinese College, where he and [William C.] Hunter were schoolmates for sixteen months. Hunter left Malacca for Canton at the end of 1826, and Yuan visited him there in the fall of 1827.' Yuan translated into English the draft of a letter composed by Commissioner Lin for the Queen of England, pointing out to her the iniquity of the opium trade; see Chang, *op. cit.,* p. 137.

9. College annual reports, 1826–29; Morrison to Fisher, 18 March 1827, 9 Nov. 1830, LMS, China personal, R. M.; Morrison to Hankey, 14 Nov. 1830, LMS, S. China; Kidd to Hankey, 1 May 1827, LMS, Malacca; and Hunter, *Bits of old China*, pp. 237–64. For J. H. Moor, William C. Hunter, and J. R. Morrison, see Appendix II, *c*., p. 193.

10. Morrison, *To the public*, p. 5; and To the Christian public, July 1823, LMS, China personal, R. M.

11. College annual report, 1834.

12. *Ibid.* One graduate (Kee-cheang) was head of an American mission school in Rangoon, Burma, in 1831 (John Taylor Jones to Morrison, 2 Oct. 1831, LMS, S. China).

13. James Bone: most probably a son of A. B. Bone, Penang merchant and publisher of the *Prince of Wales Island Gazette*, whose death in 1815 had left his family in destitute circumstances; see Byrd, *Early printing in the Straits Settlements*, p. 3.

14. Milne to Morrison, 29 Jan. 1822, Morrison, *Memoir*, II, p. 149; and Milne's testimonial for James Bone, 12 May 1821, LMS, Malacca.

15. Lovett, *History of L.M.S.*, II, p. 449; LMS, *Reports of directors*, 1844; and H. E. Legge, *James Legge*, p. 17. See Appendix II, c.

16. See Appendix II, *c*., p. 194; Carl T. Smith, 'A register of baptized Protestant Chinese, 1813–1842', *Chung Chi Bulletin* (Hong Kong), 48 (1969) 23–26; and 'Dr. Legge's Theological School', *ibid.*, 50 (1971) 16–22.

17. *Missionary sketches*, Jan. 1848; Cook, *Sunny Singapore*, p. 19; Song Ong Siang, *One hundred years' history of the Chinese in Singapore*, pp. 76–78.

CHAPTER SIXTEEN
Mission Schools (pages 132–143)

1. Morrison, *To the Public*, p. 5.
2. Hill, *Hikayat Abdullah*, pp. 38–56.
3. *Ibid.*, pp. 52–3.
4. *Indo-Chinese Gleaner*, 10 (Oct. 1819), pp. 215–17. *Pice:* East Indian copper coin; 4 pice = 1 anna; 16 anna = 1 rupee. Malay *duit:* small coin, cent; *hari Khamis:* Thursday (fifth day).
5. *Ibid.*, 11 (Jan. 1820), p. 265.

6.   Milne to Directors, 30 Dec. 1815; Evans and Dyer to L.M.S., 1 Oct. 1836, 2 Oct. 1838, and 1 Nov. 1839, LMS, Malacca.

7.   Laird, *Missionaries and education,* pp. 6–11; Milne to British and Foreign School Society, 5 May 1821, LMS, Malacca.

8.   San Tsze-king: the Three Character Classic, a digest of classical writings for schools. 'The Trimetrical Classic was the first *hornbook,* or digest of classical writings, to be put into the hands of a Chinese child, a primary book of tuition to be learnt by heart.' See S. Wells Williams, *The Middle Kingdom,* I, p. 480.

9.   Medhurst, *China,* p. 312; Morrison to Burder, 24 Jan. 1819, LMS, S. China; Milne to Dutch Government, 31 May 1819, LMS, Malacca.

10.   *Indo-Chinese Gleaner,* 7 (Jan. 1819), pp. 46–47. The managing committee of the school *pro.tem.* consisted of J. A. S. Parve, Collector; J. Carnegy, Master Attendant; H. Kraal, Captain of the Burghers; the Kapitan China, and the Kapitan Kling.

11.   Humphreys to Directors, 20 Oct. 1822, and 8 March 1823; Milne to Directors, 15 Feb. 1822; and Humphreys and Collie to Directors, 13 June 1823, LMS, Malacca.

12.   Moor to Arundel, 20 Sep. 1825, 4 Jan. 1826; Humphreys to Orme, 3 April 1828; Humphreys, Collie and Kidd to Directors, 28 April 1827; Miss Newell to Arundel, 18 Feb. 1828, LMS, Malacca; and Garling to Ibbetson, Dec. 1830, SSR, series W 1. The managing committee of the Free School in November 1829 consisted of Samuel Garling, Deputy Resident; A. M. Bond, Wm. Scott and J. Hendriks; in December 1830 the members were Samuel Garling, W. T. Lewis, A. M. Bond, A. Minjoot, and Thos. Neubronner.

13.   Report of School Managing Committee, 3 Nov. 1829, SSR, vol. 169.

14.   *Ibid.;* Fullerton to Governor-General, 13 Nov. 1830; Garling to Ibbetson, Dec. 1830, SSR, series V 4, W 1; College annual report, 1835; and Begbie, *Malayan Peninsula,* pp. 1–2.

15.   Humphreys, etc., to Garling, 4 Sep. 1826; Garling to Humphreys, 14 Sep. 1826; Garling to Anderson, 18 Sep. 1826; Report on Schools, 10 Jan. 1827, SSR, vol. 165; and Humphreys to Directors, 28 April 1827, LMS, Malacca.

16.   Humphreys to Garling, 16 Feb. 1827, SSR, vol. 165; same to Orme, 3 April 1828; Kidd and Hughes to L.M.S., 12 Nov. 1831,

LMS, Malacca; Medhurst, *China*, p. 319; and Abeel, *Journal of a residence*, p. 273.

17. Hughes to Arundel, 5 Dec. 1830; and Kidd and Hughes to L.M.S., 12 Nov. 1831, LMS, Malacca.

18. The British and Foreign School Society was formed in 1819 by a group of friends of the English educationist Joseph Lancaster.

19. Humphreys to Burder, 21 July 1827; Miss Newell's diary, 19–29 Aug. 1827; Miss Newell to Arundel, 16 Nov. 1827, and 18 Feb. 1828, LMS, Malacca.

20. Miss Newell married the German missionary Karl Gützlaff (see chap. 11, note 11) earlier in 1829, went with him to Siam in Feb. 1830, but died there barely twelve months later. See Gützlaff, *Journal of three voyages*, p. lxxxiv; according to Waley, *The Opium War*, p. 223, she left Gützlaff 'a considerable sum of money.'

21. Mrs Garling to L.M.S., 11 Dec. 1830; S. Dyer letter, 22 Oct. 1831; Kidd to L.M.S., 7 March 1831; and Miss Wallace to L.M.S., 22 Oct. 1831, LMS, Malacca; *The Chinese Repository*, I, 3 (July 1832), pp. 104–7; Eliza Reed to L.M.S., 1834, LMS, S. China.

22. Hughes and Evans to L.M.S., 1 Jan. 1835; Evans and Dyer to L.M.S., 6 April 1836, 1 Oct. 1836, and 2 April 1838, LMS, Malacca; Begbie, *Malayan Peninsula*, p. 467.

CHAPTER SEVENTEEN

Retrospect (pages 144–158)

1. David Laurie, *Hints regarding the East India monopoly*, pp. 5, 51; quoted in K. E. Knorr, *British colonial theories, 1570–1850*, p. 247.

2. Morrison to Hankey, 12 Nov. 1822, LMS, S. China. The Baptist Missionary Society was founded in 1792.

3. *Cambridge history of India*, VI, pp. 98–99; Laird, *Missionaries and education*, pp. 61–63; and S. P. Carey, *William Carey*, p. 355.

4. Mackenzie, *The Christian task in India*, pp. 85–102; and Laird, *op. cit.*, pp. 95, 142.

5. S. P. Carey, *op. cit.*, p. 351.

6. Laird, *op. cit.*, p. 149; Begbie, *Malayan Peninsula*, p. 368; Hill, *Hikayat Abdullah*, p. 126 n.; Turnbull, *Straits Settlements*, p. 224. The College building was in fact assigned by Morrison to the L.M.S. in 1824.

7. Morrison to Fisher, 9 Jan. 1831, LMS, China personal, R. M.; Morrison, *Memoir,* II, p. 445; Morrison to Rev. Craknell, 19 Dec. 1820, LMS, S. China; and Laird, *Missionaries and education,* p. 149.

8. Milne, *Retrospect,* p. 204.

9. See Gottfried Wilhelm von Leibnitz (1646–1716), *Novissima Sinica.* 1697; and Francois Quesnay (1694–1774), *Le déspotisme de la Chine.* 1767.

10. *The Chinese Repository,* I, 8 (Dec. 1832), pp. 326–29.

11. E. J. Hobsbawm, *The age of revolution, 1789–1848,* p. 278; Morrison, *To the British public,* p. 7.

12. Milne to Timmerman Thyssen, 12 July 1821, Jakarta, *Buitenland,* 22.

CHAPTER EIGHTEEN

Postscript *(pages 159–162)*

1. G. F. Hudson, *Europe and China.* Boston, 1961, p. 308.

2. E. C. Carlson, 'Obstacles to missionary success in nineteenth century China', *Asian Studies,* IV, 1 (April 1966) 16–28.

3. C. P. Fitzgerald, 'Religion and China's cultural revolution', *Pacific Affairs,* XL, 1 & 2 (Spring-Summer 1967) 124–29.

4. The Chinese nationalist leader, Sun Yat-sen, speaking at a public meeting in September 1912 said: 'Where did the idea of revolution come from? It came because from my youth I have had intercourse with foreign missionaries. Those from Europe and America with whom I associated put the ideals of freedom and liberty into my heart.' Quoted in Donald W. Treadgold, *The West in Russia and China,* II, p. 96.

Appendix I

ANGLO-CHINESE COLLEGE, MALACCA, STAFF, 1818–1843

A. Missionary teachers

Robert MORRISON, President 1818–34. B. nr. Morpeth, Northumberland, Jan. 1782; entered Hoxton Academy (later Highbury College), London, 1803; trained at L.M.S. seminary at Gosport, Hampshire, 1804–5; ordained Jan. 1807; arr. Macao, Sep. 1807; Chinese secretary to East India Company at Canton, 1809; interpreter on Amherst mission to Peking, 1816–17; D.D., Glasgow, 1817; visited Malacca, Feb.–July, 1823; in England, 1824–26; F.R.S., 1825; d. Canton, Aug. 1834. *Dictionary of the Chinese language*, 6 vols. Macao, 1815–23; *The Bible in Chinese* (trans. with William Milne), 21 vols. Malacca, 1823; etc.

William MILNE, Principal 1818–22. B. at Kennethmont, Aberdeenshire, 1785; trained at L.M.S. seminary, Gosport, 1810–12; ordained July 1812; arr. Macao, July 1813; toured Java, 1814; started mission at Malacca, May 1815; D.D., Glasgow, 1820; d. Malacca, June 1822. *The sacred edict* (trans.). London, 1817; *Retrospect of the first ten years of the Protestant mission to China*. Malacca, 1820; etc.

Claudius Henry THOMSEN, 1818–22. B. in Holstein, Lower Saxony, 1782; arr. Malacca, Sep. 1815; moved to Singapore, 1822–34; resigned from L.M.S., Oct. 1829; returned to England and Holstein, 1834. *Malay spelling book*. Malacca, 1818; *Vocabulary of English, Bugis and Malay languages*. Singapore, 1833.

Walter Henry MEDHURST, 1818–20. B. London, 1796; educ. St. Paul's School and Hackney College; joined L.M.S., 1816; arr. Malacca, June 1817; served as missionary at Malacca, Penang (1820–21) and Batavia, Java (1822–); toured east coast of

Malaya (1828), Java and Bali (1829–30) and China coast (1835); in England, 1836–38; in Shanghai, Dec. 1843–Sep. 1856; d. London, Jan. 1857. *Dictionary of the Hokkien dialect*. Macao, 1832; *English and Japanese vocabulary*. Batavia, 1830 ('the first . . . English work on the Japanese language'—A. Wylie, *Memorials of Protestant Missionaries* . . . , p. 37); *China, its state and prospects*. London, 1838; *Chinese-English dictionary*, 2 vols. Batavia, 1842–43; *Ong Tae-hae, or the Chinaman abroad*. Shanghai, 1844; *The Shoo King or Historical classic*. Shanghai, 1846; *English-Chinese dictionary*, 2 vols. Shanghai, 1847–48.

John SLATER, 1818–19. Ordained Liverpool, Aug. 1816; arr. Malacca, Dec. 1817; moved to Canton for health, Aug. 1818, then to Batavia, April 1819; resigned from L.M.S., 1823.

Thomas BEIGHTON, 1818–19. Arr. Malacca, Sep. 1818; moved to Penang, 1819 and started a new mission there including Malay and Chinese schools. *Christian catechism in Malay*. Malacca, 1824; *Arithmetic in Malay*. Malacca, 1825.

John INCE, 1818–19. B. 1795; trained at L.M.S. seminary, Gosport; ordained in London, 1818; arr. Malacca, Sep. 1818; moved with Beighton to Penang, 1819; d. Penang, April 1825.

Saumel MILTON, 1818–19. Ordained at Exeter, Jan. 1818; arr. Malacca, Sep. 1818; moved to Singapore, Oct. 1819, and started a Chinese school; resigned from L.M.S., 1825; d. in Singapore, 1849.

Robert FLEMING, 1820–21. Trained at Gosport; ordained at London, 1818; sailed from England with Beighton, Ince and Slater, but stopped for a time at Madras to study Tamil and Sanskrit; arr. Malacca, Jan. 1820, and began study of Chinese; suspended 'for acknowledged adultery and for derangement of mind' and returned to Madras, 1821.

George Henry HUTTMAN, 1820–24. Arr. Malacca Sep. 1820 as superintendent of printing; made no progress with study of Chinese and left the college 1824.

James HUMPHREYS, 1821–29, Principal, 1822–24. B. Glasgow; trained at Gosport; ordained in London, Feb. 1821; arr. Malacca, Sep. 1821; studied Chinese at first, then Malay after 1824 when he resigned from post of Principal; left the college for health reasons and returned to England, 1829.

David COLLIE, 1822–28, Principal 1824–28. Trained at Gosport; ordained at Bristol, Sep. 1821; arr. Malacca, June 1822; designated professor of Chinese, 1823; d. at sea en route to Singapore, Feb. 1828. *The celestial mirror*, 2 vols. Malacca, 1826; *The Four Books* (trans. and ed.). Malacca, 1828.

Samuel KIDD, 1824–32, Principal 1828–32. B. at Melton nr. Hull, 1804; trained at Gosport, 1820–23; ordained at Hull, April 1824; arr. Malacca, Nov. 1824; designated professor of Chinese, 1827; returned to England for health reasons, 1832; pastor of Congregational church at Manningtree, Essex, 1833–37; professor of Chinese language and literature, University College, London, 1837–42; d. London, Aug. 1843. *The thousand character classic*. Malacca, 1831; *Catalogue of the Chinese Library of the Royal Asiatic Society*. London, 1838; *China, or illustrations of the philosophy, government and literature of the Chinese*. London, 1841.

Jacob TOMLIN, 1828, Principal 1832–34. B. 1793; B.A. Cambridge; appointed missionary by L.M.S., April 1826; arr. Malacca, Feb. 1827; moved to Singapore, April 1827; assisted at Anglo-Chinese College, March–April 1828, on Collie's death; visited Malaysian tin mines with Humphreys, April–May, 1828; travelled in Siam, Java and Bali between Aug. 1828 and Jan. 1832; returned to Malacca as college Principal, 1832; left in 1833 and opened a new international school

in Malacca, 1834; returned to England, 1836. *Missionary journals and letters*. London, 1844.

John SMITH, 1828–29. M.A., Glasgow; appointed L.M.S. missionary with Tomlin, April, 1826; arr. Malacca late in 1826; moved to Singapore with Tomlin, April 1827; assisted at the Malacca college, April 1828; returned to Singapore, March 1829 and left for health reasons the same year, arriving in England in Feb. 1830.

Josiah HUGHES, 1830–35. Arr. Malacca, Nov. 1830; Malay specialist; left the college, Oct. 1835; d. of cholera in Malacca, Nov. 1840.

John EVANS, 1833–40, Principal 1834–40. B. 1803 (?); 'for many years a teacher in England, . . . trained a number of pupils for Cambridge and Oxford universities, having been successively professor of classics, mathematics, Hebrew and Arabic' (A. Wylie, *Memorials . . .*, p. 76); ordained as missionary at Hertford, Dec. 1832; arr. Malacca, Aug. 1833; succeeded Tomlin as Principal, May 1834; d. of cholera in Malacca, Nov. 1840. *Malay reading book*, Malacca, 1837.

Samuel DYER, 1835–42. B. at Greenwich, 1804; educ. Woolwich and Cambridge University; trained at Gosport, 1824–27; ordained in London, Feb. 1827; arr. Penang,

Aug. 1827; specialized in Chinese printing with moveable metal type; joined Anglo-Chinese College, Oct. 1835, with special charge of the press; returned to England on account of wife's health, 1839–41; arr. Singapore, Feb. 1842; left July 1843 to attend missionary conference in Hong Kong, August 1843; d. in Macao, Oct. 1843.

James LEGGE, Principal 1840–43. B. Huntly, Aberdeenshire, Dec. 1815; educ. Aberdeen Grammar School; King's College, Aberdeen (M.A., 1835), and Highbury College, London (1837); joined L.M.S., 1838; ordained at Brompton, London, April 1839; arr. Malacca, Jan. 1840; succeeded Evans as Principal, Nov. 1840; arranged sale of L.M.S. mission property and college building, April 1843; left for Singapore, May 1843; arr. Hong Kong, August 1843; head of L.M.S. Theological Seminary, Hong Kong, 1843–56; minister of Union church, Hong Kong, 1844–73; returned to England, 1873; professor of Chinese, Oxford University, 1876–97; d. Nov. 1897. *The Chinese classics*, 5 vols. Hong Kong and London, 1861–72; *Life and works of Mencius*. London, 1875; *The religions of China*. London, 1890.

B. Instructors

Abdullah bin Abdul Kadir, 1818–22, and irregularly 1823–40. B. at Malacca, 1797; writer-copyist on staff of Stamford Raffles, 1810–11; occasional Malay tutor, translator and press assistant at Anglo-Chinese College, 1818–40; moved with C. H. Thomsen to Singapore, 1822; d. on pilgrimage to Mecca, 1854. *Kesah Pelayaran Abdullah*. Singapore, 1838; *Hikayat Abdullah*. Singapore, 1849.

Lee, 1818–30 (?).

Chu Tsing, 1820 (?)–32. Baptized by Morrison at Canton, Dec. 1832. Later employed under new British administration in Hong Kong but was dismissed (being an opium smoker) in Oct. 1843.

Nunsid (Siamese), 1823.

Yaou, 1824–34.

Yim, 1827.

K'o, 1834–35.

Chuy Gwan, 1835.

C. Printers

Leang Ah Fah, 1818–43. B. nr. Canton, 1787; trained as printer; went with Milne to Malacca, 1815; baptized by Milne, Nov. 1816; printed *The Bible in Chinese* (trans. Morrison and Milne), 21 vols., Malacca, 1823; ordained by Morrison, 1824; moved with Legge to Hong Kong, 1843; left Hong Kong for Canton, 1845; d. 1855.

Kew Ah Gung, *alias* Wat Ngong, 1818–43. B. Canton, 1785; came to Malacca c. 1815; in Macao c. 1830, where he was baptized by Morrison and then journeyed with Leang Ah Fah from Canton for 250 miles into the interior of China distributing Christian tracts; printed for Morrison in Macao, then returned to Malacca, 1836; moved with Legge to Hong Kong, 1843, and served for many years as a preacher for the L.M.S.; d. 1867.

Ah Chaou, ?–1824.

Ah Tsieh

Ah Sun, or Ho Ah Sun, *alias* Ho Ye-tong. Accompanied Legge to Hong Kong in 1843; d. 1869.

Appendix II

STUDENTS, 1818–1843

a. From Morrison's 1823 list.

Yaou, Oct. 1819–24.

Loo, Jan. 1820–?

James Bone, Feb. 1820–May 1821.

Chang Chun, March 1820–.

Tsze Hea, March 1820–. [Baptized by Kidd in April 1829 (A. Wylie, *Memorials…*, pp. 47–48)]

Ma King Tseuen, August 1820–.

Woo Tuy Pe.

Tsang Kow Gan, Sep. 1821–May 1822. Went to Singapore.

Woo Heun Chan, Sep. 1821–.

Kow Kwang Tih, Sep. 1821–.

Soo Yuen Tseuen, Feb. 1822–.

Teen Sang, April 1822.

Mang Teen Yin.

b. From 1834 list of graduates.

Cho Hay, pensioner on the College funds.

Keung Tshoong, shopkeeper.

Tseang Tshoon, government interpreter in Singapore.

Ke Seeng, commander of a vessel.

Teen Seeng, captain's clerk.

Gan Tsheung, merchant.

Hoon Tsheung, writer in the custom-house, Singapore.

Lang Tsheung, writer in the custom-house, Singapore.

Ho Han, government interpreter at Malacca. [Governor Bonham of Hong Kong enquired in January 1842 whether Malacca could provide educated Chinese interpreters to join the British expeditionary forces on the China coast. He enquired in particular whether Ko-han [sic] was 'disposed to take service as a linguist in China'. (SSR, vol. U 8, 27 Jan. 1842)]

Ang Kew, merchant's clerk.

Yim Seeng, shopkeeper.

Kim Seeng, merchant's clerk.

Shaou Tih [Yuan Te-hui, 1823–27], interpreter at Imperial court, Peking [see pp. 126–27].

Yoh Seeng, shopkeeper.

Pai Yang, merchant's clerk.

Tsing Kei, merchant.

Tsing Yang, merchant.

Tsing Sung, merchant's clerk.

Teen Yin, merchant.

Teen Yu, no situation.

Soo Seeng, commander of a brig.

Teen Sung, deceased.

Tsing Sung, no situation.

Tsing Han, no situation.

Yih Sam, shopkeeper.

Tong Hae, merchant's clerk.

Kung Tih, shopkeeper.

Tsing Seng, merchant's clerk.

Sim Seeng, medical assistant.

Kung Hae, navigator.

Teen Tsheung, deceased.

Sam Chae, shopkeeper.

San Hae, shopkeeper.

Yoh Seeng, deceased.

Ma Soon, deceased.

Ah Yu, Chinese doctor.

He So, independent.

Ang Sim, no situation.

Lim Chwuy, no situation.

c. Other students.

John Henry Moor, 1825–27. B. Macao, Dec. 1802; educ. Trinity College, Dublin; arr. Malacca, 1825; student-tutor at Anglo-Chinese College, 1825–26; founder and headmaster, Malacca Free School, 1826–29; founder and editor, *Malacca Observer*, 1826–29; editor, *Singapore Chronicle*, 1830–34; editor, *Singapore Free Press*, 1835–37; teacher at Singapore Free School and Singapore Institution, 1834–43; d. May 1843. *Notices of the Indian Archipelago.* Singapore, 1837.

William C. Hunter, 1825–27. Joined the American trading firm of Russell & Co. at Canton, 1827, and was later associated with Augustine Heard & Co. in Macao and Hong Kong; retired in 1868 and moved to France; died at Nice, 1891. *Bits of old China.* London, 1855; *The 'Fan-Kwae' at Canton before treaty days, 1825–1844.* London, 1882.

John Robert Morrison, 1827–30. Son of Robert Morrison, founder of the College; b. 1814; Chinese translator to the English East India Company at Canton, 1830; Chinese Secretary to the British Superintendent of Trade, Canton, 1834; interpreter during Anglo-Chinese treaty negotiations at Nanking, 1842; nominated member of legislative council,

Hong Kong, 1843; d. Macao, aged 28, Aug. 1843. *A Chinese commercial guide.* . . . Canton, 1834.

Ho Tsun-cheen (or -shin), *alias* Ho Fuk-tong, 1840–43. Worked and studied in Calcutta as a youth; entered the College, 1840; went to Canton and Hong Kong, 1843; ordained, 1846; d. 1871; father of Ho Kai (1859–1914), prominent Hong Kong medical doctor and lawyer, C.M.G., 1892, knighted 1912, founder of Alice Memorial Hospital, 1886, in memory of his English wife, and one of the founders of the Hong Kong Medical College which opened in 1887 with two students, one of whom was Sun Yat-sen.

Ah Sou or Ng Mun-sou, c. 1840–43. This student and the two following joined Legge in Hong Kong for a time, accompanied him to Scotland in 1845, and attended school and were baptized at Huntly in Aberdeenshire, Oct. 1847. Returning to Hong Kong, Ah Sou became at various times preacher, interpreter, and member of the Chinese Maritime Customs service until his death in 1881.

Kim-lin or Li Kim-lin, c. 1840–43. After his return from Scotland became a teacher and printer for the L.M.S. in Hong Kong; returned to Malacca, 1855, and died there in the following year.

Song Hoot-kien (or -kiam), c. 1840–43. B. Malacca, 1830; returned from Scotland to Hong Kong with Legge in August 1848; went to Singapore, Feb. 1849, and became a teacher in the Singapore Institution; in 1853 joined the P. & O. Co. which he served as cashier until his retirement in 1895; d. Oct. 1900; father of Song Ong Siang (1871–1941), prominent Singapore lawyer, educ. Raffles Institution, Middle Temple (1889), and Downing College, Cambridge; called to the English bar, 1893; author of *One hundred years' history of the Chinese in Singapore.* London, 1923.

Appendix III

PUBLICATIONS (1815–1840) OF THE MISSION PRESS/ ANGLO-CHINESE PRESS, MALACCA

WILLIAM MILNE (ed.), *Chinese Monthly Magazine* (Ch'ai shih su mei yueh t'ung chi ch'uan), 7 vols., 1815–21.

CLAUDIUS HENRY THOMSEN, *The Ten Commandments* (in Malay), 1817.

—, *Dr. Watt's second catechism* (in Malay), 1817.

—, *A Malay spelling book*, 1818.

—, *The Gospels* [part] *in Malay*, 1818.

WILLIAM MILNE (ed.), *The Indo-Chinese Gleaner* (quarterly), 3 vols., 1817–22.

—, *A catechism for youth* (in Chinese), 1817.

ROBERT MORRISON and WILLIAM MILNE, *General plan of the Anglo-Chinese College forming at Malacca*, 1818.

WALTER HENRY MEDHURST, *A geographical catechism* (in Chinese), 1819.

WILLIAM MILNE, *Exposition of the Lord's Prayer* (in Chinese), 1818.

—, *Sacred history* (in Chinese), 1819.

—, *A retrospect of the first ten years of the Protestant mission to China*, 1820.

—, *Commentary on the New Testament* (in Chinese), 1820 or 1821.

—, *Essay on the immortality of the soul* (in Chinese), 1820 or 1821.

—, *Practical exposition of the Epistle to the Ephesians* (in Chinese), 1820 or 1821.

—, *Brief sketch of all the kingdoms of the world* (in Chinese), 1820 or 1821.

CLAUDIUS HENRY THOMSEN, *Vocabulary of the English and Malay languages in the Roman and Arabic characters*, 1820.

—(ed.), *Malay Magazine* (in Malay and English), 1821.

ROBERT MORRISON and WILLIAM MILNE (trans.), *The holy Bible in Chinese*, 21 vols., 1823.

ROBERT MORRISON, *To the public, concerning the Anglo-Chinese College* 1823.

—(trans.), Joyce's *Scientific dialogues*, 1823.

—, *Lectures on the sayings of Jesus*, 1823.

—, *Notices concerning China, Canton, the affair of the frigate 'Topaz', and fire of Canton*, 1823.

—, *Memoirs of the Rev. William Milne*, 1824.

THOMAS BEIGHTON, *Christian catechism in Malay*, 1824.

—, *Arithmetic in Malay*, 1825.

JOHN HENRY MOOR (ed.), *The Malacca Observer*, Sep. 1826–Oct. 1829.

DAVID COLLIE, *Abridgment of sacred history*, 1826.

—, *The celestial mirror* (in Chinese), 2 vols., 1826.

—, *The English and Chinese students' assistant, or colloquial phrases*, 1826.

—, *Bogue's essay on the evidences of Christianity* (in Chinese), 3 vols., 1827.

— (trans. and ed.), *The Four Books*, 1828.

SAMUEL KIDD (ed.), *The Universal Gazette* (T'ien hsia hsin wen), in Chinese, monthly, 1828–29.

— (trans.), *The thousand character classic*, 1831.

JOSEPH HENRI MARIE DE PRÉMARE, *Notitia Linguae Sinicae*, 1831.

[P. J. BEGBIE], *A narrative of the late Nanning expedition . . ., 6–25 August, 1831*. By an Officer of the expedition, 1831.

ROBERT MORRISON, *Domestic instructor* (in Chinese), 4 vols., 1832.

JACOB TOMLIN, *Missionary Journal kept at Singapore and Siam, May 1830–January 1832*, 1832.

ANON., *The twelve tables, being the inter-exchange of the government currency at the British Settlements in the Straits of Malacca*, 1833.

SAMUEL DYER, *A selection of three thousand characters*, 1834.

JOHN EVANS (ed.), *The periodical miscellany and juvenile instructor*, 1836–38 (?).

—, *Malay reading book*, 1837.

CLAUDIUS HENRY THOMSEN, *Vocabulary of the English and Malay languages in the Roman and Arabic characters* (1820); new edition enlarged and improved, 1837.

ANON, *Malacca weekly register*, 1839–40.

Bibliography

I.   CONTEMPORARY SOURCES

(i)   LONDON MISSIONARY SOCIETY RECORDS

(a)   Manuscript

Incoming letters, China-Ultra Ganges:
  South China (4 boxes), 1807–1847;
  Malacca (3 boxes), 1815–1843;
  Singapore (2 Boxes);
  Penang (2 boxes);
  Batavia.

Outgoing letters, China-Ultra Ganges (3 boxes of bound manuscript volumes), 1822–1854.

South China journals, 1807–1842.

Ultra Ganges journals, 1813–1841.

China personal, R. Morrison (3 boxes).

(b)   Printed

Reports of the directors (12 volumes), 1795–1846.

Transactions of the Society (4 volumes), 1795–1818.

Quarterly Journal of Transactions of the Society (4 volumes), 1815–1832.

Anglo-Chinese College annual reports (some bound in *China Pamphlets,* vols 12 and 69; others loose in *China personal,* R. Morrison, Box 2).

Missionary sketches (2 volumes), 1818–1868.

(ii)   ENGLISH EAST INDIA COMPANY RECORDS, STRAITS SETTLEMENTS

India Office Library, London: vols. 49, 54, 55, 66; vols. 165, 168, 169 (Malacca Diary).

National Library, Singapore:
Series I 18   (Penang miscellaneous letters out);
O 3   (Malacca Resident's diary);
U 3, 6–8 (Governor's letters to Resident Councillors);
V 2–3   (Governor's misc. letters out);
W 1–3   (Governor's misc. letters in);
EE 8, 11 (Malacca Resident Councillor's letters to Governor).

(iii) NETHERLANDS EAST INDIA COMPANY RECORDS

Arsip Nasional, Jakarta: *Buitenland* 22, 29 (Duplicaat Missiven van Malakka).

Arkib Negara, Kuala Lumpur:
Malacca Church Records:
Resolutie Boek, 1773–1825;
Kerk Boek, 1809–1822.

(iv) PRINTED BOOKS AND JOURNALS (see also Appendix III)

Abdullah bin Abdul Kadir, *The Hikayat Abdullah*. Trans. A. H. Hill. Kauala Lumpur/London, 1970.

Abeel, David, *Journal of a residence in China and the neighbouring countries from 1829 to 1833.* New York, 1834.

Begbie, P. J., *The Malayan Peninsula*. Madras, 1834; Kuala Lumpur, 1967.

The Chinese Repository. Canton, 1832–1851.

Crawfurd, John, *Journal of an Embassy . . . to the Courts of Siam and Cochin-China,* 2 vols. London, 1828; Kuala Lumpur, 1967.

First report of the Singapore Christian Union (formerly called Singapore Committee) formed in September 1827 for extending the benefits of education and the knowledge of Christianity in Singapore and other parts of the Malayan Archipelago . . . Singapore, 1830.

Gützlaff, Charles, *Journal of three voyages to China in 1831, 1832 and 1833 . . .* London, 1834.

Hunter, William, *Bits of old China*. London, 1855.

Laurie, David, *Hints regarding the East India monopoly*. Glasgow, 1813.

Malcom, Howard, *Travels in South-Eastern Asia, embracing Hindustan, Malaya, Siam and China, with notices of numerous missionary stations, and a full account of the Burman Empire.* 2nd ed. (2 vols. in one). Boston, 1839.

Medhurst, Walter H., *China, its state and prospects.* London, 1838.

——, *A glance at the interior of China.* Shanghai, n.d.

Milne, William, *A retrospect of the first ten years of the Protestant mission to China.* Malacca, 1820.

—— (ed.), *The Indo-Chinese Gleaner, containing miscellaneous communications on the literature, history, philosophy, mythology, etc., of the Indo-Chinese nations, drawn chiefly from the native languages, Christian miscellanies and general news.* Published quarterly. Malacca, 1817–1822.

Moor, J. H., *Notices of the Indian Archipelago.* Singapore, 1837; London, 1968.

Morrison, Elizabeth, *Memoir of the life and labours of Robert Morrison, D.D.* Compiled by his widow, with critical notices of his Chinese works by Samuel Kidd, and an appendix containing original documents. 2 vols. London, 1839.

Morrison, Robert, *Memoirs of the Reverend William Milne, D.D., late missionary to China and Principal of the Anglo-Chinese College, compiled from documents written by the deceased, to which are added occasional remarks.* Malacca, 1824.

——, *To the public, concerning the Anglo-Chinese College.* Malacca, 1823.

——, *To the British public, interested in the promotion of Christianity, morals, and useful knowledge, among heathen nations, this account of the Anglo-Chinese College is respectfully addressed.* London, 1825.

Newbold, T. J., *Political and statistical account of the British settlements in the Straits of Malacca.* 2 vols. London, 1839.

Philip, Robert, *The life and opinions of Rev. William Milne, D.D., missionary to China.* London, 1840; New York, 1843.

Raffles, Sir Thomas S., *Minute of the establishment of a Malayan college in Singapore.* Singapore, 1823.

Tomlin, Jacob, *Missionary journal and letters written during eleven years' residence and travels among the Chinese, Siamese, Javanese, Khassias and other Eastern nations.* London, 1844.

——, *Missionary journal kept at Singapore and Siam from May 1830 to January 1832.* Malacca, 1832.

Tyerman, David and George Bennet, *Journal of voyages and travels by Rev. D.T. and G.B., Esq., deputed from the London Missionary Society to visit their various stations in the South Sea Islands, China, India, &c., between the years 1821 and 1829*. Compiled from original documents by James Montgomery. 2 vols. London, 1831.

Williams, Samuel Wells, *The Middle Kingdom; a survey of the Chinese Empire and its inhabitants* . . . 2 vols. 2nd ed. New York/London, 1848.

Williamson, G. R., *Memoir of the Rev. David Abeel, D.D., late missionary to China*. New York, 1848.

II. LATER PUBLICATIONS

Barnett, Suzanne W., 'Silent Evangelism: Presbyterians and the mission press in China, 1807–60'. *Journal of Presbyterian History*, 49, 4 (Winter 1971) 287–302.

Blythe, Wilfred, *The impact of Chinese secret societies in Malaya: a historical study*. London, 1969.

Boardman, E. P., *Christian influence upon the ideology of the Taiping Rebellion, 1851–1864*. New York, 1972.

Box, Rev. E., 'Morrison, Milne and Medhurst'. *Chinese Recorder and Missionary Journal*, (Feb.–March 1904) 79–89, 117–26.

Broomhall, Marshall, *Robert Morrison, a master builder*. London, 1924.

—— (ed.), *The Chinese Empire: a general and missionary survey*. London, 1907.

Buckley, C. B., *An anecdotal history of old times in Singapore*. Singapore, 1902.

Byrd, Cecil K., *Early printing in the Straits Settlements, 1806–1858: a preliminary enquiry*. Singapore, 1970.

Cambridge history of India. Cambridge, 1922–.

Carey, S. Pearce, *William Carey*. London, 1934.

Carlson, E. C., 'Obstacles to missionary success in nineteenth century China'. *Asian Studies*, IV, i (April 1966) 16–28.

Chang Hsin-pao, *Commissioner Lin and the Opium War*. Cambridge, Mass., 1964.

Cheeseman, H. R., 'Dr. Robert Morrison and Malaya'. *British Malaya*, XXV (3) (1950) 52–53.

Chelliah, D. D., *A history of the educational policy of the Straits Settlements*. Singapore, 1947.

Cook, Rev. J. A. Bethune, *Sunny Singapore; an account of the place and its people, with a sketch of the results of missionary work.* 2nd ed. London, 1907.

Cordier, Henri, *Bibliotheca Sinica.* Paris, 1904–1908. *Supplément,* 1922–1924.

Dictionary of national biography. London, 1908–1909.

Eliot, T. S., *Notes towards the definition of culture.* London, 1948.

Endacott, G. B., *A History of Hong Kong.* London, 1958.

Fairbank, John K. (ed.), *The missionary enterprise in China and America.* Cambridge, Mass., 1974.

——, *Trade and diplomacy on the China coast.* Cambridge, Mass., 1953.

——, E. O. Reischauer and A. M. Craig, *East Asia, the modern transformation.* Boston, 1965.

Fay, Peter W., *The Opium War, 1840–1842.* Chapel Hill, N. Carolina, 1975.

Fitzgerald, C. P., 'Religion and China's cultural revolution'. *Pacific Affairs,* XL, 1 & 2 (Spring-Summer 1967) 124–29.

Gibson-Hill, C. A., 'The date of Munshi Abdullah's first visit to Singapore'. *Journal of the Malayan/Malaysian Branch of the Royal Asiatic Society,* 28(1) (March 1955) 191–95.

——, 'The Singapore Chronicle'. *Journal of the Malayan/Malaysian Branch of the Royal Asiatic Society,* 26(1) (July 1953) 175–99.

Gray, Charles, 'Journal of a route overland from Malacca to Pahang across the Malayan Peninsula'. *Journal of the Indian Archipelago and Eastern Asia,* VI (1852) 369–75, reprinted from *The Malacca Observer,* 27 Feb. 1827.

Greenberg, M., *British trade and the opening of China.* Cambridge, 1951.

Gregg, Alice H., *China and educational autonomy: the changing role of the Protestant educational missionary in China, 1807–1937.* Syracuse, N.Y., 1946.

Gulick, Edward V., *Peter Parker and the opening of China.* Cambridge, Mass., 1973.

Haines, Joseph H., *A history of Protestant missions in Malaya during the nineteenth century, 1815–1881.* Unpublished thesis, Princeton, N.J., 1962.

Hardy, T. J., 'Catalogue of Church records, Malacca, 1642–1898'. *Journal of Malayan Branch Royal Asiatic Society,* XV (1) (1937) 1–24.

Harrison, Brian, 'The Anglo-Chinese College and early modern education', in Kernial Singh Sandhu and Paul Wheatley (eds.), *Melaka: the transformation of a Malay capital, c. 1400–1980*. Kuala Lumpur, forthcoming.

——, 'The Anglo-Chinese College at Malacca, 1818–1843', in C. D. Cowan and O. W. Wolters (eds.), *Southeast Asian history and historiography: essays presented to D. G. E. Hall*. Ithaca/London, 1976, pp. 246–61.

Hobsbawm, E. J., *The age of revolution, 1789–1848*. New York, 1962.

Hough, G. G., 'Notes on the educational policy of Sir Stamford Raffles'. *Journal of Malayan Branch Royal Asiatic Society*, XI (2) (1933) 166–70.

Hudson, G. F., *Europe and China*. Boston, 1961.

Ingham, Kenneth, *Reformers in India, 1793–1833: an account of the work of Christian missionaries on behalf of social reform*. Cambridge, 1956.

Kitzan, Laurence, 'The London Missionary Society and the problem of conversion in India and China, 1804–1834'. *Canadian Journal of History*, V (2) (Sep. 1970) 13–41.

Knorr, K. E., *British colonial theories, 1570–1850*. Toronto, 1944.

Kopf, David, *British orientalism and the Bengal renaissance*. Berkeley, 1969.

Laird, M. A., *Missionaries and education in Bengal, 1793–1837*. Oxford, 1972.

Latourette, K. S., *History of Christian missions in China*. London/New York, 1929.

Legge, Helen E., *James Legge, missionary and scholar*. London, 1905.

Legge, James, *The Chinese classics*. 5 vols. 2nd ed. Oxford, 1893; Reissue, Hong Kong, 1960.

Leibnitz, Gottfried Wilhelm von, *Novissima Sinica*. Paris, 1697.

Lo Hsiang-lin, *Hong Kong and Western cultures*. Honolulu, 1963.

Lovett, Sir H. V., 'Education and Missions to 1858', in *Cambridge history of India*, VI, pp. 95–120.

Lovett, Richard, *History of the London Missionary Society, 1795–1895*. 2 vols. London, 1899.

Lutz, Jessie G. (ed.), *Christian missions in China: evangelists of what?* Boston, 1965.

Mackenzie, John (ed.), *The Christian task in India,* Chap. VI, pp. 85–102, 'Higher education'. London, 1929.

Mills, L. A., *British Malaya, 1824–1867.* Singapore, 1924; London, 1960.

Needham, Joseph and Wang Ling, *Science and civilization in China,* IV, pt. 2. Cambridge, 1965.

Neill, Stephen, *Colonialism and Christian missions.* London, 1966.

—— (ed.), *Concise dictionary of Christian world mission.* London, 1970.

Noorduyn, J., 'C. H. Thomsen, editor of a code of Bugis maritime laws'. *Bijdragen tot de Taal-Land-en Volkenkunde,* 113 (1957) 238–51.

Potts, E. Daniel, *British Baptist missionaries in India, 1793–1837: the history of Serampore and its missions.* Cambridge, 1967.

Quesnay, Francois, *Le déspotisme de la Chine.* Paris, 1767.

Ride, Sir Lindsay, *Robert Morrison, the scholar and the man.* Hong Kong, 1957.

——, 'Biographical note on James Legge', in Legge, J., *The Chinese classics,* I. Hong Kong, 1960.

Rowbotham, Arnold H., *Missionary and Mandarin: the Jesuits at the Court of China.* Berkeley, 1942; New York, 1966.

Sen Gupta, K. P., *The Christian missionaries in Bengal, 1793–1833.* Calcutta, 1971.

Smith, Carl T., 'A register of baptized Protestant Chinese, 1813–1842'. *Chung Chi Bulletin* (Hong Kong), 48(1969) 23–26; and 'Dr. Legge's Theological School', *ibid.,* 50(1971) 16–22.

Song, Ong Siang, *One hundred years' history of the Chinese in Singapore.* London, 1923.

Townsend, William J., *Robert Morrison, the pioneer of Chinese missions.* London, n.d.

Treadgold, Donald W., *The West in Russia and China.* London, 1973.

Turnbull, C. M., *The Straits Settlements, 1826–67.* London, 1972.

Waley, Arthur, *The Opium War through Chinese eyes.* Stanford, Cal., 1958.

Whitehouse, John O., *Register of missionaries, etc., of the London Missionary Society, 1796–1885.* London, 1886.

Wijeysingha, Eugene, *A history of Raffles Institution.* Singapore, 1963.

Williams, Frederick Wells, *The life and letters of Samuel Wells Williams, LL.D.* New York/London, 1889; Wilmington, Delaware, 1972.

Wong Lin Ken, *The Malayan tin industry to 1914.* Tucson, 1965.

Wurtzburg, C. E., *Raffles of the Eastern Isles.* London, 1954.

Wylie, Alexander, *Memorials of Protestant missionaries to the Chinese: giving a List of their publications, and obituary notices of the deceased. . . .* Shanghai, 1867.

Yip Yat Hoong, *The development of the tin mining industry of Malaya.* Kuala Lumpur/Singapore, 1969.

Index